Behind the Scenes:
Hollywood to Broadway

RAY KLAUSEN
Award-winning
Designer & Art Director

For

John S. Harrington and HR Nicholson

Table of Contents

Foreword

When I first met Ray, I was already a successful agent and had been since 1960. At the time, I was running the TV/Lit department at Ashley Famous Agency. I had decided to expand our roster by adding more clients who were involved in the creating and execution of television entertainment. It was through a mutual acquaintance that I decided to meet with a young Ray Klausen, a recent Yale graduate with little to no actual experience. I was immediately intrigued by his unique designs, which incorporated many of the new materials and looks that were beginning to capture the attention of a younger generation.

I had never represented art directors or set designers before, but knew through my contacts with directors, producers and stars that people were ready for Ray's unique new approach. I was particularly taken by a design for a play at the Mark Taper Forum that was literally done at a cost of $500 and yet was as creative and visually exciting as anything I'd seen. I quickly consulted with a colleague and we decided to give it a try.

Once Ray entered the world of Bing Crosby, Perry Como, Frank Sinatra, Sammy Davis, Jr. and Dick Clark, and producer/directors such as Bob Finkel and Marty Pasetta, the rest was television history. Most will recognize Ray's iconic "Elvis-in-lights" design as the most-watched show of its generation. Ray's "Elvis Aloha from Hawaii" and his "Sinking of the Titanic" set in the long-running "Jubilee" at the MGM Grand in Las Vegas are also iconic. Just hearing some of the stories of these shows and Ray's involvement brought back many memories. I hope it will give readers an insight into a very creative and interesting business.

Ultimately, it was Ray's work ethic and enthusiasm for his work that inspired me to represent him for more than 25 years, and lead him to win three Emmy Awards, the highest honor bestowed in television. Many of you reading this book will recognize the important place of Ray's work in television history and its contribution to society. In addition to all the other lessons it brings, this book truly shows us how hard work and dedication are a major part of one's career.

For an idea of the extensiveness of Ray's work over the last half century, I suggest that you turn to the section of the Appendices and look at his amazing list of accomplishments. You will enjoy this book!

Sandy Wernick

Preface

I wrote this book to share with you how my life surpassed all my hopes and dreams with hard work and the help, love and support of others. My story also serves as a record of a fascinating period of time in television and theatre history.

You will discover that I'm a mixture of many things. I've been fiercely ambitious and driven, a lover, an artist, a risk taker, a raconteur, and a very appreciative student of the world I found myself in. In many ways, I'm a self-made man who dreamt big, and in seeking my goals, encountered some amazing people and had some extraordinary experiences.

When I look back at my more than a half century of work in theatre and television, I'm filled with a sense of pride and amazement that I was able to fuse a lifetime of designing, friendships, romance, and personal growth leading to a level of attainment that was a mere dream in the beginning.

When friends started finding internet videos that include sets I produced for a wide variety of shows, and when they told me how amazed they were by them, and peppered me with "How'd you do that?" questions, I began to see value in writing this book. I had no idea that *Youtube* alone would be full of examples of my work from decades ago. The reader will be able to find via an online search many of the television sets I created, and be able to see them "in action." Watching those videos is a re-living of my career that I did not even imagine when I was designing those sets. Try it and enjoy!

As for how I've recalled so many of the episodes in this book, well, that goes back to 1976 when I was working on "The Andy Williams" series with Carl Gibson, the gifted lighting designer on the show. We were sitting in the control booth talking about how fortunate we were to have such interesting and rich lives working in the media, and I remember saying "We ought to start keeping a journal of these adventures." The next day, that's exactly what I did, and so I now have a useful record of my many experiences over the years up to this day.

I hope my words disclose how much I loved designing for television and theatre, and how deeply grateful I am for the special life I've had. It is with great pleasure that I share it with you.

Ray Klausen

rayklausen.com

August 14, 2021

Chapter 1

Early Days

L ooking back, here's what I see: a shy kid, kind of a misfit who somehow ended up designing the scenery for more than 400 television shows including series for Cher, the Smothers Brothers, Andy Williams, and Pearl Bailey. It was a career I can't believe happened, one that also included designs for 10 Academy Awards shows, 26 American Music Awards shows, 10 American Film Institute Tributes for stars like Bette Davis, James Cagney, Orson Welles, and Fred Astaire, sets for Michael Jackson, Madonna, Barbra Streisand, Kenny Rogers, and my all-time favorite, Miss Piggy, not to mention Elvis, plus nine Broadway shows that encompassed such celebrities as Bea Arthur (what a remarkable lady and friend), James Earl Jones (great actor and nice man), Lauren Bacall (what a difficult lady), Rosemary Harris (loved her), and Liza Minnelli (really remarkable).

How did this happen? It surprised me for sure. Let me try to explain: It all started with my two hardworking parents who emigrated from Denmark to the United States. Their story, like all such stories is, I think, unique. My mother, Ane Kathrine Jensen, was born in Roskilde, Denmark, in 1904 and was the first of five children in what was considered to be a wealthy family, since hers was the only family in town to have a piano. At 16, her mother died and Kathrine was made to take care of her four siblings. At a young age, she became engaged to a banker, and together they applied for visas and planned to learn English in Canada, England, or America. One day, the president of the bank for which my mother's fiancé worked visited my grandfather and told him, "You must not let your daughter marry this man." When my grandfather asked for an explanation, the bank president revealed that the man had syphilis. Since there was no such thing as penicillin in those days, my mother sensibly broke off the engagement. Soon after, a visa for America arrived and she, being the adventurous woman she was, left Denmark for a new life on April 24, 1929, on the *S.S. United States.* On board she met a fellow Dane of the same age named Jens Klausen, who was from Logstrup and would become my father. In short, if penicillin had existed, I would not be writing this book.

My father's visa was for Canada, so he was obliged to disembark in Nova Scotia separately from my mother. However, the two kept in touch by writing, and eventually he got a visa for America. They were married June 1, 1930, in a Lutheran church in Jamaica, N.Y. The ceremony was simple, without any friends or family. While the ceremony was going on in the nave, a different gathering was taking place simultaneously in the church basement. When the congregation in the basement heard about this couple getting married, they invited the newlyweds downstairs for an impromptu wedding lunch.

At that time, my father, a talented carpenter, had just finished a large job and was owed $500–a lot of money in the 1930s. Before he was paid, the man who owed him the money suddenly died. My parents decided to forgive the debt; they had their whole lives ahead of them, they reasoned, and the man's widow needed the money far more than they did. I always admired my folks for that.

This was during the Great Depression, and my father ended up unemployed. My mother worked as a beautician, supporting my father as well as a friend who was also without work for more than a year. Times were tough. Their big outing was to walk a mile every Sunday to a nearby town and treat themselves to an ice cream cone. Because of the dire economy they put off having the child Mom wanted.

But then, on Nov. 22, 1937, my brother was born. There was a disagreement about what to name him, as my mother wanted one name, my father another, and my aunt Mickey (Mom's sister), the baby's godmother, wanted a third name. They ended up putting the three names in a hat and drew the name James. I suspect "James" had been my mother's choice, as she tended to get her way. I was born a year and a half later, on May 29, 1939, and named after my godmother, Rae, a family friend. (I kind of wish my mother had held off until January so I could say I was born in the '40s.)

Of my early recollections, when I was two or three I remember wondering what dirt tasted like and trying a handful. Last time for that! Memorable too (and this is probably more information than you need) was a pale blue pull-toy of a large cannon that stuck straight up and on which I accidentally sat while in my crib. James, who had been given a toy doctor's kit (Why? What four-year-old kid needs or wants a doctor's kit?), tried to bandage my torn scrotum. Needless to say, I ended up looking like a mummy on speed. Eager to show off his handiwork, he called out to our mother who took one look and rushed me to our local doctor. I remember vividly the embarrassment of having that private area stitched and patched up. No wonder I don't like guns! I'm not too crazy about doctors, either.

A little later, when I was seven or so, the family was meeting some friends for a Sunday afternoon picnic at a campground not far from our house on Long Island, in Valley Stream, N.Y. As we drove by the playground, a group of men were playing baseball, and their ball flew into an open window in our car and hit Mom in her right eye, shattering her glasses. It was very traumatic for me to suddenly have her rushed off to a local hospital and to not understand how she could be so quickly taken away from us. How could this happen? Early that evening, she returned home wearing an exotic black eyepatch and a reassuring smile for James and myself. It was a shock and a surprise to see how life could change irrevocably for no apparent, logical reason.

Whenever James or I acted up and crossed the line, Mom had a system way ahead of its time. She established a "time out" space, actually the six- by five-foot entryway to our house, and told us to stand there until we could behave. James would last about 10 minutes. Mom would ask him if he was ready to behave himself, James would readily agree, and off he'd go to play with his friends. Not me! I had to win. When asked if I could behave myself, I would insist, adamantly, "No!" And there I would stand for more than two hours. Mom would finally win and I would reluctantly agree to behave, but as I made my exit I would mutter, "Well, anyhow." I always had to have the last word. What Mom didn't realize was that my active imagination made it possible for me to entertain myself in that small entryway. I could look at the shapes on the rough plaster walls and imagine all sorts of animals and the stories that went with them. Standing there wasn't bad at all.

Mom had a pretty, intelligent face but was stuck with a plump body that refused to respond to diet or exercise. She wasn't a great beauty. In our family, that role went to James, who was an extraordinarily beautiful child. He had platinum-blond curls and an angelic face. Those were the days of home permanents and the "Which Twin Has the Tony?" campaign that promoted curls for women, all of whom went wild for James's hair. The ladies simply couldn't keep their hands off him. James hated the attention and became a bit of an introvert, while I was jealous and launched my own campaign to get people to notice me. James and I were clearly not alike and handled life in different ways. We were not close and really didn't play much together. What older brother wants to be bothered by a younger brother, especially one that's a bit of a sissy? I do remember once playing with James in the goat field near our house. We had our bows and arrows and were lying on our backs when suddenly James, holding the bow with his feet, shot an arrow high into the air. Well, the arrow went really high and I was sure it would return to Earth and hit me. I yelled, "James! It's going to hit us!"

"Don't move," my brother ordered. Well, I did move just a few feet and darned if that arrow didn't land just where I had been kneeling. One of those strange, and unforgettable, close calls.

The first sign of my future career came at age eight when a family friend named Else Klamer gave me a Christmas present of a small mannequin and a kit to make dresses for it. Else may have thought the gift was a joke, but I took it seriously. The next day I began designing clothes for the doll. A few weeks later I designed a real dress for a girl named Julie who lived down the street. Mom was pleased and tried to set me on a course toward becoming a fashion designer, but Dad had a different opinion. As a macho carpenter and construction worker, he was quietly appalled. However, he didn't dare contradict my smart, controlling mother.

My father had his reasons. Born a simple peasant in Denmark, on a farm where the indoor plumbing consisted of just a hand pump in the kitchen, he was forced at age 14 to leave school and choose between being a farmer (like his father before him) or learning to be a carpenter. A quiet man, he had hated being raised on the family farm, so he opted for carpentry. His apprenticeship was long and hard and included working with other macho, simple boys constructing crude pine coffins for days on end. Wood shavings placed in the coffins made them comfortable enough for lunchtime naps. He certainly was tough and physically strong. He lived for a time in the wilds of western Canada, where he suffered an appendicitis attack. Fourteen miles from the nearest doctor, he rode most of the way on horseback. When his appendix burst, he walked and crawled the remaining two miles, reaching the doctor just in time. All his life he was around other equally tough men–tough and homophobic and clearly uncomfortable about anything gay. Not good for me.

As far back as I can recall, dinner was served at home promptly at 6 p.m. For the first 15 minutes James and I weren't allowed to talk, as Dad turned on the radio and everyone had to listen to the news. After the program was over, war would break out at the dinner table. By that I mean Dad would proceed to verbally attack both James and me. It was awful. James would clam up and refuse to talk, but I would fight back. In a bizarre way it made me strong but, God, it was painful. Dad was never supportive of us, ever. Neither James nor I can remember our father ever saying he loved us or was proud of us. Forget about ever getting a hug. Heaven knows I spent a good part of my life trying, and failing, to please him. In a way his rejection was a gift, as it made me work hard to achieve recognition.

Dad had a mean side. He always stirred his very hot coffee with a heat conducting silver spoon–his calloused hands never felt the intense heat. With delight he would wait until we weren't looking and then place the spoon on our hands. How he would laugh as we screamed in pain. James and I were hurt not only by the burns but from the confusion as to why our father would want to cause us pain. Wasn't a father supposed to love his sons? This haunted me my entire life.

While Dad did little to provide any growth experiences for the family, Mom took advantage of every opportunity to encourage us to be independent and adventuresome. From the time I turned seven and my brother turned nine, we would be put on a local bus and allowed to travel by ourselves to visit our family friend Eldora King in Oceanside, N.Y., a 20 to 30 minute bus trip. Mom would call up Eldora and let her know which bus we'd be on, and she would meet our bus. We felt very gown up and responsible. Later, when I was 11 and James was 13, we announced that we wanted to visit our cousin Ole, who was 15 and lived in Albuquerque, N.M.–quite a bit farther than Oceanside. Our parents agreed. As long as we could earn the money for the tickets ourselves, we were free to go. I was too young to get a paper route, but James was able to land a huge one. All through the cold, rainy winter we rode our bikes with their heavy canvas bags brimming with the folded *Newsday* papers and threw them up on the doorsteps of the neighborhood houses. When school vacation arrived, James and I confidently boarded a Greyhound bus in New York City. Three days, two nights, and seven transfers later we arrived in

Albuquerque happy, proud of ourselves, and in need of a shower.

Going to Albuquerque was a natural outgrowth in teaching us to be independent and resourceful. The next year, when I was 12, Mom instigated a trip to Denmark for the summer, to help us understand our heritage and to meet our Danish relatives. Mom, James, and I sailed on the Polish ship *S.S. Batory*, a second-rate (cheaper) ocean liner. But we traveled first class. Dad joined us a month later. What an adventure! Mom told me once about how as a young girl whenever she had a temper tantrum her father would say to her, "If you can't control yourself, how do you expect to control others?" My mother took this advice to heart, something made clear by the "time out" space she created for James and me. When it came to controlling my father, she operated in a subtler fashion. The next trip took two years of planning on Mom's part so that Dad would think it was his idea. In 1954 we traveled by car for two months seeing most of the continental United States. For me, the trip was not pleasant, as Dad constantly picked fights with me.

Despite my father's evident disapproval, my creative urges did not stop. In grade school I made a puppet of Snow White and played the part in a school puppet play (yup, my voice hadn't yet changed). Later, at age nine, my mother took me to Radio City Music Hall. I fell in love with that stage. Mom had Dad make a puppet version, complete with arched proscenium. I loved the stage he created but hated the curtain, because even at that young age I knew the fabric didn't drape properly. If only my parents could have seen the future, when later in life I would be designing shows for that venue and setting the trim of that marvelous curtain.

Soon, though, I learned there was a stigma against boys who enjoyed such activities. I hid my creative inclinations and shifted over to designing the scenery for proms, plays, and other school events. Back then, I was somewhat socially withdrawn. It didn't help that I had a stubby front tooth that made me feel unattractive. To cover the tooth, I developed a lopsided smile that must have looked odd. Fortunately, Dr. Hammond, our family dentist, understood my embarrassment and agreed to make a cap for that tooth. Knowing our family's financial situation, he charged just $50, since cosmetic improvements were not in the family budget. Suddenly I had a smile and became more extroverted.

As a teenager, I joined the Boy Scouts and did well with that organization. In truth, they provided the paternal guidance I never got from my father. Motivated by my mother, who was ambitious for me (and because I lacked any encouragement, or love, from my father), I became highly competitive. Trying to please her and to win his love and respect, I worked hard with the Boy Scouts and before turning 16, earned an Eagle Scout award. I remember being afraid to mention to my parents I was to receive the award on a Friday, as my parents always played cards on Fridays. My fear was they wouldn't come to the awards ceremony: They would opt for cards over me. But as it turned out, they did in fact attend. One has to keep in mind that my foreign-born parents didn't understand America's customs or way of life. Sad to say, but they had no way of knowing that getting that award was such an honor and terribly important to me. All my life I've been highly motivated to succeed, and back then I worked hard for their recognition.

Eventually, at 16 years of age, I worked at my Boy Scout camp where I was in charge of nine other boys and ran the Craft Lodge. I also became the Lodge Chief of the Order of the Arrow, a prestigious national organization. My lodge had more than 2,000 members, adults as well as teenagers. It was quite an honor for a 16 year old to be its president, an accomplishment that added a great deal to my self-confidence. Around that time, I was also selected by the American Legion to represent my high school at the Boy's State countrywide jamboree, which taught young men how politics and government work. It was also in my sixteenth year that my father announced to me in a loud voice at a large Thanksgiving dinner, "You were an accident."

"Serves you right for being careless!" I quickly replied in an even louder voice and kept right on eating. He never crossed me again. Not long after, a Scout master pulled me aside and pointed out that my sarcastic attitude, which really was a defense mechanism, wasn't very appealing. I had a real mouth on me at the time. I took the man's comment to heart, as I wanted desperately to be liked, and tried to curtail that flippant part of my personality. It's sad that the Boy Scouts of America (BSA) was, until recently, homophobic, as the BSA did a great deal of good for me. I would have loved to have been a financial supporter of the Scouts, but I could never contribute to any organization that was anti-gay.

Looking back, I can see that Mom did everything possible to treat her sons equally, to educate us and open doors for us. The fact that dad clearly never wanted children, and that he only agreed to have James to please my mother, hurt. Remember, I was "an accident." Sadly, he resented James and me because of the attention we received from Mom. However, he was certainly a hard worker, and while we were never wealthy, we always felt secure financially.

Typically, after a full day at a job site, Dad would often come home with his hands cracked and bleeding from working outdoors in the cold. He never complained. After our six o'clock dinner, he would go out to his workshop in the garage and work on various free-lance carpentry jobs to earn extra money for the family. I truly believe I got my drive and strong work ethic from the example set by both my mother and my father. It was a wonderful gift.

Chapter 2

Summer of '48

The year was 1948, and the hit song was "You Made Me Love You"–at least it was for Grace, the beautiful lady who lived next door to us. Oh, how I loved to hear her sing that song in her clear, sweet, anxious voice! I was nine years old that summer. The leaves had just turned from a brilliant lime green to that lush rich green that signaled our passport out of school. We were free–free to sit in the grape arbor playing cards and monopoly. I can still hear Grace's voice drifting over our backyard: "You made me love you, I didn't wanna do it, I didn't wanna do it," as she cracked her gum.

She was, as my brother put it, "Some dish!" Not sure if he really understood what those words meant, but looking back I'd say he was right. Grace was a real bombshell of a package. A Petty Girl come to life. Even at that time, I knew what a Petty Girl was because Mr. Bailey, who owned the local barbershop and cut my hair, was a big fan of that look. In fact, he had what appeared to be a zillion Petty pinups plastered all over the walls of his shop: drawings of beautiful ladies in skimpy, skin-tight outfits, often transparent, coyly posing behind balloons, or busy in activities such as walking cute little dogs, peeking around a small heart-shaped box of Valentine's Day candy, relaxing sexily in a negligee while speaking on the phone, and so forth. Real teasers. The pinups were everywhere except on the wall behind the barbershop chairs where the many-colored hair tonics in bottles stood row upon row on shelves at attention, perhaps in response to the enticing pictures. But what would I know about such things?

At the end of my haircut Mr. Bailey would always spin me around with a flourish, sometimes one and a half times if I was lucky, and order me to "Pick ya poison," and once again I'd pick out one of the hair tonics–maybe the green one with hopes that it would turn my hair green. Ha! No such luck. It was too much to wish for and, after all, changes sadly weren't easy to come by in my life then. Little did I know that years later when I was designing a set for Cyndi Lauper on the American Music Awards, I would be visiting her in her dressing room and she would have her hairdresser put a bright red streak in my hair (more to come on this).

Now, Grace was something you didn't want to change. She was a strawberry blonde with a face full of sunshine and laughter to match. As one of the men down the street said, "She sure knows how to fill a sweater!" She did, in fact, wear mostly tight sweaters and shorts that showed off her amazing legs. She was something else.

We seldom saw Grace's husband, John. He worked as a delivery man for UPS in one of those big brown trucks that have never seemed to change over the decades. All I knew was that the neighbors used to say, "John must not deliver 'cause Grace sure was lookin' around for something else."

Grace and John lived in the house next to ours in Valley Stream, N.Y., on Ocean Avenue, which was in fact the county line between Queens and Nassau. The two counties seemed oceans apart as they could never agree on the right time to repair their side of the avenue, and the road was usually in great disrepair on one side and in good shape on the other. As time passed, the quality of the road switched sides. Same thing with some of the people on my block. Things changed slowly but over time sometimes for the better, sometimes not. But then again, sometimes change happened fast! Strangely enough, Grace and John's home was exactly like our house, right down to the last detail. Even the color of the tiles in the bathrooms was identical, but while everything was the same it was also the opposite, as Grace and John's home was the mirror image of ours.

Our nearly identical houses were close to each other, and we as families were close too. Grace and John and my parents helped each other out on a regular basis with whatever needs popped up or when things didn't go right. I remember that Grace had a friend from out of town named Nancy. This friend was a rather plain woman, which was unusual as Grace tended, with the exception of my mother, to make friends with just men and children. One day Grace came running over to our place all excited. It seemed that Nancy, who had been severely depressed, had locked herself in the front bedroom and wouldn't answer when Grace asked if she was all right. No amount of banging on the locked door would produce a response, so Grace had come to Mom for help. Now Mom was a very smart and resourceful woman, and there was a small pitched roof over the front door, which went part way up and under the window to that front bedroom, and so Mom climbed up on it and gained access through that window. I heard years later that apparently Mom had found Nancy passed out on the floor with a bottle of sleeping pills still clutched in her frail hand. An ambulance was called, and Nancy was taken away to the hospital. That night Grace was too shaken or afraid to visit her friend, so Mom went in her place. Nancy looked wearily at Mom and said, "Why didn't you let me do it?" That fall we heard that Nancy had tried again, and this time no one had stopped her.

I loved our house and Grace's mirrored version of it. Our homes were maybe 30 or 35 feet apart and were separated by a five foot tall hedge that ran down the length of the two properties. In the middle of the hedge was a beautifully arched opening, which allowed for a well-worn path to connect the stoops to our two kitchen doors and our two families. Our lives were joined in a special way. Both families shared laughter and at times, like with Nancy, tears.

It was arranged that Grace would teach my brother and me to play the piano. We both hated it. Forget about practicing. Whenever James heard that Grace was on her way to our place, he would be desperate to avoid her and her usual request that he play a piece or two for her. James and I had been taught to climb out our bedroom window and slide down the roof if ever there was an emergency such as a fire, and having to play for Grace was in James's eyes a real emergency, so whenever he heard that Grace was downstairs, out the window he'd go.

Grace had better luck teaching us to play cards, mostly Go Fish and Canasta, which I loved. Pinochle and poker were the games preferred by adults, and Mom and Dad played with John and Grace religiously every Friday night after dinner with a highball or two. These Friday night sessions alternated between the two houses and seemed to be the only occasions when my father relaxed and enjoyed himself. On nights when the grownups met at our house, James and I would lie on our beds and hear much laughter coming from below. John was always on the quiet side, but Dad seemed to be more animated than normal during those card games. After they played, they would share one of mom's terrific homemade cakes.

Grace never baked. However, one could always count on some cool lemonade and store-bought cookies over at her place on a hot day, or any day for that matter. There she would be sitting in the kitchen in her tight sweater, reading a movie magazine, licking her index finger as she eagerly turned each page, and singing or humming "You made me love you, I didn't wanna do it..." It made for a wonderful, fun-filled summer of playing cards and Monopoly and sometimes making kites. Mom insisted that James and I make our own kites. No store-bought kites for us. Ours often didn't fly, but when they did it was a terrific feeling of success. We didn't have a lot of money in those days but, as I said, Mom was very resourceful. When we were younger, on rainy days, we drew horse heads on cardboard, cut them out and nailed them to dad's sawhorses, then added shredded rags for tails to the other end. Presto, we had our own steeds, which we rode for hours.

All was golden that summer. The war was over, and everything looked so hopeful and promising. Our family friend Charlie was back from the war with stories of India that thrilled us, and no scars, physical or emotional to frighten us. He did, however, show us a 15-inch Kukri knife he had brought home. It had a huge, curved blade and also a small four-inch blade attached at the hilt, which Charlie said was used to cut off the victim's ear as a souvenir. Exciting and frightening. He and his wife, Eldora, had joined in the Friday night card sessions, and even more laughter could be heard drifting up on the summer nights from below, or from Grace's house over to ours.

All was perfect, all so peaceful. But a new war was brewing. One morning I awoke to the sound of digging. I looked out my bedroom window to see Mom standing on our kitchen stoop, both arms folded sternly across her chest while she supervised. And there was Dad, digging up parts of the hedge at the far end of the yard and transplanting them into the opening in the hedge that connected the two houses. Symbolically as well as physically, he was cutting off Grace from our family. Evidently, Grace's roving eye had landed on Dad. Over the sound of Dad's shoveling, I could hear Grace's sweet voice, now tinged with sadness: "You made me love you, I didn't wanna do it, I didn't wanna do it."

Chapter 3

Fran Dwyer: An Example to Live By

In the autumn of 1955, I was about to have one of those pivotal moments in life. As I started my junior year at Wantagh High School on Long Island, I was 16 and shy, a dreamer and a misfit. Mrs. Dwyer was to be my English teacher for the next two years, and what a teacher she was. In her mid-20s, she was beautiful in a Maria Callas sort of way, with a posture that showed great confidence and assurance, and a smile that made her even more beautiful. And she smiled often.

On Day One, Mrs. Dwyer took us teenagers and went to work. First, she had the class read some poems, including one that talked about a ship yearning for the sea yet afraid of it. We discussed how life has to be grabbed and explored no matter how frightening it might appear at first. How I related to that! I desperately wanted a future yet had no insight or self-confidence. Mrs. Dwyer's class was the beginning of a metamorphosis for me. From then on, I just took a deep breath and dove into life.

At the time, I had never owned a book of my own—never really ventured into a bookstore. Mrs. Dwyer encouraged me to read, and soon I discovered a shop that sold used books for 50 cents a copy. That was the start of what was to become my own library. Next, she taught us the importance of staying informed about the world around us. In class we read the *New York Times* each morning, something I still do.

But the most telling lesson–the one that changed my life–came that winter when she took our class to the theatre. "Li'l Abner," my first Broadway show, was a life-altering experience. I remember looking down from my balcony seat at the voluptuous Tina Louise playing Appassionata von Climax and saying to a buddy sitting next to me, "That's the business for me!" (Years later, when I was working with Alvin Colt, the costume designer who had won a Tony for "Li'l Abner," he came to our house for dinner. I told him about my teenage impression of Miss Louise's breasts, to which he replied, "You have no idea how hard I had to work to give her those breasts!")

After seeing this Broadway show, a small voice inside me said, "Wouldn't it be wonderful to design scenery?" A dream was born. From then on, I started going into Manhattan every Friday night on the Long Island Railroad and heading to Broadway. While on the train, I would take the *Times* theatre section, circle the three shows I wished to see, One, Two, and Three, in order of preference, and try for standing room, which was $5.50 in those days–a real stretch for my financial resources but worth every penny. If I couldn't get into my first choice, I'd go on to my second choice. Rarely would I have to settle for my third. Imagine seeing the original "West Side Story" with Chita Rivera, Larry Kert, and Carol Lawrence; Franco Zeffirelli's "Romeo and Juliet"; the original "Music Man" with Robert Preston and Barbara Cook; and Julie Andrews and Rex Harrison in "My Fair Lady." Later, a friend got me backstage at "My Fair Lady," and I sat on the scenic steps off stage left to watch the show until the steps were rolled on stage for the song "On the Street Where You Live." It was thrilling to be backstage. Little did I know that eventually I would get to work with Carol, Chita, and Julie. It was a wonderful, illuminating time for me and a pivotal period in my development, all thanks to Mrs. Dwyer.

One day Mrs. Dwyer came into class with a smile even broader than usual. Naturally, the class was curious to know what was up. Finally, we got her to tell us: It was her anniversary. She was so clearly in love with her husband. I'll never forget her saying, "Don't let anyone ever tell you marriage is 50–50. It is 100 percent and 100 percent."

Years passed. I was a three-time Emmy winner as a production designer in Hollywood and living with John Harrington, my partner of 23 years. I was no longer the shy kid with a dream but a successful man with much to be thankful for. As I reflected on my good fortune, I thought of Mrs. Dwyer and the seismic change she had brought to my life. And so I decided to find her, thank her, and let her know the results of her teachings.

Tracking her down was not easy. She had changed schools and was now a guidance counselor, but finally, in that pre-Internet era, I got a letter to her through someone who knew where she worked. After a lively correspondence it was agreed that she and her husband, Marty, would join John and me for dinner when they came to Los Angeles to visit their daughter, who happened to live in Malibu. This new adult friendship blossomed with visits both in LA and back East, whenever I worked there. Once during dinner at the Dwyers' home on Long Island, I told the story of Mrs. Dwyer (now Fran to me) coming into class beaming and commenting on marriage being 100 percent–100 percent. I watched as she and Marty reached across the table, held hands, and sighed their agreement. On another trip back East, I was designing sets for the Miss America pageant, and Fran and Marty came down to Atlantic City for a visit. I don't know who smiled more, Fran or me, as I walked her down the Miss America runway before one of the rehearsals. I saw this wonderful, sophisticated lady flash her trademark smile.

At one point I discovered that Fran and Marty would be celebrating their 40th anniversary around the time that John and I would be honoring our 25th, so we decided to celebrate together–in India. Now, India was not an easy country to explore, and there were many hiccups along the route–flights canceled and hotels that were pre-paid and suddenly had no available rooms. Nonetheless, it was a great adventure. Just to see a flock of green parrots fly in front of the Taj Mahal as the sun came up and to share the moment with Fran, well, it doesn't get any better.

To our delight Fran and Marty also enjoyed a cocktail or two, which helped mellow out any frustrations that India might have to offer. One morning we had an early wake-up call, as we were to go out on the Ganges and see all the religious ablutions as the sun rose. While it was still dark, there was a knock on our hotel door, and when I answered it, there stood Fran, my favorite high school English teacher, handing me a bottle of bourbon. "You left this in my room last night." I smiled and thought, "Anything is possible." If anyone had told me when I was 16 years old that Mrs. Dwyer would one day hand me a bourbon bottle (in India no less), I would have laughed in disbelief. I was so glad that I had made the effort to contact her and to try in some small way to give back at least a little of what she had given me.

Years later, Fran developed breast cancer and had a double mastectomy. Did she mourn the loss? At the time there was a book out about overcoming similar crises entitled, *First You Cry*. Not Fran. She said, "Nonsense. You just strap on another pair." Then, a number of years after that, Fran and Marty were at a cocktail party at our apartment in New York City. Fran and I were having a nice chat when Marty came over and suggested that Fran explain about a new health issue she had. With a smile more subdued than usual, she said uncomfortably, "I have a health issue but I can't remember what it is." It turned out she was in the early stages of Alzheimer's.

The last time I saw Fran she was on another journey and was slipping away from us all. There sat this marvelous woman playing with a tea bag in an empty cup and not relating to anyone in the room. While the scene was extremely sad and distressing, I had the comfort of knowing I had made the effort to thank her for all she had done for me. Fran Dwyer is now gone but lives on in countless life journeys of students like me.

Chapter 4

Sex

In 1955 at the age of 16, I discovered two things about myself. First, I realized I was attracted to men, an attraction that was dangerous and best kept hidden. Second, I found out I had a clever side. One day I bought a male physique magazine at a local candy store and saw an advertisement in the back for photos from France of hot male body builders. Intriguing! What was a 16-year-old kid to do to get some of those?

My solution: I went to the local post office, rented a mailbox, and sent off a money order to buy some of those photos. Several weeks later an envelope from France landed in my rented box. Inside were photos of some very sexy guys. Too bad they were wearing posing straps (also known as G-strings). However, the photos came with a warning in English not to get the images wet, which, of course, I quickly did. I sprinted to the bathroom, locked the door, and ran the photos under the faucet. Surprise, surprise, the posing straps washed off, and I now had a collection of handsome guys totally nude. *Very* exciting for a young man who was just awakening sexually. With the photos came a new awareness that I could manipulate "the system" and get things my way. All I needed to do was be bold and clever.

That same year I had my first gay experience, with a classmate named Gary. It felt like a natural fit for me, but I was afraid of the stigma and continued to hide my inclinations. At one point I found myself alone in the boy's locker room with one of the class bullies. After he made some smart, sarcastic reference to my being gay, I responded, "What's the matter– don't you have someone better to bully?" He backed off. At times it was handy to have this emerging assertive personality.

At 19 I met Howard, my 32-year-old English teacher at Hofstra College. Howard seduced me– or did I seduce him? I've never been sure. Unimportant. Anyway, just like Hester Prynne, I earned a scarlet "A" that year in English. It was a remarkable period in the drama department at Hofstra, which had not yet become a university. Among the students in the department were Madeline Kahn, Lainie Kazan, Elizabeth Wilson (who was later in the Broadway show "Waiting in the Wings," for which I designed the sets), Francis Ford Coppola, and Susan Sullivan. I tried acting and had a small part in the college's production of "Romeo and Juliet." After just 10 performances I realized I had absolutely no talent as an actor. I wasn't just bad. I was awful.

Howard and I started seeing each other, going to Broadway and Off Broadway shows, and had sex for the next three years. This was a formative period for me. With Howard I learned how to relate to another person intellectually and sexually. I could not have had a kinder, better teacher. Thanks to Howard, I saw many impressive productions including Judy Garland's legendary concert at Carnegie Hall, which remains the greatest performance I have ever seen, and I've seen thousands of them. Much later I was hired to do the sets for her daughter's show on Broadway, "Liza's at the Palace." Interesting how things come around.

Howard was smart and a remarkably talented writer, a dazzling man who lacked ambition. He was also terrified of failure. This was an important lesson for me, as I realized that one had to overcome the fear of failure if one was to accomplish anything in life. My attempts to help Howard came to nothing, which was deeply disappointing. I would gladly have been a supportive partner, like the one Noel Coward reportedly had. But I was too inexperienced to know how to fulfill that need. Eventually we broke up, since I had lost any sense of having a future with him. Also, not having ever had sex with a woman, I was curious to see what that was all about. I do believe it is rare for a person to be 100-percent gay or straight. And I was certainly attracted to women–but to what degree? That was something I needed to explore.

After earning my Bachelor of Arts degree from Hofstra, I took a job teaching art at a very rough junior high school on Long Island. Around this time, when I began wondering what it would be like to have sex with a woman, Carol (as I will call her) was a gorgeous fellow teacher at the same school and had just had a fight with her boyfriend. I got lucky on the rebound. The experience was just okay. In truth I had no experience in this area and most likely didn't do much to replace the boyfriend.

Nonetheless, I continued to date women. One summer while working in theatre stock my roommate and I connected with two chorus girls who came through with a production of "A Funny Thing Happened on the Way to the Forum." They were typical good-looking dancer types, and we enjoyed them onstage and off. I was still a novice when it came to women, and I remember the woman I was bedding saying how refreshing it was to be with a guy who just did it "the old-fashioned way." Needless to say, that intrigued me.

At one point, just before I entered Yale, I was frequently dating a very attractive lady I met while pursuing some extra courses in commercial design. One night I took her out in my tiny MG convertible. The car was so small that in the midst of some heavy necking I got my foot stuck in the glove compartment. When the time came to drive her home, I had a devil of a time getting both feet back on the floor. Later on, I came close to getting engaged to that same lady. This happened after I had entered Yale and was called off when the lady in question decided I was more devoted to my studies than to her. She handed me an ultimatum: "Choose Yale or me." Without hesitation I chose Yale, as I intended to make something of my life, and Yale was the ticket. Without a doubt, being married to a woman would have made life easier, but I could not have handled a steady date and Yale at the same time. Besides, partners of the same sex were beginning to be a better fit for me. Hey, men were more fun, much less complicated, and easier to understand. We seemed to share equal rhythms. Confirmation came the summer of '66 when I was working at the John Drew Theatre in East Hampton, N.Y. One day on my afternoon off I decided to explore a gay beach. While there, I met a handsome guy. We went back to his place and had a wonderful time. I knew from then on that my orientation in life would be just gay, and I remember being unbelievably happy and at peace with the idea, and with myself.

In my third year at Yale, when it became clear I would graduate, I felt a new confidence and continued to think about dating men. In the beginning of my time at Yale the work was so intense and demanding that any form of social life was out of the question. I had to focus all my attention on making it through that three-year Master's program. However, toward the end of year three, my mind did begin to wander. Just to be sure I was on the right track, I consulted the school psychiatrist to see if I could change my orientation and fit into "normal" life better.

"Why would you want to do that?" the psychiatrist asked. "You're okay as you are." My decision had been validated. And a good thing, too, because just after graduation I would meet the man with whom I would spend the next 50 years. Looking back, I can see that I was in the right place, at the right time. What luck to be headed toward the television business, where being gay was generally well accepted. Over the years, most people, both men and women, accepted me for what I was. It was also my good fortune to be reasonably pleasant to look at. While never handsome, I was good looking enough that I could enter a room for a meeting, flash a smile, and have a fairly easy time charming people. I felt sorry for the really handsome gay men I knew. For them, as with many beautiful women, a feeling of genuine loss comes with the passage of time. I watched as many great-looking gay men of my acquaintance in Hollywood and New York began to feel invisible to younger gay men and ended up beneath the surgeon's knife having facelifts, etc. As I've grown older, my looks have certainly faded, and while I miss having that physical advantage, the loss has been well compensated by the wonderful men in my life.

Chapter 5

Army Time

One day my good friend Dawna O'Brien came up with the statement that she thought there ought to be a draft. "Everyone should serve for two years," she said. Her thinking is that many of the social problems we have here in the States with our young people would not exist if everyone was given the discipline of Army life. Many of our problems, she pointed out, are non-existent or greatly diminished in countries like Israel where there's a draft. When she finished speaking, something snapped in me and I started yelling that it was fine for her to say, "All kids should be drafted," but she had no idea what she was suggesting. For me, going into the Army had been comparable to being sent to jail. I topped off my outburst by storming out of the room. I *hated* the Army. And yet, did Dawna have a point?

In 1962, before I went to Yale, I joined the Army. In many ways it was a dividing line in my life. I was 23 years old, teaching art in a tough junior high school on Long Island, and not the happiest of men. I had been raised by a mother who expected great things from her sons, but I had yet to find my niche in life. Up to this point I was drifting in what seemed to me to be a black-and-white world, no color, comparable to a ship without a rudder on a gray day.

I had graduated from Hofstra with a split major in psychology and economics, with enough art courses to qualify to teach art in public school but was unhappy with the whole lot. The window of opportunity appeared to be closing quickly.

I had a vague dream of working in the theatre but knew the chance of success in that area was close to zero. To get a better salary at the junior high where I was teaching, I started attending New York University in the evenings, but with the exception of one course in set designing, the work was turning out to be rather useless. Was I wasting my time? Did I really need a Master of Fine Arts degree just to get a slightly better salary? On top of all this unhappiness was the threat of the draft. I knew that quite possibly I could end up in Vietnam, and dead, just like my good friend Dick Harper, who had been the Lodge Chief in the Boy Scouts the year after me. And so, to avoid being drafted for two years, I entered the Army's reserve program, which meant six months of active duty and seven years in the reserves. I was in for a shock. Even in that smaller dosage, the Army felt like prison.

At Fort Dix in New Jersey, where I was sent for basic training, we were issued khaki uniforms, housed in khaki barracks, and got three colorless meals a day. My unhappiness was now complete. In the Army, one is told what to do, what to wear, what to eat, and when to sleep, then forced to participate in pointless activities for endless hours. The only benefit I could see was that, thanks to the Army, I now knew I needed only seven hours of sleep a night. I had always thought I had to have a minimum of eight hours every night. (That extra hour of awake time was to serve me well in years to come.) Just to be sure we didn't get any ideas about breaking out of our gray existence, we were told to mail back the civilian clothing we had worn onto the base. As I packed up my bright-red sweater, I realized that one of the reasons I was so depressed had to do with the near-total lack of color. I actually made a promise to myself that when I got out, I would add as much color to my life as I could.

After basic training I was sent to Kentucky, where after extensive tests at Fort Knox it was determined I might make a good tank driver. What a laugh. The joke was on both me and on the Army. The classes were boring, as well as insulting, as was the treatment of the trainees. Let's face it: It's all downhill when your day starts at 5 a.m. and by 5:30 a.m. everyone is lined up in front of the barracks and the sergeant yells out, "Good morning, gentlemens!" Not "gentlemen" but "*gentlemens*," to which we were to reply, "Good morning, Sergeant!" I found myself encouraging the company to respond, "Good morning, *Sergeants*!" He never caught on.

I soon learned there was a bit of Sergeant Bilko in me– the smart-ass and manipulating non-com played by Phil Silvers in the 1955 television series "The Phil Silvers Show." I discovered I could play his game in spades. The first stunt I pulled off was to get out of class by telling the sergeant I had a toothache and needed to see the dentist. I made an appointment for 9 a.m. thereby escaping the first class at 8 a.m. I finished with the dentist around 10:30 but didn't sign out. Instead, I went to the library and read until about 2 p.m., then returned to the dentist's office and signed out. When I finally rejoined the company (too late for afternoon classes), the sergeant(s) barked at me, demanding to know what had taken me so long. I replied, "Well, I waited an hour and a half [believable], then they took some X-rays, which took close to an hour to get the results. But there wasn't any film in the X-ray machine [totally believable], so I didn't get out until just now." This scam was a good one and worked more than once. No one thought to check up on me. And I was very convincing.

One time our company, along with about 10 other companies, was going to be entertained by some visiting performers. Our company commander was upset with us because we had messed up our drill. In fact, we were the lowest rated group on the base, so to get even with us, he delayed our arrival to the rec hall. By the time we got there, all the seats were taken. Up since 5 a.m., we were dead on our feet and would be forced to stand for the show. Well, at this point I knew the Army never questioned anyone who acts with authority, so I turned to my buddy Pete and said, "Follow me." We marched into the officers' lounge and I said, "That one, and that one," pointing to two large chairs. Pete and I took the chairs and marched down the audience aisle, set the chairs by the first row, and seated ourselves comfortably. That night I learned the key to Army life was this: Make your move and then *blend in*.

Tank driving wasn't quite so easy to pull off. This is probably not surprising, since no one really taught me how to drive one of those massive pieces of equipment –not even how to start it. Those vehicles were so big and heavy they took two gallons of gas to go a single mile. It also wasn't very reassuring to know that once the enemy hit you with an armor-piercing shell, the projectile would have just enough power to get inside the tank but not enough to go all the way through. Instead, it would ricochet around the inside of the tank an average of 300 to 500 times. Not a happy thought.

The week they taught the company to drive the damn tanks I had been laid up in bed with a legitimate cold. When I got well enough to return to class, it was time to take the driving test. I was informed that if I didn't pass, I would be held back and have to go through the whole training program again, all six weeks' worth. No way for this soldier! I decided to fake it.

The test was a riot. They drove us to a mud flat, an area that had been used for years to test tank drivers. The "flat" was in fact a series of steep, muddy hills and water-filled gullies. We trainees were divided into two-man teams, with each team assigned to a tank and a sergeant who tested us. The sergeant rode up on top, his body sticking halfway out of the hatch while we remained down in the guts of the tank in the driving compartment (or whatever it was called–I never did find out). We were therefore out of the sergeant's line of sight and could communicate only over a faulty set of headphones.

I convinced my partner to go first, so starting up the tank was no problem, as he had done the work for me. The test, however, was terrifying. The inside of the tank was painted bright white, and buttons, gauges, and dials were everywhere. Riding in one of those things was like being inside an active washing machine without the water. What would happen if I got jostled into some of those damn buttons and switches? Well, my partner finally finished his drive and passed the test. Now it was my turn. I told him to leave the motor running and carefully climbed into the driver's seat (not easy), put on the headphones, and waited to fail. Through the static I heard the sergeant say, "Move out, soldier, and go up that hill in front of you." So there I was, sitting in this huge machine with its tiny steering wheel, maybe 11 inches across, kind of like one of those in a bumper car. It was freezing outside, but my hands were sweating profusely. "Please don't let me screw up," I prayed.

Suddenly, the sergeant said through the headphones, "Now shift into high," to which I thought, What the hell. I took my foot off the gas for a second and then floored it. "Very smooth!" the sergeant commented. Hey, maybe this wasn't so hard after all. "Now go up the hill to the top," was his next command. Well, the hill was a good 40 to 50 feet high and very slippery with all that mud, so I had no choice but to inch my way up. When I arrived at the top, I heard again lots of static before the sergeant's voice came through. "Step on it!" Which, of course, was what I did.

Well, we barreled down that hill and hit the water at the bottom so hard we tore halfway up the hill on the other side. It turned out that the static part had contained this warning: "Go down the hill *very* slowly, and when you get to the bottom step on it." That's what all the other tanks did, and they hit the water so slowly that the water and mud from the recent rains poured into their tanks. Everything inside the other tanks was covered with mud. Those poor drivers had to spend hours in the freezing weather cleaning up their tanks, but our tank was its usual spotless white. How lucky can you get? The best part: I passed!

That was the upside. The next day at the tank motor pool I was told to go inside one of the tanks and rev up the engine. No big deal–the engine was already running, so all I had to do was step on the accelerator. The only problem was no one had told me that if you were in neutral and you moved the wheel, the tank would move as well. By just nudging the wheel one way or the other, the tank would pivot. Not knowing this, I grabbed the wheel to ease myself into the tight driver's area, and without even stepping on the gas the whole tank pivoted–and I nearly smashed a guy who was standing between my tank and the tank parked next to me. I don't know who was more frightened. No wonder so many noncombatants get hurt in the Army. We were both lucky that day.

One day I wasn't so lucky. Because I hated the way the Army wasted men's minds, I always carried a book in my hip pocket. The first night I spent in the Army at least half the company was in their bunks reading, and another 15 to 20 percent were writing letters. My last night I was the only one reading. It was a real battle to stay mentally active. In very short order, the Army becomes mind-numbing. Anyway, one day my luck ran out, or so it seemed, when we had a surprise inspection. Now, our footlockers provided our only storage space; items inside the locker had a *specific* location, with no room remaining for anything else. Well, the sergeant conducting the inspection was not happy with this soldier when he took a look at my footlocker and saw 17 books, some paperwork, and drafting equipment. This was certainly not up to Army regulations, which clearly stated that all our gear must be Army-issued. The company commander overheard the ruckus and asked what the problem was. The sergeant pointed to my locker and did a three-minute meltdown. After he was through, the company commander asked why I had so many books. I told him that I was studying for my Masters at NYU and also taking a mail-order drafting course. To my relief, the commander said to the sergeant, "Leave him alone." Close call, that one.

And so, with this company commander as my new ally, I had two new schemes brewing. Knowing how competitive the companies were, I smoothed things over with the sergeant by mentioning that in real life (he never got the humor of that) I was a graphic artist, and if he ever needed any posters or signs, I would be glad to help. Well, three hours later I had my own office with an assistant of my choice (my buddy Pete). Together we cranked out signs in a warm, cozy room while the rest of the company dealt with their tanks in the freezing cold.

The best was yet to come. One day I made an appointment to see the company commander. Remembering his respect for my desire to study, I told him that if I could get released six weeks early, I could make it back to NYU in time to start my last semester. Wonder of wonders, he agreed, and that is how I did only 18 weeks of active duty rather than the minimum of 24.

But the Army has a way of getting even. After my release from active duty, I was required to attend reserve meetings that took place one night a week for seven years. Eventually, when my evening work as a set designer made attendance impossible, I was able to get those weekly meetings waived. Well, one day, toward the end of my seven-year Army obligation, the phone rang. It was the Army calling from Washington. Because I had not been attending my reserve meetings, the brass had reconsidered and decided I would be called back to active duty. Remember, this was the middle of the Vietnam War. Frightening news, to say the least. I tried to explain that I had been excused because of my work, but the guy on the other end of the line could not have cared less. Thinking quickly, I asked if the Army would allow me to complete my reserve obligation in lieu of active-duty orders. I would look for a unit in Los Angeles, where I was then living. "After all," I said, "I have only three months to go to complete the seven year obligation." Reluctantly, he agreed. But I couldn't find a unit willing to take me in! The amount of paperwork just wasn't worth the short period I would be with them. I finally found a reserve unit in Long Beach in need of a graphic designer that agreed to admit me. But my relief was short lived.

The next morning, I got another phone call from Washington. This time it was the brass saying they had changed their minds–again. Orders for active duty would be issued immediately. Just as I was taking this in, my other phone line rang. I put Washington on hold and picked up the second line. It was the Long Beach unit calling to say they had changed *their* minds and decided not to accept me. Again, thinking quickly, I said, "But I've already told Washington you accepted me," to which the Long Beach guy reluctantly responded, "Well, okay, we'll take you." I then reconnected with Washington and said, "But I found a unit in Long Beach that has already started the paperwork to take me in," to which the Washington guy muttered with a sigh, "Oh, well. Okay."

Three months later I was out of the Army for good. I was also finished with my Sergeant Bilko personality. Or was I? Following my active-duty period, I had continued my studies at NYU, taking courses in set design from Patton Campbell. With Mr. Campbell's encouragement and help, I had quit teaching and entered the three-year Masters program at Yale Drama School. Because of the Army I became motivated to move forward. My unfocussed self had been left behind, and the survival skills I had learned in the Army helped me flourish in the highly competitive atmosphere at Yale.

Would I recommend a draft? Absolutely not. No one should be forced to live even briefly without freedom. But for me, military service became a springboard to positive growth. It can happen. And it did.

Chapter 6

Yale

Wh#en Patton Campbell, a Broadway designer and my theatre design instructor at NYU, suggested I apply to the Yale School of Drama, I thought the idea was utterly ludicrous. First of all, I didn't think I was smart enough to go to Yale. Moreover, I had only enough money to see me through a year and a half of the three-year program. Nonetheless, at Mr. Campbell's insistence, I sent in an application that included three of my best set designs. In short order I was turned down. Refusing to accept this, Mr. Campbell contacted Donald Oenslager, a highly regarded Broadway designer and head of Yale's set-design department. Mr. Oenslager had a policy of never interviewing applicants, but he made an exception for me. Three days later I received an acceptance letter. It was the happiest moment of my life up to that point.

And so, in 1964, I entered the Yale School of Drama. I was 25 years old and saw this as my one and only chance to build the basis for a special life as a set designer. I was excited but also terrified. The odds of making it through Yale were not good. The school typically accepted 17 set design students and expelled half of them at the end of the first year. Many simply did not come up to Yale's seemingly impossible standards. The school dropped still more students at the end of the second year. The year before I arrived, only two design students had made it through the three-year program. Terrifying, but in truth the school's policy had a great deal to do with the reality that students would later face in the world of set designing.

We design students were expected to arrive at Donald Oenslager's class every Thursday with the completed assignment for that week. Fondly referred to as "The O," this formidable instructor called everyone by his or her last name until they made it through the second year.

Our first assignment didn't seem too tough. We had a play assigned to us that required just one simple box set. As the year progressed, however, the plays required two, then three sets. At the end of the third year, we were expected to design the sets for a play with up to six different looks each week. This was a brilliant approach because it taught us to design fast and to give each show a unified style. However, this meant that every Wednesday night I would sit down at my drawing board and try to nail the assignment in a way that demonstrated I was good enough to belong in the school and shouldn't be dropped. (For years I had bad feelings about Wednesday nights.) Great pressure, and great training.

One of many lessons I learned from The O was that great design has its origins in the world around us. It extends beyond one's work and into how one lives one's life. This basic principle was brought home the day The O passed around a box of seashells. He told us to select a shell and take it home, then use it to develop a set for "Ring Around the Moon," a Christopher Fry play. From that single shell I learned to see shape, color, and texture everywhere I looked. From then on my eyes were greedy to find new design ideas to incorporate into my assignments, and into my life.

Typically, after an hour of student presentations, we'd have an hour-long lecture from The O on the history of theatre and how it affected the evolution of set designing. I took notes using a shorthand system I had developed during my undergraduate days, but the lectures were so tedious and we students were so exhausted that staying awake became a challenge. Luckily, there were no written exams about the content of the lectures. My worry was that The O would think I was not paying attention and therefore not worth his time. I finally came up with a solution: I discovered that as long as I was eating, I wouldn't fall asleep, so I started to bring a small box of raisins to class and slowly would eat one raisin every three minutes or so during the lecture. Problem solved.

Other tricks to survival included the use of decoys to camouflage a less than stellar effort. For instance, a flashy mat with a bit of gold-tape edging was enough of a distraction to cover a rendering that might be great in concept but mediocre in execution. Another trick included the use of found objects in my presentations. I learned to keep an eye open for second-hand objects that cost little but could help me get my ideas across. An old phonograph, for example, purchased for $3 at a secondhand junk shop, became a revolving turntable in one of my sets.

Exhaustion was the norm, as I never slept on Wednesday nights. Often, I would come into class with my renderings still wet with fresh paint and my hands shaking from a night of too much coffee and fear of failure. Once, in a daze of creative exhaustion, I was cutting a mat to frame one of my sketches and the mat knife slipped; suddenly, the tip of my thumb was gone. I looked at the wound in disbelief and slowly realized there was indeed cause for concern. I dragged myself to the medical center and got patched up. That day my renderings were not beautifully matted, and so I told the class the saga of my mishap and got everyone laughing. The saga broke the tension and got me through the presentation. That day I learned a useful lesson: Humor helps.

Coming up with impressive sets week after week was only half of it. We students also had to learn to pitch our work, and to make the pitch in a limited amount of time. The training worked: I learned to sell my concepts quickly and succinctly, a skill useful at Yale and beyond. By the time I entered the business I could sell almost any idea to some of the biggest producers in Hollywood or New York.

During my time at Yale, I augmented my training in other ways. Realizing I knew little about the acting world, I approached the head of the acting department, a dynamic teacher named Connie Welsh, and asked if I could audit some of her classes. She graciously agreed to allow me to observe. I also enrolled in Lester Polakov's Studio and Forum of Stage Design in New York City. Every Sunday morning for a year I took the train to the city to study scene painting. In those days one was expected to take the United Scenic Artists Union exam to be able to work as a scenic artist. We practiced our painting by standing over a canvas that was stretched flat on the floor. Using long bamboo sticks fitted with brushes, we would dip our stick-brushes into premixed cans of paint and try to create the desired image. Not easy. In fact, when I finally took the union exam, I failed by two points (later, the rules were relaxed). Since I didn't need to join the Scenic Artists Union in Los Angeles, this wasn't a problem. The insight I gained into the limits and possibilities of scene painting proved useful for years to come and made the class well worth the effort.

Even though money was always tight I still managed to see Broadway shows. My system worked like this: After selecting a show, I would find out the exact time of that show's intermission, then arrive with a rolled-up Playbill in my hand and my coat over my arm. I'd walk into the theatre, grab an empty seat, and see the second act. Did I feel guilty? Well, yes, but I swore that someday I would pay back the theatre community by contributing my talents to it. And I did. One time I augmented my funds by following the advice of some Yale undergrads, who clued me in to a TV game show called "Password." There was a way to get onto the show and win some much-needed cash. I phoned the number the undergrads gave me, made an appointment for an interview, dressed in my best preppy outfit, and took the train into New York. Apparently, they liked me, because they asked if I could be on the show the next day. I stayed overnight at the YMCA and the following day won $400 and a cheap typewriter. What did I do with the money? I bought a TV set and a used tuxedo. Shades of things to come.

Once, after designing a set for "Amahl and the Night Visitors," Mr. Oenslager, who rarely handed out compliments, said, "That's a wonderful sky, Klausen, but why did you paint it in green?" I replied with much embarrassment that the sky was green because I didn't have any blue paint. Unlike some of the more affluent students, I simply couldn't afford the needed supplies. I never forgot that moment. Later, when I had reached a degree of success, I set up a small scholarship fund at Yale for students who needed money for supplies.

When I finished my first year at Yale in the spring of 1965, the exhaustion was total. Would I be asked back by Mr. Oenslager for the second year? Finally, the day came when the names of those who had made it through Year One were posted on the bulletin board in the Drama School green room. When I saw that my name was included on the list of students who would be asked back for Year Two, the relief was indescribable. It was after reading that announcement that my roommate told me that the previous year two students from other parts of the university had committed suicide by jumping off the library roof after learning they had failed. In fact, several of my classmates didn't make the cut, but did well nonetheless. Carrie Fishbein Robbins became a costume designer and ended up doing numerous Broadway and Off Broadway shows, and Michael David became the co-founder of the producing company Dodger Theatricals and produced "Jersey Boys," "Into the Woods," and many other Broadway shows.

When I arrived at my parents' home in Wantagh, N.Y. for a short break, I crashed on the chaise on the lanai and read one James Bond book a day for seven days. To my parents' credit they never said a word. It had been a tough time, since in truth I had no backup plan. Well, actually, I had one possible option and that was Frank Beven, head of the costume department, who liked me a lot. He and I wore the same size jacket. The only difference was that his wardrobe was sensational and mine was threadbare. When Frank discovered we shared the same size, my wardrobe suddenly improved. As I said, Frank liked me, and possibly I could have transferred over to the costume department if The O had dropped me from the program. But who knows?

After the visit with my parents, it was time to get to work. This meant going up to Fitchburg, Mass., to apprentice in summer stock at the Lake Whalom Playhouse. Summer stock turned out to be different from Yale in that the stress factor was practically nil. The hours, however, were roughly the same: 70 or so per week, with no days off.

In those days, what would happen in summer stock was a star would arrive and perform in a play or musical for a week and then move on to make room for the next star. The producer at the Whalom Playhouse was Guy Palmerton, and he had been putting on shows there since 1934. He was the boss and in reality, we were his servants. The theatre was an outdoor affair, with a roof and open sides, and a capacity of about 900 spectators. We put on eight performances every week.

Each star had a manager who would arrive at the site ahead of the performer and lay out what was needed for that particular production. So if, say, Dorothy Lamour was the star that week, the manager would make sure that the sets and all props were ready and waiting and her personal needs were met before she arrived. A set designer and lighting designer on staff at the theatre ensured that all the technical details were carried out. As part of the house staff, I helped build the sets and secure the props. This was all fascinating to me and great, if exhausting, fun.

I remember seeing Miss Lamour arrive on a rainy day, looking like a middle-aged housewife; she really should have a shopping cart in front of her, I thought. No glamour to that gal. The next day, when we were to open her show, which was a musical called "Du Barry Was a Lady," I heard with a certain horror that she was going to open the show in her trademark sarong, worn in her movies with Bing Crosby and Bob Hope.

She was then 51, overweight, and quite frankly dumpy. "How embarrassing to have to go out on stage looking like that," I thought. Well, I was so wrong. Standing in the wings as the overture played, I watched a magical transformation. As her posture straightened, I saw pounds and years fall away, and when the curtain went up there stood a glamorous, 30ish-looking woman and a star. Years later we met again when she appeared in a TV special I designed called "Night of 100 Stars." I mentioned to her that I had worked on "Du Barry Was a Lady" when she had come through Guy Palmerton's theatre. She tapped me on the shoulder and said, "You must have been a *baaaaby!*" I loved it. I loved *her*.

Other stars who came through the Whalom included Martha Raye, who I remember talked for hours to the guys on the crew in the communal kitchen about how important the Vietnam War was and how we should all go there. I wondered afterward how many men she talked into enlisting and how many of them might have lost their lives.

Then there was Jayne Mansfield, who appeared in "Nature's Way." I was allowed to design the living room set needed for her show. I decided to make the walls all white, not realizing the need to "tech down" (darken) the white so the walls wouldn't flare and outshine the star. I'm happy to say Miss Mansfield held her own, even against that overly bright background. She was terrific in the show. She was also very kind to everyone. At the time, she was six and a half months pregnant, but as tired as she must have been after doing the show, she agreed one evening to have her photo taken individually with each kid on the crew as well as the local actors on the show. Snobbishly, I turned down the chance to have my photo taken with her. Stupid. How I would like to have that photo now! Sad to say, not long after, on June 29, 1967, at the age of 34, she was killed in an awful auto accident along with two other people who were with her in the front seat. Her three children in the back seat were seriously hurt but survived. Terrible.

Another star to come through the Whalom was Maureen O'Sullivan. She appeared in a one-set show that included a fully operational kitchen. I remember her going through the set when she first arrived at the theatre and looking at the rubberized dish drainer next to the sink and asking what it was. I was fascinated that anyone could be so ignorant as to how a kitchen operated. Hey, she started out as Jane in the Tarzan movies, so how was she to know?

The Whalom had its oddities, including a kiddy train that started at a nearby mini amusement park and traveled around the theatre. On some occasions, we'd be in a serious moment in a play and suddenly we'd hear the train chugging and even tooting its whistle as it made its way around the theatre. Crazy.

Working at the Whalom Playhouse also had its dangerous side. One day backstage I had to climb a 30 foot wooden ladder that extended from the ground floor to the scenic loft. When I had barely reached the top, the last two rungs broke loose and I started falling back while still clutching the two loose rungs in my hands. Luckily, my head and shoulders had made it through the opening into the loft. I narrowly escaped falling down the full 30 feet and landing on the pinrail (a series of vertical rods used for tying off flying set pieces). It turned out that the producer's dumb nephew knew the ladder was falling apart but hadn't bothered to tell anyone.

On the silly side, there was a curved road that went up between the theatre and the barn where we painted the scenic drops. One day, just for the hell of it, one of the apprentices took a prop toilet, put it in the middle of the road, dropped his pants, sat on the john, and opened up a newspaper, as if he were reading while relieving himself. Well, the first car to come around the bend almost ran off the road at the sight.

On another occasion, I was recruited to man one of the follow spots. As the audience arrived, I decided to get a feel for the follow spot and aimed it around the theatre. I hit a nest of bats. The bats responded to the heat of the light and started flying toward me. Quickly, I moved the spot and stayed safely away from that area of the theatre for the rest of the night.

And so I had a summer rich with experiences that helped round out my education in theatre. The Whalom Playhouse, alas, went dark in 1968 and burned to the ground in 1975. End of an era.

During the following school year, I continued to learn my craft. In the second and third years, the weekly assignments grew larger, with more and more scenes and with the design solutions even more challenging. Again, no sleep on Wednesday nights for this guy. But my financial situation improved the last year and a half when Yale picked up my expenses. They also gave me housing at Jonathan Edwards, one of the undergraduate colleges. I loved the dining room, an immense wonder of peg-and-groove paneling constructed without a single nail. The students who used it were required to wear ties and jackets. Most of us followed the rules, but there were always a few exceptions who rebelled by wearing their ties and jackets but with just T-shirts. Dinner was the one time they could let off steam. I remember seeing a pat of butter fly past and land on that fabulous wood paneling. Food fights were tolerated, as the pressure on the kids was tremendous. While being a bit older and under my own set of pressures, I didn't resort to getting into the fights, but in retrospect participation might have provided relief. The college also lent me a studio, which was a terrific help. Strangely, the room turned out to be too big. I discovered that I worked best in small spaces where my creative energies could be better focused.

On top of the heavy classwork, I occasionally worked on shows outside of the drama school. One job was designing the sets for the charming Gershwin musical "Oh, Kaye!" which we did in the Jonathan Edwards School dining room. Fun and challenging. There was also a show called "The Revenger's Tragedy" at a nearby college, for which I was set, lighting, and costume designer. A ridiculous amount of work. A dark Elizabethan drama, the play proved to be an even greater challenge than "Oh, Kaye!" At least eight different looks were required. My scenic treatment featured distinct backdrops for every scene. Each 24-foot-tall by 36-foot-wide drop of muslin was covered with large sheets of crumpled aluminum foil coated with orange shellac and watered-down black paint, which made a richly textured surface that to my knowledge had never been done before. In addition to being affordable, it was highly reflective, taking the light in the most amazing ways. Various details like windows were worked into each drop and helped define the location and atmosphere. Years later I used this same technique for an Academy Awards set when we staged a song from "The Omen" in the Best Song category. All my life as a designer I would try out new materials, and if the results were good, I would use them in ever more elaborate ways.

The lighting for "The Revenger's Tragedy" was really bad as I had little training in that area (and as that nest of bats could testify). I did my best, which was not good at all. One reviewer entitled his piece, "The Lighting Designer's Revenge." Enough said about that. The costumes, however, were another matter. I did some really nice work and enjoyed that part of the assignment the most, not least because there were a number of attractive young men in the play who were required to wear cod pieces (decorative fabric pads used in Elizabethan times to cover and protect the groin area). I was, of course, responsible for the look of each costume—including its cod piece. One day, one of the wardrobe ladies came to me and said that she and her fellow seamstresses were uncomfortable fitting the young actors with the cod pieces. Would I take over the fittings? *Hmmm.*

The summer between my second and final years at Yale I was able to secure a job at the John Drew Theatre at Guild Hall in East Hampton, N.Y., only this time I was the full-fledged set designer. Again, we presented a new show every week, which, of course, was great training for what I would ultimately face when my career took off. In 1968, the John Drew was a charming 381-seat theater with a festive, circus-like atmosphere that featured a striped tent for a ceiling and a chandelier of internally lit "balloons." The crew, myself included, lived in a ramshackle house next door. We'd grab as much sleep and fun as we could and work like crazy the rest of the time, building scenery, painting drops, and running eight performances a week as each new production came through. That summer I designed sets for 10 shows, including "The Fantasticks" and "Gypsy." We worked hard and learned a great deal.

One night after the show my roommate and I were entertaining a few ladies in the ugly house where we lived next door to the theatre, and I very nearly burned the place down. To make the atmosphere sexier, I had placed a towel over one of the living room lamps. After a while we headed up to our bedroom with the ladies. Sometime later I went downstairs to get a drink of water and discovered the towel on the lamp had caught fire and was burning merrily away near some highly flammable upholstered furniture. The old place was a tinderbox. Quickly I pulled the towel off the lamp, tossed it into the kitchen sink, doused it with water, and threw the towel away. No one was wiser. Close call, that one.

The John Drew Theatre catered to the ritzy East Hampton crowd, so occasionally I would get invited to someone's extraordinary home. One house featured a roof made from the dome of an old metal silo. What that would sound like in a rainstorm was anybody's guess. Another property turned out to be the family summer home of a theatre intern who invited me to a party. When I arrived, a good 60 cars were parked on the lawn in front of the 30-room house, which was perched on a bluff overlooking Long Island Sound. The place was stunning–pure Gatsby. All the walls on the first floor were white, as was the carpeting, with accents of lime, lemon, and raspberry provided by French chairs and sofas, plus a number of three-foot-tall bouquets of zinnias in the same colors. To this day I don't know if those flowers were real or the best fakes I have ever seen. That house was beyond sensational and made a great impression on me. The boathouse contained three vessels varying in size from a small powerboat to a large yacht. The daughter was clearly interested in dating me, but she was way too young and way out of my social league. And so, after a terrific summer, I returned to Yale for my third and final year. I worked hard but felt less pressure now that I knew the chances of being kicked out were slim. During the year, my knowledge and skills grew, as did my knowledge of life. I was ready to face the world and design my future.

Chapter 7

John

After graduating from Yale in 1967, my plan had been to go to Japan on a Fulbright scholarship and write a book on Japanese set design. But first I had to learn to speak Japanese. This proved impossible, owing to my workload at Yale as well as my lack of language-learning skills. But good fortune came my way once again when Yale offered me a Bates Travel Fellowship, sponsored by Jonathan Edwards College, which was a six week, all-expenses-paid trip to Europe to study theatre. So, at 28 years of age, off I went in search of adventure. For guidance, I relied on the bestseller *Europe on $5 a Day*, plus, I have to say, the kindness of strangers.

Quite truthfully, I chose to start my adventure in Amsterdam because after my largely celibate time at Yale, I wanted some action, and Amsterdam had a reputation for being a great place for making sexual connections. Looking back, this was one of the wisest decisions I ever made.

On my first night in Amsterdam, on a bridge over the Singel Canal, I met John Harrington, my future partner of 50 years. The encounter was completely accidental. John would later refer to our meeting as "a cheap street pickup." I was wandering around the area when a guy stopped John and asked directions to a certain canal. John didn't have a clue but stopped me and asked if I could help. Being fair haired I guess I kind of looked like a native of the area.

58

"Well," I said, "I don't know. I'm new in town and looking for a place to go myself." The stranger replied, "There's a bar around the corner, but you wouldn't be interested. There are just guys there." John got a mischievous smile on his impish face and said, "Honey, that's just what he's looking for." He grabbed my arm, and as we walked toward the bar, I looked back at the guy and he was scratching his head in confusion. John was not confused at all.

After a beer at that bar, which, of course, turned out to be a neighborhood gay bar, John and I decided to go to his hotel room (remember, these were the carefree days before AIDS). As we were walking out the door, I said to John, "We haven't paid for our beers." "That's okay," John replied. "The bartender and I have been tricking [having sex] all week. I'm sure he'll cover the cost of the beer." Well, we spent the night together and I discovered him to be intelligent, masculine, sexy, and *fun*. The next morning, John flew back to Los Angeles, where he was a highly regarded negative-film cutter at Paramount Studios. And that, it appeared, was the end of that. With John in LA and me in New York City, what chance was there of any kind of a relationship?

I had a wonderful time the next six weeks making up for not having had much of a social life at Yale. I met some great people, saw a lot of Amsterdam, Paris, and London, and even was offered the London production of Arthur Miller's "After the Fall," which unfortunately never moved forward. At the end of my trip, I arrived back in Manhattan and settled into my Upper West Side apartment, a place so tiny that if I had put a bed in the "bedroom" there wouldn't have been any floorspace on which to walk (I slept on a convertible sofa in the living room). Barely an hour after I walked through the door, the phone rang. I answered, and a voice on the other end of the line said, "Hi. It's me." At first I had no idea who "me" was, but quickly John and I became reacquainted–at least on the telephone.

John was impressed with my Yale degree and clearly smitten. He started putting on the pressure for us to get together. As the film cutter on the original Paramount shows "Star Trek," "Laverne and Shirley," "The Brady Bunch," "The Magician," and "Mission: Impossible," he was at the top of his field. He also had his own company, through which he cut all of Lucille Ball's shows after she completed "I Love Lucy." He was very well off, a bit compulsive, and wanted to send me an air ticket to Los Angeles. To me this was not acceptable, as I had no emotional attachment to him, and I would not accept a gift like that from someone who was basically a stranger. But we continued to phone back and forth, and eventually I got to know this interesting man.

Work in New York was scarce, but I managed to get an interview with a top set designer who will remain nameless. Attractive and gay, he was looking for someone to be his assistant on "Androcles and the Lion," a television version of the George Bernard Shaw play, starring Noel Coward. He asked that we meet at the New York Athletic Club, and when I arrived, he suggested we take a swim. Naively I said I was sorry, but I hadn't brought a suit, to which he replied, "We don't wear suits here." Uh, oh, I thought. I know where this is going. When he made his move, I said, "You know, if I didn't want to work for you, I would have you in bed so fast it would make your head spin. But more than anything I want to work for you, since I know I would learn so much from you." I got the job.

The taping of the show, at a huge Brooklyn studio, was an eye opener for me. The director was the remarkable Joe Layton, with whom I would work years later designing sets for the national tours of Kenny Rogers, Julio Iglesias, and Lionel Richie. Over the following six weeks, I did, indeed, learn a great deal. I also saw what pressure there could be on the talent. In one scene, Noel Coward, dressed as an emperor, was required to sing a complicated song while descending a grand staircase into a court filled with dozens of extras all costumed in period Roman attire. Richard Rogers had written the music and lyrics. I have to say, in my limited experience, the lyrics were pretty lame, and poor Mr. Coward had to deliver these nonsensical verses without tripping over his toga on the staircase. Well, he kept flubbing his lines, and we did take after take as the clock ticked away and the producer's money flew out the window. Finally, the star made it down the stairs with the lyrics intact, only to have Norman Wisdom, the other star of the show, flub the next line. The cast groaned. We thought the scene was blown but, thanks to editing, the director was able to save the number.

Years later, at a Hollywood brunch, I ran into the set designer who had hired me and took him aside to tell him how much it had meant to me to be introduced into television art production by him. He appeared to have had a fair amount to drink. In a slurred voice he said to me, "Oh, Ray, you're so full of shit!" Sad that he couldn't believe he had helped me and that I honestly appreciated what he had done, the encounter made me glad I had never developed a drinking problem, nor a drug problem for that matter. My attitude was, life is so exciting, who needs outside stimulation? Besides, I always wanted to be in control.

After "Androcles and the Lion" I found it extremely difficult to get work in New York, so I signed on to do two out of three shows in repertory at the Loretto Hilton Theatre in St. Louis, Mo. As my two shows were winding down, a rumor reached me that the producer wanted me to do the third show as well. So, I started my own rumor: I was going to Los Angeles for meetings. I was deliberately vague about this but indicated I would be interested in doing the third show. At that time, I didn't have an agent, and so I had to push myself forward and negotiate my own deals. Normally, this is not easy but, hey, I had just made it through Yale and was full of confidence–and, sorry to say, full of myself as well.

Brazenly, when asked to do the third show, I requested they pay me my usual per-show fee and throw in my airfare to LA and back. After all, anyone they hired would most likely need to fly in from one coast or another. They agreed. Now I would have three shows under my belt: "The Miser," "The Caucasian Chalk Circle," and "The Time of Your Life." But more importantly, I had free airfare to see John, and off I went. We had a great 10-day visit at the end of which I knew I really liked him. (Later, John confessed that, not wanting to take any chances, he had invited only unattractive friends to the party he threw for me on that visit. No fool, that man.)

After my visit to LA and at the conclusion of my work in St. Louis, I returned to New York where job opportunities, especially for newcomers, remained scarce. I was close to starving. Christmas was very lean that year. I had no money for gifts for my family, and my scrawny Christmas tree was a pathetic 20 inches tall. I decorated it with matchbooks covered in tinfoil and made to look like little holiday presents and with lights repurposed from one of my old Yale set models. Clearly,

I had to return to Los Angeles where there was work in television. The question was, how could I get out to the West Coast without taking the air ticket John wanted to send me? My solution: a bank loan. I went to Bankers Trust, held up my Yale diploma, and said, "I'm going places and I need $500 to get there." To my delight, they lent me the money, which I dutifully paid back as soon as I could. I then phoned John and announced that I liked him but did not love him, and that I was coming to LA. "Let's see what happens," I said. Three days later, on January 5, 1968, I boarded a plane and never looked back.

When I left New York for Los Angeles, the move was a total gamble. My career had not yet started, and I didn't even have a job lined up. Two weeks later I got a job painting scenery at CBS. But how was I to get to work, since I didn't have a car? Despite his own busy schedule, John drove me to and from the studio, and anyplace else I needed or wanted to go. In those early years I was impressed by his willingness to welcome me into his life. He was so caring and giving. Plus, as mentioned, he was great fun. Watching him in action helped me lighten up. When I entered John's life, I was unsophisticated and a bit of a loner. I simply didn't know how to socialize and had little or no sense of humor. That didn't last long. Thanks to John, I grew to find a lot of humor in life and to enjoy life's experiences. These were wonderful gifts he gave me and much more valuable than the free airplane ticket he had originally offered.

John enjoyed making people laugh. One time when we were out with friends everyone wanted to know why he started using a straw to drink his cocktails. "My doctor says I need to stay away from alcohol," he explained. Not infrequently he had me in stitches. I would be talking to my mother on the phone (back then we spoke every weekend) when John, stripped down to his birthday suit, would appear in the room and perform a few pirouettes before vanishing as suddenly as he had arrived. Of course, Mom would want to know what was going on–why was I laughing so hysterically? Flustered, I would try to explain my way out of the situation.

John was also one of the most amazing-looking men I had ever seen. A bit taller than me, he had a great build and a face filled with smiles that could charm anyone, along with twinkling, intelligent brown eyes. His hair was a beautiful, shiny dark brown, almost black. The lopsided grin that captivated everyone featured a snaggle tooth, which he tried to convince a dentist friend to fix; the friend wisely dissuaded him. That tooth was key to his roguish look and changing it would have been a grave mistake. What a contrast to my own childhood dental issues!

John's face exuded humor and laughter and hinted at the imp inside. He certainly didn't look his age. In fact, one day early on we were sitting in Nickodell's, an "in" place to have lunch for the Paramount crowd, when the subject of age came up. John asked, "By the way, how old are you?" "Twenty-eight," I answered. "How old are *you*?" "Forty-two," came the startling response. I was dumbfounded and dropped my spoon in surprise, with a loud *clang* on the Formica tabletop.

His work in those days was demanding and involved long hours and thousands upon thousands of feet of film that needed to be precisely cut and spliced together to form a finished reel of film that could be duplicated and eventually released for distribution. He was proud that over the many years he was in charge of negative-film cutting at Paramount he had lost only one piece of film, which was found two years later in a storage can in some remote part of his office.

John Spencer Harrington, Jr., grew up in Perth Amboy, N.J. At age 17 he left high school in his senior year to join the Navy, to fight in the Second World War. His father, John Sr., had advised his son to avoid the Army. Memories of his own experiences in the muddy trenches of the First World War were still painfully fresh. He shared some of these experiences with us during occasional visits at his Hollywood home and at ours. One story, in particular, impressed us greatly. One night in France, John Sr. had been asleep in his tent when he awoke with the urgent need to visit the latrine. He decided against making the long trek down the endless rows of tents and instead decided to squat outside his own abode. While there, he heard a thud. The next morning he saw with a certain horror that a German bomb had, indeed, landed just a few feet from where he had been doing his business the night before. Fortunately, the bomb had been a dud. If it hadn't been, John Jr. would never have existed and I might well have not written this book.

To escape the mud and bombs, John Sr. came up with a plan. He would take his government-issued handgun and shoot a toe off his foot. The gun had never been fired, and when he pulled the trigger, it exploded and blew off three of his fingers. Alas, his trigger finger remained intact, so the Army just patched him up and put him back into action. No, John Sr. was not a fan of the Army.

After John Jr. finished his stint in the Navy, he worked for a while in New York City as a photographer but eventually found himself in Hollywood, where John Sr. was a producer

65

in the movie business. He asked his father to help him get a job. His father refused. John Sr. hated nepotism, as it was rampant in those days, and still is. Finally, John pleaded, "Please, Pop, make one call, just one," and John Sr. relented. The result was that John landed a job in one of the labs, and the rest was just a matter of time before he made his way up to the top. He ran a challenging department in a smart but friendly way. He was much admired, and his staff of nine loved him. John Harrington, I soon found out, was no push-over. He was strong willed, self-made, and smart. *Very* smart. He also had a volatile personality. The first time he blew up I was upset for two weeks. As the outbursts continued over the months and years, the amount of time I was upset lessened to a week, then three days, etc. Toward the last part of our relationship, I'd just roll with the outbursts, knowing they would soon blow over and usually were meaningless.

Once on a trip to Europe, John bought a new Jaguar XKE and soon came to the conclusion that the automobile was "a piece of crap." A convertible, the car leaked when it rained. We ultimately had to stop at a drugstore and buy some surgical tape so that we could secure the roof to the windshield to keep the water out. Control buttons on the dash would pop off and fly across the front seat for no reason at all. Finally, John lost it. We had just checked in to a smart hotel in Rotterdam, and I was up in the fourth-floor room when I heard John swearing up a storm down in the parking lot. I looked out the window and saw that he had reached the limits of his patience and was attempting to push the Jaguar into a nearby canal. Luckily, I was able to stop him. John's strong personality posed a problem for me early on, as it was clear that if I didn't stand my ground, his persona would run right over me. The result was that I developed a strong character of my own, one of John's many gifts to me.

The bottom line was that John was an enigma, someone who was never boring. Over the 50 years we were together, his personality didn't change much. From the beginning, what I saw was what I got. The only hobby he explored in any depth was cooking. There he had a keen interest, going so far as to purchase a stove that had once belonged to James Beard. I, on the other hand, evolved over that half-century, as I was always learning something new and trying to improve. It's amazing that we were able to stay connected the way we did, but then we were fiercely devoted to each other and had certain rules that helped to keep us together, such as this: It's okay to go to bed mad at each other, but it isn't okay to go to sleep mad. In short, we never carried over any unhappiness to the next day. We also operated under the motto, "If there's no solution, there's no problem." Clearly, we both wanted our relationship to work and were committed to creating an environment in which we could both thrive professionally and socially. Never once did we consider or discuss that maybe we should have a trial separation or leave each other. I deeply loved this special man.

We had a method to defuse conflicts we called "The Map of Florida." John recalled a time years before when he had observed a mother and her eight-year-old, who was hell on wheels. They were in a supermarket, and the kid was pulling items off the shelves, opening boxes of cereal, and leaving a trail of food along the aisles. All this time the mother would say, "Billy, please don't do that," or "No, no, Billy. Don't do that," to which the kid would respond by doing more of the same in an effort to further provoke his mother. Finally, the little monster pushed his mother over the edge, and she said, "Okay, Billy. When your father gets home, you're going to see the map of Florida!" Billy froze, then clutched his mother's skirt in terror. John never did find out what, exactly, the "map of Florida" was, but for us it became a code for "Danger! Do not cross this line!" If a disagreement ever escalated into the danger zone, one of us would say, "Map of Florida," and the discussion would have to stop then and there. Sometimes "Map of Florida" had to be invoked more than once, but the system worked, preventing us from ever letting a discussion get to the point of hurting the other person.

One time John did something that really upset me–I can't even remember what it was, which shows how unimportant it must have been. I stormed out of the house, slamming the front door good and hard and stayed away for three hours. When I came home, he was so upset and concerned about me that I realized I had crossed a line and had best never do that again.

In 2005 my 65th birthday was approaching, and I knew exactly what I wanted: to get married to John. So, I decided to ask him if he would, as a birthday gift, marry me. To my delight, he readily agreed. Gay marriages were very new in those days, and Massachusetts was the only state that condoned such a union. We drove north from New York City, where we were then living, to Cape Cod. On May 29th we were joined at our friend Ward Cromer's waterfront summer house in North Truro. A beautiful setting and event, and the best birthday gift I ever received. But now every time I had a birthday, I had to get John an anniversary gift! A great joke on me, with a price I was delighted to pay.

When I look back to the time I started living with John, each year, right up to the last, was better than the one that preceded it. Together we created the environment we aimed for in which we could thrive. With such a committed, joyful partner, how could life be anything less than a grand adventure?

Chapter 8

Hollywood

Within two weeks of my arrival in California in 1968, I was painting scenery at the CBS Scenic Paint Shop in Los Angeles. My job was devoid of any sort of glamour. Every morning while it was still dark, John would drive me to the studio on Beverly Boulevard, then pick me up after the sun had set. With the exception of the occasional day off, I never experienced "sunny California." I did get to work on shows for Carol Burnett, the Smothers Brothers, and others, but rarely saw these celebrities, as I was painting the scenic pieces in the shop before the sets were rolled onto the assigned stage to be graced by the appropriate star or stars. Mostly, I used a paint called Dino White, named after a grayed-down white that didn't flare when the cameras viewed it under the strong studio lighting. If only I had known about this color when I did that set for Jayne Mansfield!

In addition to painting scenery in the CBS Scenic Paint Shop, I did some work at the Mark Taper Forum, mostly small experimental theatre projects with miniscule budgets. One show, "The Dance Next Door," required a set that consisted of an entire house–kitchen, living room, bedroom, the works. I solved the low-budget problem by going to a company that produced large paper billboards and talking them into giving me some old, unused examples, which I cut up and wallpapered onto sheets of plywood so they could stand up. I then cut those out to create the various parts of the set. All this was done in John's driveway. When it came time to put up the

70

set, I strapped all the parts onto the roof of an old Plymouth I had bought for $50 and drove them down to the theatre. The car had been souped up with a large Chevy V-8 engine and was powerful! I guess I was speeding a bit, because the set nearly blew off onto the middle of the freeway. But I got it there, and the scenery worked great. This was a big success for me. Years later, Gordon Davidson, who headed up the Mark Taper Forum, saw "Big River," a show I had done gratis for the Deaf West Theatre out in the Valley, and moved it to the Taper. Eventually "Big River" went on to Broadway, then toured nationally and internationally (more on "Big River" to come). The lesson here is, as a designer you've got to be willing to work hard and often for little or no pay with the hope that a show might possibly move forward.

Back then, in the late '60s, I was determined to once again make my own luck. While I was working as a scenic artist at CBS, I researched all the set designers who came through the shop. Jim Trittipo, or Trit, as he was called, was the best in the business. He designed most of the top shows and had won three Emmy awards for excellence in set designing. Clearly, he was the one I should work for. With a little more research, I found out that John and I, along with Trit, had a mutual friend named Bob Lawrimore. John and I soon talked Bob into having a dinner party for us that would include Trit. The evening of the party, I made sure to sit next to Trit and did my best to charm him. Finally, I mentioned that I would love to show him my portfolio, to which he replied, "I don't look at portfolios." Now, two things that every designer who graduated from Yale took away from that school were an exceptional portfolio and an aggressive approach to getting work. "Not for a job," I responded, "just for your opinion."

This was one of the few times I out and out lied, as I wanted and needed to work for Trit. Reluctantly, he agreed to see my portfolio.

One week later, Hub Braden, Trit's assistant of seven years, fell while hiking on a glacier and ended up in a hospital for four months. I filled in for Hub and remained with Trit for two years. In those days, unless you worked for a specific studio like ABC, CBS, or NBC, a designer and his assistants typically worked freelance from show to show. Most designers had agents who helped them get work, negotiated their contracts, and hopefully got as good a fee as possible. Assistants like me were hired without contract by the set designer, and so, for the sake of future jobs, it was essential to be the best assistant possible.

Soon I was working on two of Trit's television specials, one featuring Frank Sinatra and the other a showcase for Mitzi Gaynor (a terrific and rather bawdy gal loved by all), plus the television variety show "The Hollywood Palace," noteworthy for the quality of its talent which included Jimmy Durante, Groucho Marx, the Rolling Stones (in their first television appearance), Diana Ross, and Ethel Waters. "The Hollywood Palace" ran for six years and was a great place for making valuable contacts. I remember seeing the then-matronly Miss Waters looking at the super-slim Miss Ross and saying, "*Humph*, in my day they called me String Bean." Kind of like saying, "Your day will come, honey."

It was while working on "The Hollywood Palace" that I got my first chance to design for television. Trit let me create a set for Diana Ross and the Supremes. By now, I knew a few people in the business, including Michael Travis, who in addition to designing the costumes for "Laugh In" and Elvis, did the wardrobe for Diana Ross and the Supremes. I was able to go to Michael's studio and get a swatch of the beautifully beaded fabric (a sea-green that ombred, or blended, into silver) from which the group's gowns would be made. Using the swatch as the key to the color and texture of my set, I created an Art Nouveau butterfly, 20 feet wide by 16 feet tall, that was flown in on cables. Additionally, very thin cables that the camera could not see operated the wings. When the cables were pulled, the butterfly opened, revealing the ladies, who walked down toward the audience. The butterfly then closed up behind them. Very theatrical, as well as successful. Trit seemed pleased with my first solo performance, and I was thrilled.

One day I found Trit laughing as only he could. He had just returned from a meeting with Joan Crawford, who was to be the next week's hostess on "The Hollywood Palace." The meeting had taken place at Miss Crawford's home. We had all heard about what a cleanliness nut she was, and so Trit had been amused to see that she had indeed covered everything in clear plastic–*everything*, right down to the toss pillows on her sofa.

Another week, the producers had decided to book the 20-year-old Bernadette Peters on the "Palace." She was performing in "Dames at Sea" up in San Francisco, so a group of us, including John, flew up to see this new star in the making. She was adorable and marvelous. Little did I know our paths would cross again when I designed the 54th Annual Academy Awards in 1982.

Because Trit was a great designer but not a good artist, he asked me to do the renderings of his designs for the upcoming Frank Sinatra special. Trit's designs were wonderfully innovative but difficult to put on paper, as they were to be made mostly from sheets of reflective brown Plexiglas–something that had never been done before. The sets were technically sophisticated and hard to illustrate, but I was able to draw them, thanks to the skills I had learned at Yale.

When the day came to show Mr. Sinatra the set designs, Trit announced that he couldn't attend; the meeting conflicted with the installation of the scenery for the Mitzi Gaynor special. Would I go to the Sinatra meeting in his place? "Yes," I replied, delighted but nervous. Off I went to Mr. Sinatra's bungalow on the Warner Bros. lot. It was exciting to drive up to the studio gate, give your name to the guard, and then be ushered onto the studio lot. Numerous large stages filled the Warner's lot, each with a large number emblazoned on its side. A wide assortment of extraordinary cars and animals soon came into view, along with actors in exotic costumes. All exciting and head-turning for me. I located Mr. Sinatra's bungalow, walked in, and announced myself. Almost immediately I was presented to the man himself. Meeting Frank Sinatra in person was intimidating, to say the least, but he could not have been more charming or gracious. As I was introduced to him, he shook my hand and said how glad he was that I was part of the team on the show. There I was, fresh out of school, still very young and inexperienced, and in a meeting not just with the producer and director but with Mr. Sinatra himself!

During that meeting, per Mr. Sinatra's instructions, all incoming calls were held except for two: One was clearly from a family member (daughter Nancy, I think). All we could hear was Frank saying, "Now, we haven't been together as a family for a long time. We need to have dinner together. I don't care how busy everyone is." Impressive. The second call was from one of Sinatra's men. After a long period during which Sinatra listened intently, he finally said, "Now listen. He's a friend, a good friend. He's in trouble now, and anything, and I mean *anything*, he needs from us is his for the asking." Now that, I thought, was really amazing. What a terrific guy to have as a friend. But then, at what price?

I have seldom met a man as charming as Frank Sinatra, but that first impression was destroyed the day before the taping when he disappeared. He simply could not be located. The morning of the scheduled taping (actually, two tapings: an afternoon "dress" performance, to be used just as backup, would precede the evening "air show"), he was finally found passed out in a parking lot, sleeping off a bender. As luck would have it, the first act in the show took place in a bachelor's pad, so the fact that his famous blue eyes looked like two blueberries floating in tomato juice kind of fit for the party animal he was portraying.

The second act was forgettable. I simply don't remember it. The third and final act was a concert with a 60-piece orchestra. It was a big deal. In the first taping (the "dress" performance), Mr. Sinatra was sensational. In fact, the afternoon "dress" performance had gone so well that he decided he would simply not bother with the evening air show. This second taping was the one that really mattered. It had a VIP audience who had been waiting patiently for hours in line outside the studio. He didn't care that he had stiffed his fans and frustrated his producers. I could never understand how, with all his gifts and charm, he could be so irresponsible and thoughtless toward the show and the people who worked so hard to make him look good.

Trit, my new boss, was amazing in his own right but in a much different way. Towering at a good six feet three inches, Trit, like Frank, was a charmer with a great sense of humor and a zest for life. Working for him was an invaluable learning experience, and I was a sponge in those days. It was all so intimidating at first. Not only was Trit a brilliant designer, he was also a terrific cook. We worked out of his house on Gloaming Way, off of Coldwater Canyon in Beverly Hills, and one day he made a small, excellent lunch for the two of us. After many compliments from me, he started making lunch every day, thereby giving us a much-needed break from the intense work we were doing. These lunches also gave me time to get to know him better and to understand how he had become such a success. From Trit I learned that one had to be almost obsessed with one's work to be the best. He taught me to pay attention to every detail no matter how small, and to put your own personality and experience into the creative process. This was the only way to make a design uniquely your own.

One of the projects we were working on during this time was an Andy Williams Christmas special that featured his then-wife, Claudine Longet, and their two young children in a fantasy holiday house designed by Trit. Notorious for going over budget, Trit decided to show me how to spend money. When he couldn't find the exact red and white striped wallpaper he wanted for the entry hall, we bought rolls and rolls of expensive red satin ribbon from a display house called Moskatels in downtown Los Angeles. The scenic crew at NBC then laboriously attached the ribbon to the foyer walls. At Moskatels we bought out the store. Well, not really, but we did fill up 14 shopping carts with whatever we wanted to make

Andy's "house" as Christmassy and as special as possible. It was great fun.

At one point, the script called for the family to put on a little musical show in the living room. Trit decided that the perfect curtain for the "show" would be made out of a red and white quilt. Since none could be found that suited Trit, we had the scenic department paint the pattern we wanted on a white quilt. It looked great, but God knows how much it cost. My frugal background saved me from adopting such habits. Instinctively, I knew that fiscal restraint was important. I believe that part of my success later on was due to my reputation for sticking to a budget. By the time I hit my stride as an independent set designer, money had become much tighter, and exceeding a show's budget was no longer tolerated. To keep my record of fiscal restraint pristine, I once sent Scott Webley, who owned Showbiz, the drapery rental company, a personal check for seven dollars so that I could say that my multi-million dollar budget had come in exactly on budget.

His attitude toward money notwithstanding, Trit was an easy man to respect and admire. But he had problems. Drinking was at the top of the list. He loved to work hard and party– *hard*. Part of my job, it turned out, was to be sure he ate properly when on the set, to protect him, and to make his life easier (skills they forgot to teach me at Yale). That aspect of the job was actually easy for me, as I soon grew to love Trit. I enjoyed taking care of him. He was funny and had a really big heart.

The drinking problem had its amusing side. For example, to prep for the second day of taping the Mitzi Gaynor special, I had been on the stage until 2 a.m. The next morning,

I returned at 9 a.m. only to discover that Trit was missing in action. It turned out that the night before, while I had been busy working on the set, he had gone out drinking with some of the crew. As the rowdy group left the bar, a police car pulled up and everyone scattered except Trit, who had been too drunk to run. Consequently, he was a guest at the local jail that night and didn't show up onstage until late the next morning–to tons of ribbing. The hours before his reappearance, when I didn't know what had become of him, were not fun. In fact, I was frantic, as I was new to the game and terrified of messing up while covering for him. Apparently, I did okay. No one got upset with either of us, but it was a real test for me.

At one point, when Trit was having some family problems, he told me about a big TV special called "Hooray for Hollywood" he intended to turn down so he could go to Europe to avoid his family at Christmas. "Why don't you give the special to me?" I asked. Trit refused–that is, until I wore him down. "Tell the producers I'll design the entire show on spec," I said. "If they don't like my work, they don't have to hire me." I got the job, only to read the script and discover that the show would be the largest ever produced at CBS to date. It would star Edie Adams, Don Rickles, Charlton Heston, and Don Adams. The script called for 82 scenes, which meant 82 sets, many needing to replicate looks from famous films. No problem. I was ready, full of ambition, and not afraid of hard work.

I was also eager to solve my next problem: finding an agent. Having an agent was, and is, essential in the business. An agent negotiates your deals and (if all goes well) gets you more money. Often, they find work for you. But how, exactly, would I find an agent? During one of the too-numerous-to-count cocktail parties at our house, I overheard a friend mention the word "agent." I took him aside and told him I was looking for an agent myself. Did he know of one? He said he'd see what he could do and, presto, I had an appointment to see a guy named Sandy Wernick, who was attached to Ashley Famous–a top agency in the business.

Armed with my portfolio which, thanks to Yale, was impressive, I walked confidently into Sandy Wernick's office. If I remember correctly, I was a little cocky. Well, halfway through my presentation, Sandy bellowed, "Stop!" Assuming I had messed up, I watched as Sandy walked over to his phone, picked up the receiver, and spoke into it emphatically: "You'd better come down here–*now.*" Soon another agent entered the room, and Sandy asked me to show the entire portfolio to this new guy (whose name I have sadly forgotten). After muttering together, the two offered me a contract.

"But what if we don't get along?" I asked naively. The pair told me that the contract would be good for just one year, after which we would decide if we wanted to renew it. Sandy and I turned out to be a perfect fit, and I remained with him for 26 years.

Around this time Sandy was setting up a new stable within Ashley Famous primarily for the firm's musical-variety clients, including Bing Crosby. Remember, this was the heyday of taped television variety specials, with new shows filling the small screen on a near-weekly basis. Yale had not given me any instruction about agents and how to interact with them, but common sense told me to take any work that Sandy came up with, and to never be difficult.

I wooed Sandy by giving him credit for my success as it evolved. I said to him, "Just get my foot in the door with any producer and I'll see that the door stays open."

After Sandy signed me, I was soon very busy. There were specials for Bing Crosby followed by lots of shows for Dick Clark, followed by a Pearl Bailey series and the Cher series for which I won my first Emmy. But those are stories to come.

After I won that first Emmy, in 1975, I took out an ad in *Variety* thanking Sandy. Once, as a surprise for him and his wonderful wife, Barbara, I designed a trellis and had it built and installed in their garden. I have *always* given him the credit he richly deserves for taking a chance on me and building my career. To this day I adore that man.

As for Trit, he sadly burned himself out, succumbing to a heart attack on September 15, 1971. He was much missed, especially by me. One consolation was that he got to see me as a full-fledged set designer with my first Bing Crosby special, using the many skills I had learned from him. He called and told me I had done a marvelous job. Music to my ears!

Chapter 9

Backstage with Dean and Barbra

In 1968 I worked a season under Spencer Davies, the set designer on the "Dean Martin Show." Kind and talented, Spence had superb taste and a great eye for detail. I made it a habit to study his work and emulate him. I once asked him to teach me how to use wood moldings. His elegant and handsome baseboard treatments, as well as his crown and panel moldings, made the set. Spence said it was an art that couldn't be taught. You had to learn by doing. Just work with the different shapes, he advised, and see what they could and could not do. He was right. Eventually, I got quite good at it, but it took time and determination.

While Spence was a wonderful set designer and a very sweet man, he was also quite deaf. An accomplished lip reader, he enjoyed "listening" to my stories–from across the studio floor. I would mouth my tales and off-color jokes so that only Spence could understand, and share observations of what was going on in the studio.

In many ways, working behind the scenes in TV was a marvelous position for a young gay man to be in; my orientation was accepted by almost everyone in theatre and tape television in those days. This was not the case in the film end of the business, where tradition and rigidity still ruled. The one time I had a small problem was when a prop man muttered an anti-gay slur at me. I mentioned the incident to Spence, who was also gay, and he wanted to have the man fired. I asked him to please not do anything in retaliation as this would only reinforce the man's dislike of gay men and accomplish nothing.

Watching Dean Martin perform was nothing short of breathtaking. He was the fastest study in the business–so fast he never felt the need to attend rehearsals. In fact, permission to skip rehearsals was written into his contract. While everyone else rehearsed all week, Dino played golf and worked on his tan. The day of the show, he'd arrive in the morning and sit in his dressing room and watch his monitor to see how the other performers went through the show scene after scene. If he saw something particularly complicated on his monitor–a soft-shoe dance at the end of a song, for example–he would go out on stage and quickly learn the routine, then return to his dressing room.

Every week at the start of the show, Dean made his entrance with the same bit of business: He would enter his home base–a handsome living room designed by Spence–then sit on the lid of the grand piano and enjoy a chat with pianist Ken Lane. Soon he would hop back down, walk stage left to the set door, and greet that week's mystery guest. The delight and surprise he expressed when he opened that door was genuine. He never knew who had been invited to join him on stage. Week after week his graciousness and ability to ad lib were wonderful to see.

Probably the best, and most famous, example of Dean's quick wit and ability to laugh at himself occurred that year, when the producer and writers decided to put Dean's skills to the test. With Dean's consent, we asked the NBC special effects department to make a realistic breakaway piano from balsa and had it filled with foam rubber. That night, when Dean hopped up onto the "piano," it collapsed (the foam rubber prevented any chance of injury). The effect was hilarious. Dean pulled off the combination of acting surprised and enjoying the joke. He was brilliant.

As for his drunk bits on the show, that was all an act, a total put-on. As far as I could tell, he never drank in the studio. Onstage, the beverage in his ever-present glass was fruit juice. Later in his life this would change.

Normally, Dean would do two shows. As with the Frank Sinatra special described earlier, the first show, in the late afternoon, was called a "Dress," and the second, in the evening, was the "Air" show, which was the one that would normally be broadcast after it had been edited by director and producer Greg Garrison. Dean's Dress performance was as good as that of anyone who had rehearsed all week; by the Air show you couldn't touch him. He was that good. At the end of the show, Dean would walk offstage, pass his assistant who handed him his coat, and head out the door to his waiting car. He didn't even have to take off his makeup. He was so tanned from playing golf he didn't use the stuff.

The one time I saw Dean Martin annoyed was when Kate Smith was a guest on the show. Now Kate, aside from being a *very* large woman, set her own clock. She took her time and didn't mind keeping the audience waiting while she dawdled with a costume change. Finally, to keep the audience up and entertained, Dean blurted out, "Isn't it amazing how Kate has kept her figure all these years?" Unfortunately, Kate made her entrance just as the audience was erupting in wild laughter. Of course, she wanted to know what was so funny, but Dean managed to duck the question. Quickly he moved on to her performance.

I couldn't help but recall a story my father had told me years before. He had been hired to do some carpentry on the balcony of Kate's New York City apartment. It was a hot day, and my father thought she might at least offer him a glass of water. As he worked and sweated away, he noticed that Kate's dog was relieving himself on one of Kate's prized plants. Later, when she came out to inspect the quality of my father's work, she wondered aloud why her plants were doing so poorly. My father said nothing. She offered him nothing and got the same back. The story stuck with me. Whenever I had anyone working around the house, I made sure to offer him or her something to drink.

Dean Martin was a kind, funny man, and I liked him immensely. Many years later John and I would see Dean at Hamburger Hamlet on Sunset Strip, drinking by himself, his abstemious days long past. When he got very drunk, his man would pick him up and drive him home. This was after Dean's beloved son, Dean Paul Martin, had died in a plane crash while serving in the California Air National Guard. Dean fell apart. A terrible end to a remarkable life.

As interesting and as fascinating as it was to work on "The Dean Martin Show," the best was still to come. That was the 41st Annual Academy Awards in 1969. For the first time, the show was to be held at the Dorothy Chandler Pavilion, and I was to be part of it. I couldn't believe my luck. Little did I know that I would eventually design ten of the shows myself, and earn Emmys for two of them. In fact, the Dorothy Chandler Pavilion would become almost a second home to me.

The annual Academy Awards turned out to be a wonderful playground for trying out new materials and design approaches. As Jim Trittipo's assistant in 1969, my job was to make the models for the Oscar's sets, draft up the construction drawings for the shop, and help Trit see it through the ABC carpenter's shop and onto the stage–a big learning curve for me. I loved it. I was also responsible for setting up the press area. For the first time in the history of the Awards, when someone won an Oscar, he or she would be taken to a small elevator off stage right–no agents, husbands, or wives allowed. An Academy official, and no one else, would escort the winner into the elevator and up to the fourth floor, where the process of promoting the celebrity would take place.

Using rich, hot-pink drapes, we transformed the fourth floor's large rehearsal studios into areas for specific tasks. One area, or room, housed 50 reporters who would telephone their stories to news outlets around the world. Another, larger room served as the site for group photo shoots, while a smaller room became a photo studio where the Associated Press took shots of individual winners. The effect of all that luscious fabric was sexy, festive, and amazingly chic.

In 1969, the new system for publicizing the awards went like this: When the winner arrived on the fourth floor, he or she would be shown into a small room and placed in front of an impressive 12-foot-tall golden Oscar. As soon as the photographer took the winner's picture, the film was ripped out of the camera, and a runner rushed the film down a reserved elevator at the back of the theatre. From there the film was passed on to a man on a motorcycle who then raced off to the AP headquarters–all in time for the next day's editions. My, how times have changed.

On Awards night, at the end of the show, I sat backstage and watched, for the first time, my name go by on the crawl. I was sitting between Natalie Wood and Gower Champion, with Frank Sinatra leaning on the back of my chair. Guess who had died and gone to heaven!? As soon as the crawl had rolled by, I went quickly around to thank the crew, then rushed over to the special elevator that would take me to the fourth floor.

What I saw next I'll never forget. There on the bleachers set up for the press, more than 100 photographers stood waiting. But waiting for what? Seconds after I arrived, in walked Barbra Streisand. At the age of 26, she had just won Best Actress for her performance as Fanny Brice in "Funny Girl" (she tied with Katherine Hepburn, for her performance as Elinor of Aquitaine in "The Lion in Winter"). Barbra looked fantastic, dressed in a transparent, sequined, bell-bottomed pants suit designed by Arnold Scassi. Clutching her Oscar, she suddenly tipped it toward the press, transforming it into a make-believe ray gun, which she directed at the photographers as she spun in an arc. The battery of coordinated flashes from the cameras was amazing to see, as were the photos that ran in the papers the next day.

While watching this performance, I heard a man's voice say, "This way, Elliott, this way." There was Elliott Gould with a press-agent-type guy and no one was paying any attention. He hadn't done "Mash" yet, and few had a clue who he was. I had seen him in 1965 on Broadway in "Drat! The Cat," and recognized him and knew he was married to Streisand. So, I went up to him and said, "You're Elliott Gould, right?" He nodded in affirmation. "Obviously, you're trying to get to your wife," I continued. "I set this press area up, and if you'll follow me, I'll show you how to get to her."

We three then walked past the 50 telephone operators furiously reporting away, and up to one of the pink drapes. I pulled the curtain aside and revealed a crowd control fence. Pointing to the left, I said, "If you hop over this barrier and walk 20 feet in that direction, you'll be right next to your wife."

"Go on, Elliott," hop over, hop over" the agent urged. Glancing at Elliott I knew I had never seen a man look more unhappy.

After a long pause, Gould finally said, "No. That's ridiculous." He turned around and melted into the crowd. Two years later he and Streisand divorced. Such sadness on top of so much joy.

Later that night, I found my way to the Ambassador Hotel where the official Academy Awards party was being held. Believing that nothing could top what I had just witnessed, I walked into the lobby–and immediately laid eyes on Joan Crawford. Wearing a white tulle dress with billowing skirt, she looked spectacular. She also looked spectacularly drunk as she clutched a bottle of vodka and staggered toward me. Now, in those days at a party such as this, there would be setups at each table that consisted of bottles of scotch, gin, bourbon, and vodka; obviously, she had just helped herself to a drink for the road. Well, Miss Crawford took one look at me and her eyes got unbelievably large. Clearly, I was no one, so why was she looking at me that way? In fact, she wasn't. I turned and saw behind me a dozen reporters with cameras advancing in our direction. Aha! Caught in the act. No fool she, Crawford slammed the bottle down to her side, and that voluminous skirt enveloped the bottle. She then moved confidently, if unsteadily, through the pack of reporters, with that famous smile frozen on her face. The next day in the papers all you saw was Joan Crawford looking radiant, and no bottle in sight.

And so, like Miss Streisand, I had a remarkable evening and one I'll never forget. For Barbra, it was the beginning of her long film career. For me, it was the first of many Oscar shows which, of themselves, gave me a certain cache that led to design jobs on more than 400 television shows and helped advance my career in the theatre world. It was a terrific evening and a great start for both of us.

This moment represented the opening of many doors for me. I now had a basic understanding of how the business worked, and I was beginning to understand how I might fit into this wonderful world. While I observed many talented people both on the screen and behind the scenes, I don't recall seeing anyone more ambitious than myself. I wanted to be the best, and while I intentionally never did anything dishonest or harmful to anyone, they had best not get in my way. I would run right over anyone who got in my path. Not a very nice attitude, but I was just starting to learn the ropes, and I was very focused and highly motivated. Somehow, I knew how to make my own luck and how to take advantage of opportunities when they came along. I was well trained, and well suited to the work. Only time would tell if I was in the right place, at the right time.

As for the people around me, all my colleagues and work acquaintances were savvy and highly intelligent. If they weren't, they didn't survive. My co-workers were the absolute best and consequently brought out the best in me. The first time I realized this was 1969 when I had the good fortune to be invited to a production meeting for the Oscars at Gower

Champion's house. Mr. Champion, producer for that year's Academy Awards, was smart, charming, amusing, and very handsome. We sat around the largest glass coffee table I had ever seen. I later came up with the theory that the more important the person, the bigger his or her coffee table, and Gower Champion's was huge. Much later, when I was working with Marge Champion after her divorce from Gower, I mentioned that phenomenal table. Marge told me that Gower loved the table so much that he had taken it with him. She ended up having it copied in a smaller version. I guess she didn't feel the need to impress anyone.

In any case, there I was with the best of Hollywood and I was a like a sponge, watching how everyone interacted, how people sold their ideas and got their thoughts across, even how they dressed. Later on, when I was designing on my own, I would analyze the person I was to meet. I would look for clues to his or her personality and then dress accordingly. I needed and wanted to be a good fit for each and every producer and his team. One day I had meetings with three different producers, and I had three wardrobe changes in my car. That evening when I got home, John said, "You better be careful or you'll end up not knowing who you are." Very astute of him, and a point well taken. All these lessons were duly noted and incorporated as I became part of the big picture.

Chapter 10

My New Social Life

After I arrived in Los Angeles in 1968 and began living with John Harrington, life changed totally. Before meeting John, I knew little of how to "socialize." I had never made a drink for a visitor, much less thrown a dinner party or even told a joke in a company situation. But John was very good at these things, and I studied him. How, exactly, did he get all those laughs? Basically, his method came down to this: 1) Fit a joke or story into what is happening in the room at the time. It helps to have your story move the conversation forward in a smooth manner. To change a subject requires skill –not impossible, but it can be difficult; 2) Quickly review your story or joke in your head before you start to tell it. Woe be unto him who flounders midway or, worse yet, at the end of the tale; 3) Remember to enjoy your story or joke. It helps to laugh during the telling of it; 4) Obviously, the better the story fits your audience the better the response you'll get; 5) Keep eye contact with everyone when you're telling your story– keep everyone engaged. Whatever sense of humor I have I owe to John, who brought laughter into my life.

It wasn't long before we, as a couple, were entertaining on average twice a week and going out three or four times a week. Suddenly, I was a party animal–this, on top of working sometimes 70 hours a week. Life had shifted for me, and while I had worked long hours at Yale, I was now focused on work *and* play. I have to say the new schedule agreed with me.

As I adjusted to my new life in Hollywood, it became clear that sometimes business and pleasure could be mixed, and John and I often did so in delightful ways. Fascinating people I met through work sometimes developed into lifelong friends. One problem with this mixing, though, was the impact it had on my taxes, since I was writing off a lot of expenses relating to my social engagements. Now I not only had to deal with the budgets of my shows but also with my own finances. It wasn't long before the IRS suggested they might like to take a closer look at my tax returns. In short, I was summoned to their office for an audit. I spoke with John and his tax man and remember asking, naively, "I don't suppose I can fake my way through this?" John and his accountant were both horrified. And so I spent the weekend getting my papers in order. Early Monday morning, John's accountant accompanied me to the tax bureau, where I answered the auditor's questions. When asked about my expenses entertaining out at restaurants and such, I said, "Name a date from that list I just gave you." He selected a date, and I was able to identify the person I had met for lunch or dinner, and then named the show we had discussed at the meeting and the income that had resulted from it, etc., etc. No problem. I was home free, or so I thought. John's accountant gestured for us to leave.

But I was on a roll and couldn't resist adding, "What about entertaining at home?" "Well, deductions go both ways," the auditor responded. "Okay, on February 23rd I had Carolyn Raskin to my home for dinner," I offered. "She's a producer on 'Rowan and Martin's Laugh-In,' and as a result I got a show called 'Up with People,' which was shot in Albuquerque." We then proceeded to go through a number of other dates, resulting in similar scenarios. Ultimately, I got a refund of $174. John's accountant shook his head in disbelief. What he didn't realize was that the auditor and I had been flirting with our feet under his desk the whole time. Sometimes it pays to be gay. After leaving the tax office, I called John and told him how, exactly, the episode had been resolved in my favor. He was impressed.

John and I traveled with a crowd that enjoyed life fully. They were productive and didn't do drugs, nor did they drink to excess. Sure, I had a few friends who, I heard, did some cocaine, but only once did I see cocaine used, and that was at a huge housewarming party. While wandering around, I saw an open bathroom door; inside, some people I knew were snorting coke. One of them said, "Come on in, Ray. Try some." I declined and went on my way. Because I have always been afraid of getting hooked, the most I've ever done was try some grass with John, twice. Both times the results were unremarkable, aside from the two of us getting a bit silly.

As for drinking, John had a remarkable capacity to consume alcohol, yet he never seemed to lose control. Only once did I see him drunk, and that was after he had had a fight with his mother. Ella was in her late 70s when I met her. Once a year she would fly to California from her home in New Jersey and stay with us for a month. John loved her, but they sometimes clashed, and I would end up being the referee. Ella and John enjoyed a cocktail or three. Being tiny and frail, she could get tipsy easily but usually was never less than sweet and funny.

One night the three of us left a dinner party and decided to stop at Por Favor, a bar that was usually straight but turned mostly gay after midnight. It was approaching that hour when we entered and ended up at one end of the bar with Ella. Soon

92

we spotted a few friends, checked with Ella to be sure it was okay with her if we went to visit our friends at the other end of the room. No problem. Wrong! We spotted some other friends, talked some more, and suddenly realized we had left Ella at the bar for close to half an hour. When we came back, we found her surrounded by five gay men who had each bought her a "Rusty Screw" (Ella's name for a Rusty Nail). She had polished off three of the drinks and was working on the fourth. It was clear we needed to get her out of there and home as quickly as possible. After thanking the guys, John and I took Ella under each elbow and walked (actually, carried) her out of Por Favor with her little feet pawing away above the floor, and we laid her out on the backseat of the station wagon. No surprise that she was a little late rejoining us the next morning.

In short, I loved my work, my new partner, and my new life. My motto now was, "Work hard and play hard." But how to manage it all? In some ways, Miss Annie, our housekeeper, made our lifestyle possible. She took care of the house and us five days a week. I loved Miss Annie. She was just so-so when it came to cleaning the house, but she filled it with laughter, and no one could beat her at making pies. She was a tiny thing, with a face full of laughter and she wore a big red wig. One day when she was outside feeding the birds, she walked under one of the trees and forgot to duck. Her wig got caught in one of the branches, and off it came. I saw this from inside the house, knocked on the window and pointed to the tree where her wig was swinging gaily in the wind. Was she embarrassed? Not one bit. She just laughed and laughed. She was a joy. We also had a gardener, but no pool man. The pool was yet to come.

To keep things running smoothly when we entertained, John and I often had a bartender. His name was Scotty Bowers. Even before his autobiography (*Full Service: My Adventures in Hollywood and the Secret Sex Lives of the Stars*) appeared in 2012, Scotty was a legend.

By the time he was in his early teens, Scotty had discovered that some men "of a certain persuasion" liked to fondle young boys. Scotty didn't mind. In fact, he liked it. Throughout his life he was always clear that he was the one doing the seducing. When he arrived in Hollywood in the mid 1940s, he was in his early 20s and fresh out of the Marines and the Second World War. He landed a job at a gas station on the heavily traveled Hollywood Boulevard, where it intersected with Van Ness. Lean and handsome, he had dark hair, an athletic build, and dimples. With a mischievous twinkle in his eyes, Scotty seemed to always be smiling. Guys, especially older guys, who stopped by for gas took notice. And what guys they were: Walter Pidgeon and Spencer Tracy were just two of the notables Scotty said he serviced. Later on, he provided hookups for Charles Laughton, George Cukor, and countless others. He serviced ladies as well, providing women for the bi-sexual Katharine Hepburn and others who were similarly oriented. Scotty never gossiped about his clients–at least, not while they were alive.

Word of Scotty's talents spread quickly. He eventually left the gas station and had a group of men and women who were more than willing to help service his steadily increasing clientele. To learn more, I suggest you read the book. At this point I should add that in the fifty or so years that I knew Scotty, I found him to be impeccably honest. Also, to my knowledge he never took money from anyone who turned to him for his services as a go-between. He simply never seemed to care about money.

Because he was by nature a compulsive worker, Scotty pruned trees during the day, worked as a bartender at Hollywood parties in the evening, and then provided sexual favors later in the night. One day he was trimming a tree on our property when he suddenly announced he was terribly sorry, but he had to leave. He promised to return the next day to finish the job. No problem, we told him.

"You don't understand," Scotty said. "I have a client who I've taken care of for a long time now. You know how I like to please my clients, but I don't really like taking care of this guy anymore. His thing is to get whipped. He used to have a lot of money, but now he's fallen on hard times and can only afford a small hotel room. It's almost impossible to get that whip going around such a tiny room!" It wasn't a judgment call on Scotty's part. He was simply frustrated that he couldn't do his job properly.

In addition to trimming our trees, Scotty, as mentioned, also worked as a bartender in our home. For many years, every New Year's Eve he mixed drinks for more than 100 guys at our house. He was very accommodating to our guests. Remember, in the late '70s, things were, shall we say, a bit closeted. Scotty would charm an all-gay group by stirring our guests' drinks with his sizable equipment. Always a hit with the crowd.

At one of our parties, we had a guest named Heinz Hupert, whom we had originally met at a gay bar in Vienna. Heinz was in his 40s, attractive, and successful; he sold high-end sweaters throughout Europe. The night we met him, we hit it off, and he took a fancy to us. We went back to his

95

impressive apartment–just for a drink. Heinz had worked out a deal where he swapped the use of his London apartment with a man who had an apartment in Vienna's Schonbrunn Palace. When John and I arrived, Heinz threw his car coat on a settee and John whispered, "My God–it's lined in leopard!" Overhearing this, Heinz proceeded to show us two other coats, one lined in a fantastically beautiful dark mink and the other in a mink herringbone pattern. We had never seen anything quite like that.

In the days that followed, Heinz wined and dined us all over Vienna, ferrying us from place to place in his brand-new Rolls-Royce with schmaltz-type waltz music playing in the background. At the conclusion of our visit, he sent us off on the rest of our trip with boxes of chocolates from Demel's, Vienna's top chocolatier. Only later did I find out that Heinz had suggested to John that he swap his Rolls for me. Jokingly, I said to John, "You fool. You should have gone for the deal, got the Rolls, and I would have flown back to LA like a homing pigeon."

Eventually, we three became good friends, and Heinz visited us in Hollywood. At one of our parties, we noticed that Heinz had taken a fancy to Scotty, so John and I took Scotty aside and asked him how much he would charge to stay the night with Heinz. We settled on an amount, slipped him the cash, and Scotty stayed the night. We knew that Scotty would never let on that we had hired him to "take care" of Heinz, as Scotty was always discreet and really very caring.   The next day, Miss Annie and Heinz were talking in the kitchen, and we heard the very Southern Miss Annie say in her rich drawl, "Mr. Hupert, I understand y'all hail from Vienna." The two hit it off, and when Heinz left for Vienna he had a smile on his face, an apple pie that Miss Annie had baked just for him, and some great memories.

Typically, after a party John and I would go to bed and Scotty would clean up the house to the point where you'd never know there had been any party at all. He would then poke his head into our bedroom and ask, with a suggestive leer, "Are you sure there isn't *anything* else I can do for you guys?" "Get outta here, Scotty!" John would reply. "Thanks for all the hard work," I would chime in.

After many years of benefitting from Scotty's positive outlook on life and his strong work ethic, several of us got together and decided to give Scotty a surprise birthday party. It was a fun idea, but not a particularly good one. Scotty was so into giving to others, be it as a gardener, a bartender, or anyone else, he couldn't just be the recipient. Halfway through "his" party he ended up behind the bar, mixing drinks for everyone. At that point, he could not have been happier.

And so it would go, party after party, year after year, until we moved from Beverly Hills to New York City. However, even from a distance, we felt connected to this remarkable man and made an effort to use his (bartending) services whenever we visited LA and gave a party for our friends. In return, Scotty certainly gave us a unique view of, and insight into, the history of Hollywood, always through his twinkling eyes. Scotty lived to be 96 and died on Oct. 14, 2019. He remained a workaholic, and as far as I know, he was sexually active up to the end. An amazing man.

Often, friends stopped by for a cocktail or a combination of drinks and dinner. In those days, before video equipment, we sometimes would run a movie. Through his work at Paramount, John was able to get films to show at home. Cleverly, he set up a film projector outside the living room window, which cut down on the noise that came from the motor. We would usually show our guests a three-reeler, with the entree and the dessert courses served in between reels. Others we knew had more sophisticated projection systems. One guy had a remote-control system that lowered the screen, dimmed the lights, and even turned off the gas fireplace, and then started up the movie on cue. Still others had full-blown projection rooms–all *very* glamorous.

John loved to cook. The meals he turned out were extraordinary. He would read the Wednesday *New York Times* food section, reach me on the phone, and say, "How about inviting eight friends for dinner tomorrow?" The next day there it would be -- a full meal from the *Times*. John's cooking skills certainly helped me land jobs with the directors and producers who were often invited to our home.

I remember one time we had the previously mentioned Carolyn Raskin over. She was accompanied by three other ladies, all of whom stayed for dinner. John served a bombe for dessert, which was a large egg-shaped affair with a slightly flat bottom so it wouldn't roll off the plate. The ladies loved it, as did I, and we ate the entire thing that evening. Carolyn innocently asked John how the bombe was made.

"Well," answered John, "you take two cups of whipping cream and fold in some soft chocolate for the first layer. Then you take two cups of whipping cream and fold in half a cup of pureed strawberries for the second layer, and then finally take two cups of whipping cream and fold in vanilla flavoring mixed with confectioner's sugar for the last layer." We all sat there in shock. The ladies, who were always on a diet, had just eaten a cup of whipping cream each. You never heard such screams. John sat there quietly, enjoying the commotion and wearing his trademark impish grin.

One day John decided to make Peking duck. I don't recall the process, but I know that one of the last stages in preparing this classic was to hang it up to allow the grease to drain out of the bird. Well, as luck would have it, we got a call from our friend Bob Lawrimore down in Laguna Beach asking if we'd like to join him there for the weekend. When John told Bob that he was preparing a Peking duck, Bob said, "Great. We can have that for dinner Saturday." What did John do? Being the clever man that he was, he rigged up a way of hanging the bird over a large pan placed in the back of our station wagon, and the duck drained all the way down to Laguna. Dinner that evening was delicious.

Another time John was putting together two elaborate, back-to-back dinner parties, both to be capped with Cherries Jubilee for dessert. Each party would have 14 guests. The first night John, with a flourish, rolled out a cart with the cherries bubbling away in a handsome copper pan over a burning brazier. It was quite the show–until John grabbed the pan handle without using a potholder. As he let out a terrific scream, the cherries flew through the air, hit the wall, and rolled onto the floor. Quickly, I went into action. Within moments I was cleaning up the wall and floor as John brought out the batch of cherries he had reserved for the second night and started heating them up. Was this a disaster for John? Well, no. His evening was made when he overheard one of the ladies say, "Wouldn't you know that he'd have a backup batch of cherries?"

Yes, we loved to entertain. However, on April 13, 1979, I decided it was time for a change. That night we had given yet another dinner party, and John had outdone himself. It was a terrific meal but had involved a significant amount of work. During the meal someone said they had tried a new restaurant and had a wonderful time there. Thinking of all the effort John had put into that night's dinner and so many other meals, and realizing that no one at the table had ever reciprocated, I came up with a solution, one that would allow us to enjoy these wonderful friends without our always being the sole hosts. I suggested we form a gourmet group, to be called the Fraternity of Restaurant Connoisseurs (or FORC, for short). We would try a new restaurant each month and take turns hosting. The host or hostess would select a new restaurant, let everyone know what time to appear at the host's home for drinks, what the attire should be, and then at the last moment reveal where we were going. The group lasted for more than 30 years.

Feature-length films and great food were the focus of some of our parties. So was the swimming pool we eventually installed at our house in Hancock Park in the late '70s. The pool had an unusual black bottom and was screened from view by formal gardens. Beyond the pool was a very nice house on a corner lot owned by Jameson Parker, who lived there with his wife, Bonnie, and their children. Starting in 1981 Jameson starred in the popular TV series "Simon & Simon" on CBS, which lasted eight seasons. He and his family pretty much kept to themselves and were always pleasant. Unbeknownst to us, the neighbor just to the north of their house was less than neighborly.

One night John and I had three of our gay friends over for dinner, and after dessert we all decided to take a swim. The pool was very private, so everyone stripped and dove in. We seldom drank very much, but that night we were, in fact, a little rowdy and while we knew that Jameson was perfectly straight, one of the guys, for the fun of it, started yelling, "Hey, Jameson! Come on in–the pool is great!" It was funny but no problem, as we knew the Parkers were out of town. What we didn't realize was that the neighbor, who for whatever reason didn't like the Parkers, took them to court claiming they had noisy pool parties. They cited the night when we had enjoyed our starlit dip as a prime example. The Jamesons, who had been ideal neighbors to us, were able to produce airline tickets showing they had been in Europe at the time of the so-called disturbance, and the case was thrown out of court. We toned it down after that.

Gradually, our social life extended beyond the borders of California and often beyond the continent. We started to travel whenever we could break away from work. John and I agreed that traveling was fun and something we would make sure happened. For a great many years, we flew to Europe at least once a year and, of course, those trips were augmented by business trips as a result of my work. Along with the travel came the making of wonderful friends.

One day in 1975, our good friend Michelle Pons (whom we referred to as our French Auntie Mame) called and said she had a friend named Jacqueline Seyrat coming to Los Angeles from Paris, and would we "receive" her? Not knowing if this friend would be fun or boring, we put together a small cocktail party, contacted Jacqueline and asked her to come by– kind of a wait and see situation. What we "received" was the most charming, beautiful, witty person one could hope for. That was close to a half-century ago, and she is dear to me to this day. We have typically visited each other every year as well as traveled together.

Memorable trips included one to London, when John and I were invited to Clarence House, where two of our friends, Willie and Reggie, worked for Elizabeth, the Queen Mother. We were told that she preferred to hire gay men to tend to her needs. Who knows? She was out of town at the time, and Willie and Reggie gave us a tour and showed us, among other things, a china cabinet with an amazing display of Fabergé objects, including a miniature crystal flowerpot with lily of the valley made from emeralds and pearls– incredibly delicate and beautiful. Queen Elizabeth II had played with it as a young girl, Willie and Reggie said.

We were also told that one night "the boys" (Willie and Reggie) were downstairs while the Queen Mum was upstairs watching the telly. Suddenly the phone rang downstairs. It was the Queen Mum saying, "I don't know what you queens are doing down there, but this queen needs a gin and tonic." I would have loved to have met her. We were told that on one occasion when she was annoyed by something her daughter had done, she had said, "Elizabeth, who do you think you are?"

On another trip, we were at a cocktail party given in our honor at our friend Joe Kennedy's home in Paris on the rue Saint-Honoré. Joe's handsome apartment was perfect in every way, except for one thing: A huge, over-scaled chandelier fitted with candles gave off a heat so intense that all the candles drooped and dripped molten wax when Joe had first tried to light it. I loved the apartment with its elegant French decor and beautiful antiques, but the scale of that chandelier made me a bit crazy as I'm a stickler when it comes to proportion. When I finally managed to take my eyes off Joe's antiques, I noticed something else in the room: a slender and chicly dressed woman, whose name turned out to be Fern Bedaux. This charming lady took a liking to John and me and invited us to join her that weekend at her home, the Château de Candé in Monts, near Tours. I glanced over at Joe, who was standing close behind Fern, and saw him nod his head violently in the affirmative.

So arrangements were made, and at the encouragement of Joe we went to Godiva, the famous Belgian chocolatier, and through the store's handsome convex glass display cases marveled at an amazing assortment of chocolates. Choosing which candies to purchase for our hostess was easy, as Fern was registered there. Paying for them wasn't so easy. Our large selection cost a small fortune. As it turned out, that box of chocolates was one of the best investments we ever made.

The weekend arrived and we drove about three hours south of Paris to Monts. When we arrived at a charming but rather smallish house, I thought, "Okay, I guess this will be alright." But it wasn't. A grumpy man emerged from the front door and angrily gestured down the drive when we asked, in our terrible French, "Où est Madame Bedaux?" It turned out we were parked in front of the gatehouse and that Fern's home was about three-quarters of a mile down the gravel drive. At the end of the road, we were startled to see a 55-room Renaissance chateau that took one's breath away. We later learned that this was the house where the Duke and Duchess of Windsor had been married on June 3, 1937.

We were greeted at the chateau entrance by Fern. Three maids in light blue uniforms proceeded to lug our heavy suitcases up four flights of stone stairs to our suite, which was directly over the suite the Duke of Windsor had occupied prior to his marriage. Fern later told us that when the Duke married Wallis Simpson at Candé, the press was so hungry for news that Fern's head butler had been offered $10,000 for any bit of gossip about the couple–an incredible amount of money in those days. Fern was proud that not one member of her staff ever gave any information to a single reporter. She also mentioned that she hadn't cared much for the new Duchess of Windsor. Fern and her husband, who had some business dealings with the Duke, had lent the chateau to David and Wally after a request from a mutual friend.

Soon after we arrived, I realized that my camera was still in the car, so I went down to get it. When I returned, I said to John, "Something is terribly strange here." "What makes you say that?" he asked. "Look down below, by the car. What do you see that's odd?" John went to the window and took a good long look. "Oh, my God," he said "There are no tire tracks in the gravel driveway!" Later, we found out why the man at the gatehouse had been so grumpy: One of his jobs was to rake the driveway whenever a car drove over it.

The chateau included a two-level library, its curved balcony distinguished by one of the most unusual railings I have ever seen. Hundreds of balusters supported the railing, and no two were alike; each elaborately carved spindle featured its own distinct design. Also, in the library was one of the few remaining fully operational Skinner organs in the world. In the dining room, deep-green cordovan tooled leather covered the walls. Fern told us the leather had been nearly destroyed during the Second World War when a munitions factory a mile away exploded and the chateau's windows blew in, leaving thousands of tiny glass shards embedded in the leather walls. The shards had to be picked out by hand before the walls could be restored to their former glory. The drapes didn't survive and had to be copied at great expense.

During our stay, we didn't eat in the dining room. Instead, meals were served either outdoors under a huge tree, or on the chateau's lower level, in the "guard's room," with its beautiful, vaulted ceiling made of ancient brick. During one dinner, a maid presented a meringue-topped dessert to Fern, who took one look at it and said, "Well, there's only one way to deal with this." We were riveted as this frail, elegant woman took a serving knife and swung it down violently onto the cake, making a clean cut of it. She then passed the cake back to the maid who finished the slicing and distributed the dessert. At this point we knew Fern Bedaux was not without a sense of humor.

One day during afternoon tea I mentioned that I thought I might take a bath before drinks and dinner. On my way upstairs no servants were in sight, and yet by the time I entered our suite one of the maids had drawn a bath for me. Later, Fern told us that when a new maid or manservant was hired, one of the questions the applicant would be asked was, "How good are your legs?" The place was so huge that the help covered long distances throughout the chateau, mostly in hidden hallways and staircases. Guests almost never saw the servants. However, from time to time we would hear music that was distant at first, then grew louder, and eventually drifted away. It turned out that each servant was given a portable radio to carry while working in the chateau's hidden halls to help fight the isolation.

Our weekend with Fern came toward the end of her life. She had lived what at first had appeared to be a charmed existence. Fern Lombard, as she was originally known, came from Grand Rapids, Michigan. She had been a sickly child. Her wealthy parents took her to see many doctors, but nothing seemed to help. Finally, in desperation, her parents asked the family doctor what they should do and he said, "She won't last long. Give her anything she wants." What Fern wanted, she told her parents, was to learn to speak French. A French teacher was hired, and Fern flourished.

One day, when she was 17, Frenchman Charles Bedaux came to town. This hugely successful, self-made businessman, who specialized in human-power management, had worked his way out of the Parisian slums. He now lived lavishly both in America and France. When he met Fern, she was not only beautiful but also spoke impeccable French. Charles fell in love with her, divorced his wife (a former beauty queen from St. Louis), and married Fern. He then spent the rest of his life spoiling her. During their year-long honeymoon, the chateau was refitted with indoor plumbing and central heating; pipes for hot and cold water in the 17 remodeled Art Deco bathrooms were hidden behind thick stone walls. One day early in their marriage Fern mentioned to Charles that she had taken a chill while in her bathroom. The next day a wood-burning stove was installed, lit, and never allowed to go out.

Fern and Charles traveled a great deal. Once, when Charles announced they were going on a safari, Fern insisted she couldn't possibly join him as she would miss her morning bath and her books. Charles immediately had an inflatable rubber bathtub manufactured and ordered a custom-made Louis Vuitton trunk to hold several hundred of her favorite books–anything to make her happy. (Interestingly, Charles' mistress, an Italian countess and a good friend of Fern's, joined the expedition as well. Fern was famous for saying, "Charles is fascinating. Why *wouldn't* other women be interested in him?")

In 1942, Charles, who had become an American citizen in 1917, was accused by the Americans of being a Nazi collaborator. His cross-border business dealings had crossed the line from opportunism to treason, the FBI believed. It was a charge he vehemently denied. In 1944, while incarcerated in a Miami jail, he committed suicide. To this day no one knows all the facts. Charles was buried in Cambridge, Mass., at Mount Auburn Cemetery, where Fern would join him 28 years later. She bequeathed the Château de Candé to the French government.

During our stay at Candé, we were driven around to see the various outbuildings, the golf course where only three of the 18 holes were kept up, and my favorite area: a clearing in the woods where Fern and Charles had placed a dozen five-foot-tall antique stone gargoyles facing each other in a circle. Each had a wild grin– and a huge erection. After our memorable weekend at Candé, the gargoyles weren't the only ones with smiles on their faces. John and I agreed that a box of chocolates was a small price to pay for a marvelous adventure.

For the next 40 years, trips to France became a regular occurrence. Every year on our vacations we would drive from town to town, stopping for delicious picnic lunches and staying at old chateaux, which we would find in a guidebook. These were magical times, with dinners as spectacular as the places where we stayed. High on our list of pleasures was stopping at antique shops along the way and bringing home a bit of France to the States.

John was an excellent driver, and I preferred to be a passenger. I was always content to direct the route, aided by one of many maps. On May 8, 1987, while driving on a country road near Lyon, I spotted an antique shop coming up and yelled "Antiques!" John turned left quickly–into a man on a motorcycle with a lady on the back of it, who had been in the process of passing us on the left. The motorcycle hit our car so hard that our left front wheel was nearly ripped off. We watched in horror as the motorcycle skidded forward, tipped over, and hit a stone wall. Miraculously, the woman was unhurt, but the man was seriously injured. The nightmare was compounded by our status as tourists. We were in a foreign country and had little command of the language and no knowledge of local laws. A crowd of about thirty people materialized out of nowhere, and when we attempted to move the car off the road, several onlookers stopped us. Everything had to be left in place for the police to see, they indicated.

I was concerned not only for the injured man but for ourselves. How would this crowd of locals react to two Americans who had just injured one of their own? I took off my jacket and placed in under the injured man's head, then picked out a young kid and asked him if he could speak English, which he could. The police soon arrived, and when we explained, through the boy, what had happened, we were taken to the nearest police station where a clerk phoned Euro Car to secure a replacement vehicle for us. We then took a taxi to Lyon, picked up the new car, and were on our way. My anxiety for the injured man was accompanied by a nagging doubt: Even though John claimed he had put the directional on, I wasn't so sure. If he hadn't, we could well have been the cause of the accident. From then on, I couldn't help myself; I was never again comfortable with John's driving.

One of my favorite trips was far closer to home and didn't involve any driving. One Saturday morning, after an intense week at work, John asked if I had any plans. When I told him I didn't, he replied, "Be ready to leave for a mystery outing at noon." I love surprises, and this one was the best yet. On a dock in Los Angeles, we boarded not a boat but a seaplane. Before I knew it, we were on our way to Catalina for the day. The afternoon was filled with trying to ride a bicycle built for two. Our success was limited since we both wanted to be in control, so the bike wobbled all over the place. In the end, we swapped the two-seater for individual bikes and proceeded with our adventure, which included a tour of the charming Catalina Casino. (Later, I did a version of its stage for a TV special featuring Nell Carter.) When the sun got low in the sky, we decided it would be great fun to spend the night on the island. After a considerable search, we found a small hotel with just one room left. We took it.

Next, we went shopping and bought the bare essentials: toothbrushes and two cans of margaritas. Perfect! Well, not quite. We checked in, got settled in our room, and were lying on the bed (we still had on our shorts, thank God) while sipping our margaritas when what we thought was a closet door opened to reveal seven little girls –a Brownie troop from a local school. The Brownies and their leader marched into our room, took one look at us, and without even turning around, backed up in the direction from which they had come. Clearly the room had been assigned to us, so the hotel management had some explaining to do. We thought the episode was hilarious; the Brownie leader, not so much. Ah, the joys of travel.

In hindsight I can see how incredibly fortunate we were. We loved to share our lives with others and had endless opportunities to meet marvelous people, both in business and in our private lives. I've always said my friends are where the real richness in life is. Having a partner who was not only fun and adventurous but also a terrific cook and whose values matched my own made anything and everything possible. Looking back, I would say that when one attacks life with an attitude of appreciation, it's no surprise when dreams come true.

My mother (front center) with her brother, sister, and her mother, in Denmark, 1910

My mother, Ane Kathrine Jensen at 24

UNITED STATES

Ship Name History: United States
Builder: A. Stephen & Sons, Glasgow
Length: 501 ft.
Width: 58 ft.
Gross Tonnage: 10095
Funnels: 1
Masts: 2
Engines: Two sets of three-cylinder triple expansion

In April, 1929, my mother took the SS *United States* to the USA. She met my father on this voyage.

My brother James was so beautiful
that no one noticed me. James
hated the attention but I craved it.

James and I during WWII. My immigrant
parents were very patriotic and often
dressed us in military uniforms.

James and I with the toy
tank our father made for
us in 1943. Ironically,
in 1962, I was made a
tank driver in the army.

1941

My parents in 1941, eleven years into a marriage that lasted 50 years.

As my art teacher at NYU, Patton Campbell changed my life by encouraging me to go to Yale to study set designing. My life might well have been very different if I had not had the good fortune to meet Patton and take his advice.

Fran Dwyer. What a bright, beautiful, and loving woman!

Donald Oenslager was a tall man and a giant in the field of set design. As head of Yale's set designing department, he determined which students graduated and which were dropped. I studied under him from 1964 to 1967.

Elina Katsioula was the first recipient of the scholarship I set up at Yale. She eventually moved out to LA to become one of my best assistants.

Jim Trittipo, known as Trit. I assisted him on TV specials for Frank Sinatra, Mitzi Gaynor, and the Academy Awards. It was a privilege and honor to work for this great designer.

My set for "The Dance Next Door," the first set I designed after arriving in LA in 1968

John and I with our very special friend Jacqueline Seyrat in 1999.
We met in 1973 when a mutual friend introduced us.

With my agent Sandy Wernick who signed me up as his new client in 1971.
We worked together for 26 years, as he shaped and made my career.

Fern Bedaux's Château de Candé

On my 66th birthday, May 29, 2005, John and I were legally married.
The best birthday gift I could ever receive.

John Harrington and I were together for 50 years.
Like most couples, we had our differences, but we never came close to separating.
They were terrifically happy years.

HR, John, and I, on a cruise to Antarctica in 2014.

Chapter 11

Bing Crosby

The week after Ashley Famous signed me on in 1971, my new agent, Sandy Wernick, called and asked if I wanted to design a Christmas special for Bing Crosby. Guess what my answer was! This was to be my first of seven specials with Bing, and it was to be taped in the fall at NBC. "Bing Crosby and the Sounds of Christmas," as the show was called, featured guest stars Robert Goulet and the beautiful and charming Mary Costa, a talented opera singer known for voicing Princess Aurora in Disney's 1959 "Sleeping Beauty." This was the first of many television Christmas specials I designed. By the end of my career, it is possible that I had designed more Christmas specials than any designer in the business.

Bing was difficult to define as a performer. He had a quiet, introverted personality. One never got a sense of who he truly was. Yes, he had an air of elegance and sophistication, but it's hard to say if these qualities were in the writing of the scripts or if they came from Bing himself. His public image was so well established it was impossible to see past it. We're talking about a man whose voice during the Second World War was the most recognizable in the world–even more so than Hitler's. As for his appearance, I'm not sure he really cared. He tended to wear hats around the studio and at meetings, instead of his hairpiece (which, incidentally, was one of the best I've ever seen), and he may have been a bit color blind. Getting him to change socks so that one wasn't brown and the other black was sometimes a bit of a problem; the mismatch could look really weird with his tuxedo. Bing just seemed indifferent to such things.

On the other hand, I found Mary Costa to be full of life and smiles—a total delight and consistently beautifully dressed. Bob Goulet, in contrast, had a cardboard quality. You never knew if you were seeing the real Bob, or just the silver-screen good looks. Years later when Bob was on the Andy Williams series sets I designed, he was surrounded by three mysterious men who carefully watched his every move. Who they were and why they were there remains a mystery.

The execution of a typical television special usually started with a phone call from my agent or from the producer himself asking if I was available. I had a policy to take any and all jobs, because no matter how big or small the show, there was always something to learn, and work I must if I was to grow in my craft. And so, over the years, I ended up designing some very large and also some small productions. I was paid ludicrously large fees but also small amounts of money for doing this work that I loved. Once I even got paid in fruit trees (more on that later). So I admit up front there were times I was so swamped with the complexities of my work that I was perhaps not the most observant person around, but as I worked on Bing's specials I nevertheless did notice that one of Bing's most appealing qualities was his devotion to his children Mary Frances, Harry, and Nathaniel. They were always included in the Christmas specials, and Bing and his wife, Kathryn, made sure their children were presented in a loving, nurturing manner.

The second phase of doing a special was usually the production meeting, during which we all sat around, met any new members of the creative team, and discussed the overall concept of the show, who the guest stars would be and their possible production numbers, the schedule, etc.

One time Bob Finkel, Bing's producer, called a meeting at his Beverly Hills house. We all gathered in Bob's handsome den, which featured an assortment of chairs and a sizable bar. Bob's daughter, Terry, who was maybe in her early 20s, was helping to host and asked if anyone wanted a drink. It was around 7 p.m., and Terry directed her question first to me. Not knowing what to do, I requested a scotch on the rocks. As Terry asked the others around the room, each answered, "A Coke," "Water," or "Nothing." No one asked for hard liquor. There I was, uncomfortably drinking by myself. I never made that mistake again. Ideally, one needed to find a balance between being unique in one's talent and fitting into the group's overall demeanor. I still had a lot to learn.

For Bing's 1971 Christmas special, Bob Finkel knew exactly what he wanted. He had just returned from New York, where he had seen "Company" on Broadway and was in love with the idea of a unit set in which all the production numbers could be staged. Bob was used to getting his way.

Some designers might have bristled at having a design approach dictated to them, but I found myself grateful for Bob's input, as it gave me a strong direction. I created a fantasy set of platforms connected by stairs with many beautiful vertical wood-turned columns 6 to 10 inches in diameter and ranging from 10 to 18 feet tall, each topped with a fanciful finial and with everything painted pearlescent white. Winter trees and drifts of fake snow surrounded the entire set–a frosty winter wonderland. Later I received complimentary calls from Romain Johnston, one of the top set designers at that time, and also from my hero and mentor Jim Trittipo, telling me how much they had admired my work. Their supportive feedback helped boost my confidence at this early stage in my career. I decided then and there to send notes or make calls to other designers when a compliment was in order. Remembering to say "Thanks," either through the mail or by phone, became a habit I maintained throughout my career. It was a habit that served me well and one that I continue to recommend to designers just starting out.

At the production meeting, the subject of Bing's 10-year-old daughter, Mary Frances (later known as Mary Crosby, the one who shot JR in the television series "Dallas"), came up. Because Bing and Kathryn had enrolled Mary Frances in a ballet school, we were asked to create a dance number for her. So, during the meeting Bob Finkel dropped this bomb on us (the Crosbys weren't there, thank God). Bob looked at the choreographer, Bob Sidney, who was known for his dry sense of humor and practical approach to talent, and said, "Can we do this?" I had worked with Sidney on the Dean Martin series and knew he could make talent look good even when the talent was limited, undeveloped, or not even there. Sidney scowled a moment and said, "Give me four strong male dancers and she'll never touch the floor." And that's exactly what happened. All little Mary Frances had to do was point her toes, fly and land, fly and land. She looked great.

The show went well. I was now part of the Crosby Specials team. The next one guest starred Dean Martin, and it was decided that Bing and Dean would perform a medley of "lazy" songs, including "Up a Lazy River," "I'm Bidin' My Time," and other tunes with laid-back lyrics. For the set, I took many of the graphic shapes I had designed and used

120

throughout the rest of the show and had them blown up and built and upholstered into a large and sturdy abstract set about 35 feet long, 18 feet high, and 12 feet deep. Dean and Bing could laze around, lounging all over the set as they sang their lazy songs–or so I thought. Well, either the NBC drapery department screwed up the upholstery job or I chose the wrong fabric, because the set ended up looking, well, sloppy. To be truthful it looked really awful, and I suspect I was the culprit. Bob Finkel, who was again our producer, took one look at the set in the shop and decided to throw it out–a mere half-hour before we were to tape the number.

What to do? I was in big trouble. I swallowed hard and had the crew grab a few of the set pieces from several of the other numbers (thankfully the show was visually unified), and I created a new look on the spot. The remake didn't look half bad, but then it didn't look great either. I thought this would convince Bob to never use me again but somehow I got away with it. Later I found out that Bob admired people who could think quickly on their feet and stay calm doing it–a quality that saved me several times in my career, and in my life (as you will see). But this was a *very* close call. I didn't upholster a set again for a long, long time–in fact, not until Miss Piggy entered my life (more on that sublime swine to come).

It was now 1972 and the phone rang again and it was Sandy, my wonderful agent, on the line. I had been offered yet another Bing special, this time "Bing Crosby and Friends." The show was to have three guests: Pearl Bailey, Carol Burnett, and Bob Hope. All four performers would have equal rehearsal and performance time. Five days had been allocated for rehearsals. The first day, Monday, everyone gathered except Bob, who was out of town for a charity golf tournament. The rehearsal went smoothly, almost like a family gathering; everyone was excited and involved in the creative process. Tuesday came and Bob was still absent–same excuse. Wednesday, no Bob –different excuse. And so it continued throughout the week, with everyone rehearsing except Bob.

Well, on Saturday–D-Day–it was time to start taping. I had set up a small backstage theatre set for the first scene, which involved Bob and Carol. We started blocking the scene when Carol suddenly said, "Excuse me. Who is this person next to me doing the scene with me?"

The director, Marty Pasetta, answered her over the intercom: "He's Bob's stand-in." "Where's Bob?", Carol asked, not unreasonably. She was told that Bob was in his dressing room watching his monitor as the scene was staged. Now, I cannot emphasize enough what a kind, cooperative lady Carol is. I have never heard a bad word said against her. She is the easiest, most professional performer around. Well, Carol thought about this for a moment and said, "*Hmmm*, suppose I go into *my* dressing room and watch *my* stand-in on *my* monitor." Much confusion ensued, with lots of consulting. Finally, Bob reluctantly emerged from his dressing room and joined Carol on the set. Carol had the scene down pat, and as the blocking unfolded, Bob was frantically trying to read the cue cards and getting no response from the crew. Carol, meanwhile, was mopping up the stage, getting laugh after laugh. The crew was eating all this up. After a while, Bob stopped a moment and said to Carol, "Tell me, Carol, when you do a show like this, do you always memorize your lines?"

"Of course I do, Bob," Carol replied in her sweetest, put-on voice. "I'm a pro," to which the crew responded with a huge round of applause, cheers even. I loved her and the crew for that. What I think of Bob remains best not said.

In 1973 we were doing another show with Bing, "Bing Crosby's Sun Valley Christmas Special," with Michael Landon, the singer Connie Stevens, and John Byner, a master mimic. We were taping the show in March for the following Christmas season, and we had only one problem: no snow. There we were all set to do a Christmas show in a festival of mud. Bob Finkel, who was again producing, expressed his concerns to our star. Bing seemed unfazed by it all. He said simply, "Don't worry. I've gone to Mass and it'll all be okay." Surprise, surprise, the next morning at 4 a.m. Sun Valley was covered entirely in snow. Beautiful, and to us a miracle

In those days, TV production on location was in many ways similar to film production. We started at 4 a.m. so we could get to the taping site and be ready to shoot before the sun came up. At the end of the day when the natural light was gone, we'd move indoors and continue shooting until wrapping up around 8 p.m. or so. Then we'd go back to the production offices, repack the props and scenery for the next day, grab a bite to eat somewhere along the line, and try to get to bed no later than 11 p.m. so we could start all over again at 4 a.m. As mentioned earlier, I was used to working 70 or so hours a week, but this intensity came as a bit of a surprise. In short, it cured me of ever wanting to do film work.

Bob, as the producer, wanted the entire Sun Valley Main Street decorated for Christmas. He also wanted the largest Christmas tree possible–larger even than the typical Rockefeller Center tree. The idea was for Bing to walk down the street and end up by this giant tree, where he would sing "White Christmas" with the Crosby family and the town folk gathered around. Well, there was no way I had enough decorations to do an entire street, much less a huge tree, so I placed a call to a contact in Hollywood and had thousands of white Christmas lights shipped in. I was given a crew and a crane to decorate that darn tree.

To decorate the street, we leapfrogged the ornaments: After one section of the street was shot, my wonderfully talented assistant Paul Galbraith and the prop crew helped me rip down the decorations and race them by the armful and truckload to the upcoming set to be shot. Rip down, put up, rip down, put up, all the way down the street for blocks. What the storeowners thought, one can only imagine. Thankfully, Paul had a background in department store decorating. The whole operation was hectic, crazy, exhausting, and yes, terrific fun. Always great when a difficult design problem is solved.

At the Sun Valley Square, with that huge twinkling tree, Bing finally sang "White Christmas." At the end of the song, Kathryn leaned over and gave Bing a little peck on the cheek–a nice, warm moment, I thought. As it turned out, we had a technical problem with the sound and had to reshoot the song. As we were preparing for the second take, Kathryn, who I think is terrific, asked Bing how he liked the little kiss. Bing replied, in front of the whole town, "Not much." What an awful moment. What a thing to do to one's wife in front of the children and a multitude of strangers. It suddenly occurred to me that maybe life wasn't perfect in the Crosby household. Even mentioning this incident leaves me wondering if it accurately portrays Bing's persona. So hard to tell, as he was so distant, so cold.

On another day of taping, we were doing a scene based on an old-time movie in which John Byner, dressed in black, played an evil villain. Opposite John was Connie Stevens, costumed in a flimsy Mary Pickford-type dress and waiting in the subzero weather in front of the town bank. Not a complaint from this game gal, even when Kathryn said sweetly, "Aren't you cold, dear?"

The script called for John's character to kidnap Connie and speed away on a horse-drawn sleigh. Michael Landon played the hero, dressed all in white. His job was to pursue the villain on skis. Silly, but funny. Since John didn't know how to drive a horse-drawn sleigh (who does?), a professional driver hid under some blankets in front of the sleigh. Understandably, the driver couldn't see very well, and the sleigh, pulled by two white horses at full gallop, drifted off the road and into a gully, where the sleigh tipped over. We were horrified and concerned that our stars might be hurt. When we arrived at the scene, Connie was shaking violently–not from the cold, not from pain or fear, but from uncontrollable laughter. It seems that as the sleigh was tipping over, Connie flew through the air and landed in a snowdrift. Standing nearby were two little girls, mouths agape, as Connie screamed, "Holy shit!"

Years later, Bob Finkel told me about the first time he worked with Bing. Bob thought he would like to give Bing a special gift to express his appreciation–sort of an opening-night type gift, I guess. Bob had noticed that Bing had a leather case that was quite worn and falling apart, so Bob bought a similar one and had it monogrammed with Bing's initials. When he visited Bing at his home and gave him the gift, Bing said, "Don't ever do that again." When asked why, Bing said, "Follow me" and led Bob down into a huge room in the basement piled high with stacks and stacks of unopened gifts.

Bing explained, "If you give me a gift, then I have to give you a gift and so on and so on. So don't ever give me anything." In my mind that is one practical but very cold man. Easy to work with but not cozy or fun.

While Bing did not exude a sense of great happiness, I cannot say he was without a sense of humor. Once when I was doing a Bing special with Dean Martin and Flip Wilson, my partner John brought his mother, Ella, to the set specifically to meet Bing, her all-time favorite singer. As John was introducing Ella to Bing, Dean walked by. Ella swung around and totally ignoring Bing, said, "Was that Dino who just walked by?" Several years later John found himself alone with Bing in a Sun Valley bungalow. John reminded Bing about meeting Ella, to which Bing responded with a big chuckle, "She sure gave me the go-by."

Another time, which was unintentionally funny, Bing was playing a scene dressed as Santa Claus. At the end of the scene, the director, Marty Pasetta, released Bing so he could go to his dressing room to rest and change for the next scene. I realized that we still needed to shoot a part of the scene using Bing in his Santa Claus outfit, and so I mentioned this to Marty. "You're right!" he said. Normally a stage manager would be asked to go get Bing but I, for some reason, volunteered. When I knocked on his dressing room door and was told to enter, there was Bing with his Santa pants down and Kathryn, a registered nurse, giving Bing what I assumed was a vitamin B shot.

What made Bing the way he was? Who knows? Of course, there are times when the work can be difficult on a star. Once when Bing, at age 72, was taping a special in Pasadena, he stepped downstage toward the audience and fell 17 feet into the orchestra pit. Fortunately, he was able to grab onto a piece of scenery. As it bent, he rode it down. He could have been badly injured or killed. Instead, after just a few days in the hospital he emerged, seemingly no worse for the wear. Seven months later, though, on a golf course in Spain, he collapsed and died of a massive heart attack.

I'm very grateful for my experience with Bing. His specials were exciting, and from them I learned to interpret a script, develop a supportive style, find a unique visual approach, and deliver it on time, on budget, *and* have a good time doing it. While most of the shows were winter specials, I'll always have warm memories of them.

Chapter 12

Dick Clark

When I met Dick Clark in the early '70s, we were both young. The only problem is I grew older and Dick didn't. Well, eventually he did, but it took a long time. I was 30 when Sandy set me up to meet Dick for a small job. I can't even remember what show it was, but it was certainly small. What was my fee? That I remember because I got paid in fruit trees. That's right–fruit trees. It turned out Dick had a system going called "BX"–short for the military term "base exchange." In lieu of payment for coverage on his radio show, Dick would get BX merchandise credits, which translated into various products itemized in a catalogue. I was to be paid in any product of my choosing (within a certain price range) from this catalogue.

John and I had just bought our first house, so we now had an honest-to-God garden. From the BX catalog, I chose three fruit trees. You might think this was not an inspired choice, but in fact these were not just any fruit trees. Each had been grafted so that one tree had branches with limes, oranges, and lemons, another had nectarines, plums, and pears, etc. The trees were special but came with a slight issue: How would I pay my agent his 10 percent? The problem was solved with a check of some amount, not with fruit.

Dick was an interesting man. I was never sure if he really had a sense of humor or if he made jokes and laughed a lot as a means to charm people and to get his way. His jokes never seemed to come out naturally. Sad in a way, as I always suspected that while he lived a very interesting and rich life, I'm not sure he always *enjoyed* it. He did enjoy making money and had a remarkable ability to spot a situation that was a potential money maker.

In 1974, Dick dreamed up the idea of an awards show that would tie into his many connections with the music world. He named this new venture "The American Music Awards." The concept of an awards show was very new in those days. In the broadcast world, the major awards shows were the Academy Awards (movies), the Emmy Awards (television), the Grammy Awards (music), and the Tony Awards (Broadway). Fortunately, I had worked on the 41st Annual Academy Awards as an assistant to Jim Trittipo, so I knew how an awards show functioned. Now, here was Dick Clark putting together a real money maker, sort of a variation on the Grammys, but a show that would have greater appeal to middle America. The American Music Awards, or AMAs, as they were called, made no Grammy-like claims to high-brow culture. In those days there were not a lot of awards shows, so a large television audience sat ready and eager to watch celebrities in a live situation. With his many connections in the music business, some dating back to his "American Bandstand" days, Dick Clark was more than happy to oblige. Sandy, my ever-resourceful agent, negotiated a handsome fee (no BX) for me, which to Dick's credit increased steadily over the next 27 years. Later on, Dick could easily have let me go and hired a less expensive designer, but he stuck with me, something I always appreciated. Maybe he liked that I was always on budget and did some of my best work on that show. Who knows?

In addition to my fee, Sandy got Dick to agree to pay me a royalty of $300 a year for however long the American Music Awards used the trophy I designed for the event –a Lucite pyramid on a wooden base. Of course, my reaction was, "Sandy, by the time 30 years have gone by, I'll be able to buy an Arrow shirt with that fee." Not true, but close–maybe a Robert Graham shirt. The interesting thing was this: Dick loved to make money but hated spending it. Paying that $300 annual fee must have really irked him. The first year, I got a nice $300 check, but the next year a messenger arrived with $300 in single dollar bills. *Soooo*, being the mischievous sort that I am, I sent the messenger back to Dick with a dollar in pennies and a note saying, "You overpaid me by a buck."

That's when the fun began. The next year I got $300 in K-Mart gift certificates, and the year after that Dick requested that I come by the office. When I arrived, I was asked to wait a few minutes, then ushered into Dick's office only to discover that he had arranged for his people to cover the walls with freshly minted sheets of one-dollar bills, hot off the U.S. Treasury presses. Maybe I was wrong about Dick's sense of humor after all. The sheets made for an amazing wallpaper. They also made great wrapping paper for my nephew and niece that Christmas. The next year I started receiving one-dollar bills each day by mail–a lot of work for Dick's secretary, so, unbeknownst to Dick, she and I secretly arranged for her to send me the remaining amount in a single payment. Another year I got a $20 gold piece encased in a bottle, at that time valued at $300. In 2018 this gold piece was appraised at $3,200. I bet Dick would have preferred to keep that year's fee and substituted something less valuable. The year after that I received a $300 gift certificate to one of the restaurants Dick owned in Malibu. By the time my friends and I finished our meal, the bill came to $532, so I didn't do so well on that one. And on it went, with Dick's best stunt being three $100 bills embedded in Plexiglas, to which I responded with two pieces of Plexiglas warped and bubbled after heating them together in my home oven, with a torn piece of a dollar bill buried between the two pieces of Plexiglas along with a message from me saying, "You overpaid me again."

I remember our first production meeting for an AMA show. There we sat around a large conference table with Dick, the gifted director John Moffitt, and other members of the creative team. Suddenly I was aware that no one was speaking, and they were all looking at me as if I was the only one who knew about award shows–and they were right. Finally, I said, "Let me tell you about seat fillers." This term refers to extras who are hired by the production company so that the camera never spots an empty seat. Dressed in formal attire, the extras sit in the back of the audience. When an award is announced and the winner leaves his or her seat to go up on stage to accept the trophy and then backstage to be photographed, an extra fills the winner's seat, usually during a commercial. Hence, no empty seats and no chance the TV audience at home will think the event is anything less than a spectacular success. It was a long meeting, with me explaining all about seat fillers and everything else I knew about award shows. I smile at this, as it appears that Dick got a set designer and an awards show consultant all for the price of one.

The first American Music Awards was scheduled to be shot in the Aquarius Theatre in Hollywood. Built in 1938 during Hollywood's Golden Age and originally called the Earl Carroll Theatre, it was located at the intersection of Sunset

Boulevard and Vine Street. It was designed in the Streamline Modern style and had a stage equipped with a built-in 60-foot-diameter turntable–a wonderful toy for me to play with. This coincided with the introduction of a new material: the heat-shrink mirror, which was a Mylar "fabric" that, when stretched on a metal frame and heated with a hairdryer, became a perfect mirror four feet wide by almost any length one wanted. What I did was make a series of these mirrors measuring 4 by 30 feet and had them bolted together to form a wall 64 feet wide by 30 feet tall across the back of the stage; together with side walls of the same dimensions, the mirrors formed a large box that multiplied anything inside many times over. There was also a mirrored ceiling with slots for lights to illuminate the sets and the performers. This was 1973 and was well ahead of the famous Broadway musical "A Chorus Line" which also made a big visual impact in 1975 with the same mylar heat shrink mirrors. On the turntable was a large sculptural platform with many steps and levels for performers, and for presenters to make their entrances. There were also four multi-layered columns–one column inside another, and those inside yet another: seven layers in all, kind of like a Russian matryoshka doll, but in this case with differently decorated layers. The idea was that during commercial breaks the crew in tuxedos would strip away the layers on the columns, and the set would rotate to different positions, thereby creating a series of new looks.

Now, there were two sizable problems. The first was John Moffitt who, as director, was a bit freaked out by my whole concept. John was a clever, experienced director, having logged many years directing "The Ed Sullivan Show." I understood his concern, as there was a natural fear that the cameras would see themselves in the mirrors. I knew this wasn't a problem because I had worked as an assistant art director on a set for Diana Ross when she was on "The Hollywood Palace" and Jim Trittipo had come up with a design using mirrors. I knew that as long as the areas around the cameras were dark, they would not pick up their own image. I alleviated the director's concern by borrowing a video camera from a friend and shooting the various looks to be featured on the show in the model–a big job, but it appeared to have done the trick. John Moffitt relaxed, and we moved forward.

The next problem was tougher. It occurred after the set was installed. We had a production meeting at the theatre and during my presentation of the set, I said, "After the first number, the turntable will move a half-turn." As I made this statement, I moved the set in the model a half-turn.

"No, it won't!" Dick said suddenly. At that point, I didn't have a lot of experience working with Dick, but instinctively I knew I could not discuss this with Dick in front of the 80 or so people at the meeting. I suggested that Dick and I retire to another room for a private conversation.

"What's the problem?" I asked him. "I heard that the turntable breaks down," Dick responded. "I'm not risking my show with a faulty turntable." "Oh, the turntable was fixed a long time ago," I assured him. "It's no problem. Besides, if it breaks down you don't have to pay me my fee." Dick understood at that moment that I would certainly not risk my fee if there was any chance of the turntable not working.

After the meeting, I raced backstage, ran up to the head carpenter (the man in charge of the backstage area of the theatre), and said in a panic, "I heard that the turntable breaks down. Is that true?" He assured me that the problem had been

133

fixed. The night of the show, the turntable did, in fact, work perfectly and was a big hit. That set was one of the best designs I had done to date.

Working on the American Music Awards was a boon to my career. During my second year, Jeff Margolis took over as the director and we hit it off big time. This led to my working with him on more than 20 AMAs as well as 10 Miss America Pageants, the TV special "Happy Birthday Hollywood," the Beatrice Arthur special, "The Night of 100 Stars," and the 63rd Annual Academy Awards show. He's a marvelous director and, along with his wife, Leslie, became a valued friend. The point here is this: If you can connect with a top director, you'll have a good chance of securing important projects. In the process, you just might make a great friend.

Taking into account that I designed 27 American Music Awards shows, each featuring between 10 and 14 sets per show, I was bound to run into a few difficult moments. One that comes to mind concerns a performance by Prince in 1985. When he was booked on the show, I was sent to see his act in a large stadium in the Midwest where he was on tour. I sat through the show seated at the audio table, which was about two-thirds of the way back from the stage. The audio guy played the music so loudly that even with my fingers held in my ears throughout the performance, I could barely hear out of my left ear the next day. When I eventually needed hearing aids, I couldn't help but wonder if that particular evening with Prince had something to do with my hearing loss. One of the downsides to my work.

For his performance on the American Music Awards, Prince was to do his popular number "Purple Rain." So naturally I decided to create purple rain on stage. Obviously, this would need to be a controlled situation in which the "rain" would not land on anyone. Well, after a number of tests in the extraordinarily resourceful ABC shop, the special effects and drapery department came up with a flat, clear-plastic envelope 4 feet wide by 35 feet high with a device on top that held three gallons of purple paint. On cue, a special release mechanism would tip the device that held the paint, allowing the paint to slowly dribble down the inside of the envelope. After numerous tests with various thicknesses of paint and blocked areas inside the envelope, we got a beautiful flow of "purple rain." I then had eight of these units made and installed in the theatre for the big night. I'm still in awe over the toys I got to play with during my career. Needless to say, I was excited the night of the show.

Prince's performance was sensational, and when my purple rain was released, the audience went wild. A terrific moment for me. Prince's number was the last performance of the evening. The purple rain envelopes were then flown up high above the stage and out of sight for the closing of the show. Excitedly, I went out on stage just after the show was over to thank the crew (and to selfishly try to hear some compliments about my set). Suddenly I was hit by a drip, drip, drip of purple paint. One of my envelopes was leaking. How lucky that Prince had been the show's final performer. Not sure how we would have made it through the show with purple paint raining down on everyone. A close call, that one.

While working with Prince may have caused me some ear damage, Prince wasn't the only performer who used a ridiculously loud volume of sound. In truth, having the sound system on the American Music Awards elevated to such a dangerously high volume became a vogue. I remember the director saying to the audio guys, "I want the sound so loud that the audience's ears bleed!" Unbelievable. It got so crazy that when M. C. Hammer was a guest on the show in the old Shrine Auditorium, the volume was hyped up so high that during the rehearsal, pieces of plaster started to dislodge from the ceiling and fall down onto the audience. Fortunately, this happened during the rehearsal and no one was hit. Eventually, to protect the audience, the producers had earplugs taped to the cover of every program.

I had perks, including the use of the stage-left theatre box of the Shrine Auditorium all for myself and my guests. I could invite 17 friends to watch the show up close for free, and I could take them in small groups backstage for a tour during the show. My friends loved seeing the talent getting ready to go on or waiting in the green room.

We set designers need more than luck. We need nerves of steel, because if you ever let anyone know you have a serious scenic problem, the problem can grow and spread like wildfire through the entire production team. For example, once when I was doing a musical special at CBS for Dick, the Dick Clark production team had some scheduling difficulties. The show required an audience dressed in black tie. We had wanted to do the show on a specific night, but some of the talent was only available the night before. Dick's solution was to pre-tape the talent who could not attend the night of the actual show, and to plant dressed-up extras in the audience for the pre-taping so the pre-taped section would be interchangeable with the actual show. Everything would be edited together and then aired at a later date. It seemed like a clever solution.

Now, as a set designer I was always on the lookout for new and exciting visual elements to work into my sets. At a restaurant in Denver, I had seen 20 or so handblown, tear-drop-shaped, clear-glass globes, each with a lit votive candle inside— a wonderful, theatrical look. One of my assistants did some research, found a glassblower, and had 350 globes made for the show. Inside the ABC studio, where the ballroom set had been put into place, the globes were strung over the heads of the audience. I thought the look would be unique and terrific, and I was right. I received many compliments during the first 10 hours of pre-taping of those performers who could not be there the night of the show.

At the pre-taping, the scene looked elegant, with several hundred extras dressed in tuxedos and gowns around 22 circular tables covered with crisp, white tablecloths and topped with stunning flower arrangements. Performer after performer did his or her act. Everything was as it should be until, suddenly, I noticed a strange sight: Molten wax was seeping out of the glass globes. Over the hours of taping, the candles had liquified. Soon Dick was rushing towards me. He was frantic. Now, as mentioned before, if there was one thing I had learned early on, it was this: Never let anyone see you panic. I assured Dick that everything was under control, and the problem was already being addressed. Not true.

Quickly, I took one of the globes to the special effects shop down the hall and explained the problem. They fixed it by cementing each glass candleholder to the bottom of its globe. Of course, each globe and each candleholder had to be taken down, brought to the shop, cemented, and put back up again, but then we had planned on all the candles being replaced that night anyway. A number of stagehands made some nice money that evening.

In addition to the 27 American Music Awards I designed, I worked on many other special shows for Dick Clark Productions. Years later, after I had moved on to do Broadway shows and then finally retired, I began to see a number of Broadway musicals celebrating the lives of Cher, Donna Summer, The Four Seasons, and other music stars. If they ever do a musical based on the life of Dick Clark, who died at 82 in 2012, I would certainly be interested in participating. It would be another way that I could revisit my youth and Dick could stay young forever.

Chapter 13

Pearl Bailey

Ⅰn 1970 I was 31 years old and the youngest production designer in taped television. My first special that year was the previously mentioned "Hooray for Hollywood," a spoof of old films, starring Don Adams, Edie Adams (no relation!), Charlton Heston, and Don Rickles. The show was produced by Nick Vanoff, one of the top variety producers. I designed the sets–all 82 of them–on spec, in an attempt to convince Mr. Vanoff that I, the new kid on the block, could indeed design sets. The idea was to recreate looks from classic movies; scenes ranged from the yacht in "Some Like It Hot" to a large Busby Berkley production number choreographed by the very talented Kevin Carlisle. It was the largest television special CBS had done to date, and it required the use of all four CBS studios.

Designing the show was a challenge, and I had to wing it because while I had been well trained at Yale, my studies had focused on theatrical sets, not scenery for television. Fortunately, the only mishap occurred when we taped Edie playing the torch-wielding Miss Columbia in the famous Columbia Pictures logo. I had the CBS special effects department make a torch from a bunch of Fourth of July sparklers, not realizing wardrobe had used a highly flammable fabric for Edie's sash. When we lit the torch, one of the sparks ignited the sash, and Edie was ablaze! Quickly, we put out the fire and, to her credit, Edie agreed to reshoot the scene, this

139

time with three fire extinguishers at the ready as there wasn't time to find a different material for her sash. I sent her flowers to thank her.

I knew I had succeeded with "Hooray for Hollywood" because a short time later I got a call saying that Nick Vanoff wanted me to design sets for a new Don Knotts series. Great! Sandy started negotiating a contract. Everything was set, except for one small detail: I had yet to see or sign a contract to do the show. Assuming I had work lined up for the coming season, John and I went off on a six-week jaunt through Europe, innocently and unwisely spending some of the money that was to be coming in from the series. The last week of the trip we arrived at our hotel in Copenhagen to find a message from Sandy: "SORRY BUT PRODUCER HAS GONE WITH ANOTHER SET DESIGNER ON DON KNOTTS SERIES." No explanation. I was out and that was that.

Needless to say, I was devastated. John was very sympathetic and asked if I wanted to go home right then and there, to which I replied, "No, just give me 24 hours to mope and feel sorry for myself and then let's enjoy the last week of our vacation." I'm not much on feeling depressed, but this was a big loss for me. Luckily, it wasn't an issue of money, as John was highly successful in his own right. But the letdown hurt. I had been told I had the series, and in my mind, I was on my way. Ah, the twists and turns of building a career in Hollywood–or so I thought.

As it turned out, being free of Don Knotts made me available for something else. Bob Finkel, who knew me and liked my work, had just taken on "The Pearl Bailey Show." Bob and I shared the same agent. He, too, was part of the Ashley Famous stable, and soon a deal was set for me to do

140

Miss Bailey's series. Working with Bob was a daunting prospect. As a producer, Bob was sure of himself, intimidating, and had an aura of success about him. He reeked of wealth and achievement. He also wore the best hairpiece I have ever seen, except for maybe Bing's. The story goes that when Bob was producing the first Elvis television special, he took one look at the King of Rock on a TV monitor and called a break. "We need to talk in your dressing room," he whispered to Elvis. Once there, Bob explained to Elvis that his pitch-black hair looked phony, almost as if it had been darkened with shoe polish. Elvis didn't take this news well at all, and the discussion soon escalated to a shouting match. "What do you know about hair, anyway?" Elvis lashed out at Bob. "This is what I know!" Bob responded as he ripped off his hairpiece and threw it on the floor. Elvis had his hair re-dyed. Clearly, Bob knew how to control people. But he had met his match with Pearl.

So now we were working on "The Pearl Bailey Show," a weekly series that aired on ABC from January to May in 1971. Having missed the first meeting, I had yet to meet Miss Bailey. When I finally did, Bob graciously made the introduction. Pearl mumbled something I could not understand. What I heard sounded like, "Cum ere gim im a kass." What to do?

"Excuse me," I replied. "I didn't get that," to which Pearl again uttered something indecipherable. I sat there stupidly trying to fake my way through by just smiling. Suddenly, loud and clear she said, "Humph. He's prejudiced. He doesn't want to come here and give me a kiss."

"Oh no, Pearl, I misunderstood you," I said, and hastily went over to her and gave her a kiss on the cheek. Ducked that one.

Production meetings with Pearl were off the wall, each session as unique as she was. Pearl set the tone. While most musical-variety production meetings were intended as places to brainstorm ideas, impart information, discuss who will be in the show, the numbers that will be performed, and to talk through schedules, Pearl's meetings were conducted like children's parties. Seriously. At each person's place would be a child's placemat and party cup filled with candy and other party favors. In the center of the table, we would find other snacks, including a big bowl of fruit. Sodas and party cups were passed around. Whose birthday was this? In fact, Pearl was taking care of her brood.

In some ways, Pearl was very inclusive, and yet she also had a pecking order. At the meetings, the principal players sat in comfortable chairs around the table. The lesser participants sat in folding chairs up against the wall. Once, as a meeting was breaking up and people were leaving, one of the secretaries walked past the table and picked up an apple. When Pearl found out, she wanted to fire the woman. Fortunately, she was talked out of it, but I found all of this so very strange.

Our meetings were held in the upstairs rooms at the historic Hollywood Palace Theatre (formerly the Hollywood Playhouse and now known as Avalon Hollywood), where the show was rehearsed and taped. Pearl, who was co-producer with Bob Finkel and president of the production company (everyone's check was signed "Pearl Bailey, Prez."), sat at one end of the table, with Bob at the other end. Around the table sat the team of writers, plus Dean Whitmore, the director and one of the most charming men I have ever met. Also present were Lee Miller, associate producer, who was to become a close friend, and Pete Menefee, the brilliant costume designer whose costume sketches were witty, sharp, and smart, as was his tongue. Then there was Bob Sydney, the choreographer who, with his deeply lined face and constant scowl, looked like a character out of Dick Tracy. Beneath his downer manner and dry sense of humor was a kind, funny man.

Pearl was totally unpredictable. While Pete did the stunning costumes for the show, Pearl tended to her own wardrobe; one never knew what she would come up with next. For our first show, she had planned to wear a gold lame gown, but the video people said the dress was too "hot" (bright), so wardrobe carefully covered the entire gown with a thin black fabric (called soufflé) to tone it down, creating almost an entire new gown over the existing one. Pearl wasn't happy but this time went along with it. Typically, we used two spotlights on Pearl and one on Caucasian performers, in a quest to lighten up Pearl's skin tones (now, of course, a questionable practice). Anyway, Pearl was not happy having her dress toned down. The next week she refused to show anyone what she planned to wear for her opening entrance. This time she had on a dress of reflective silver fabric. When she made her entrance, the video man came out of his booth screaming, "My God, she's wearing Reynold's Wrap!"

Later in the show she wore a simple, beautiful deep-garnet velvet gown with a magnificent diamond brooch on her shoulder. Pearl never wore anything but the best, and one suspected that she lived inside Van Cleef and Arpels. Unfortunately, Pearl always wanted to impress people, and so she added a second, large diamond pin a bit lower, and finally

143

a third pin–right on her crotch! As time passed, Pete and I would amuse ourselves trying to guess what Pearl might wear to spoil the look we were trying for. Once she gussied up a cocktail dress, by adding a large white fur collar, which we immediately named her "toilet seat dress." There was no controlling the "Prez."

It was easy to tell when Pearl was angry because her eyes would become little slits. One day at a production meeting her eyes did just that and zeroed in on me. Pete, who was sitting next to me, grabbed my hand under the table out of concern and in support as Pearl said, "Ray, I hear you've been asking my dresser what I'm wearing in the different numbers in the show." "Yes," I replied. "What I wear has nothing to do with your sets," she fired back. "If you talk to my dresser, he'll be fired."

I looked around the production table and was greeted with a sea of faces staring at her in total disbelief. When did she enter the business? A major part of my job was to coordinate with wardrobe and lighting to make our colors and styles work together. It turned out that Pearl simply had trouble deciding what to wear and didn't want anyone to know it.

This didn't stop me. Typically in rehearsals, if her dresser was at the back of the audience during a break and I was on stage, I would walk in his direction as he walked toward the stage. As we passed each other, he would say out of the side of his mouth, "Pink in the opening number," or something similar. One time I simply could not find out what she was going to wear. Pearl loved to cook and often prepared a big supper for the cast and crew after the taping of the show. Inspired by this, she had decided that for her opening number she would demonstrate how to cook what she called "A Dish for the Masses." I created a "kitchen" that gave the illusion Pearl had been preparing this meal there. I wanted the set to echo what Pearl was wearing, so I purchased kitchen towels in every color I could find, then hid them and myself behind the kitchen counter. As the cameras focused on Pearl making her way down the aisle from the back of the theatre and onto the stage, I poked my head around the counter, saw that she was wearing yellow, quickly grabbed two yellow towels, slapped them onto the counter, and crawled on my hands and knees off stage and out of sight of both the camera audience and Pearl. This is what we did as we wanted the show and Pearl to look fabulous.

Sometimes there was simply nothing that could be done to control Pearl. On one occasion, she decided she wanted to do a number using the song "Two by Two," from the current Danny Kaye Broadway hit musical of the same name. The idea was to do it as a sweet Victorian number with the dancers all in pastels, the ladies wearing large hoop skirts and elaborate flowered hats and holding lace parasols. My set was a beautiful rattan and wicker valentine lit in soft pink washes. Very pretty. Unfortunately, Pearl chose to wear a contemporary pants suit and had just had an argument with her husband, the renowned jazz drummer Louie Bellson. Sweet and easy going, Louie was also the show's band leader. Apparently, the argument had escalated without any of the crew being aware of it.

Suddenly, in the middle of taping "Two by Two," Pearl stopped everything and said in front of the audience, "This ain't no funeral, Louie. Pick up the beat! One-two, one-two, one-two!" and we were off to the races, doing the number at breakneck speed. The poor dancers didn't know what hit them.

145

As Pearl raced through the song, the dancers frantically tried to keep pace. Hats went askew, some falling off, parasols popped inside out, and skirts got caught up in the scenery. It was a shambles and, in retrospect, unintentionally funny. At the end of the number, everyone gathered in the rattan oval of the set for a Victorian valentine pose, and what a picture it was–like a tornado had swept through, and indeed she had.

One of the great rewards of doing Pearl's series, aside from seeing a larger-than-life personality in action, was the amount I learned. For a designer, the only way to really grow is to work, work, work, design, design, design, and that is what I did. With 70- to 80-hour work weeks, I produced an average of seven sets a week. I learned to work fast, and I loved it.

It wasn't always easy. The simple fact was that I had no vocabulary, no real experience to draw on, so every set was a new challenge. At one point we were doing a top-hat, white-tie-and-tails number. I figured that in order to get the set drafted, bid, built, and on stage by Wednesday, I would need to get my designs to the producer by 4 p.m. that Friday for his approval. It was now Friday at 3:50, and I still didn't have a clue as to what to do. To my own amazement, I took a coffee break to calm down but secretly thought I was out of my mind. As I sipped my coffee from a mug my assistant had given me, I looked at the Art Deco pattern that circled the cup. Perfect! I got out my pad and pencil, drew up a version of the design, and had five minutes left over to enjoy my coffee before going in to see the producer and making my pitch. It worked, but, oh, what a close call.

One week, the show's guest star, Debbie Reynolds, was scheduled to sing a rain medley. What to do? I ended up creating several Art Nouveau tree trunks topped with leaves

146

shaped like raindrops and painted translucent white, opaque frosted white, and lime green, all on clear plastic panels. During the rehearsal, I asked the director to find out what Miss Reynolds would be wearing. "Oh, it looks just like the set," the director replied. Sure, I thought. Well, the next day Debbie performed her rain medley wearing a white gown with a full skirt covered with white, frosted, and lime-green raindrop-shaped leaves, just like my set. Pete and his crew must have been up all night creating that fabulous dress that echoed my set. Wonderful!

Pearl had a habit of annoying people, which sometimes was funny and sometimes not. Joel Thurm, who traveled from New York with Pearl as her assistant, probably had the most difficult job of anyone on the production team. One day, word came that a good friend of Pearl's had been taken to the hospital. The friend was ill enough that it was decided to not tell Pearl because she would most likely go to the hospital and make the friend even more ill with her typical carryings on. So, Joel hid the information from his boss. When Pearl found out, she confronted Joel and asked if he had known that her friend was in the hospital. When Joel confessed, Pearl promptly hauled off and slapped him as hard as she could, and Pearl was one powerful woman. Later, she apologized to Joel and gave him an expensive ring from Cartier. I couldn't resist asking Joel if the ring was worth it. He just smiled. He had been through a lot of her moods and outbursts and was used to her. The rest of us were not.

One day Pearl gave the dancers a lecture on personal hygiene. She told them that when they danced, they often would sweat, and the odor could be offensive. Pearl's solution was to suggest they wear cologne. This annoyed a Black dancer who had been in Pearl's all-Black cast of "Hello Dolly" on Broadway. Like Joel, he was accustomed to Pearl's behavior. So, the next day he showed up at rehearsal reeking. He had gone out and purchased three bottles of the cheapest cologne he could find and poured them all over himself. But this wasn't enough of a payback.

Later that week, during a run-through rehearsal, when the various dance numbers were being shown to the production team, in the middle of one of the numbers Pearl began to stagger around, holding her head. We all thought it was very funny until we realized she was, in fact, hurt. Pearl wasn't fooling around. Everyone sat down as our star was fussed over. The same Black dancer who had pulled the cologne stunt was sitting next to me vibrating–not from concern but from uncontrolled laughter. When I asked him what was so funny, he replied, "I got her! I got the Black bitch!" It turned out he had made a fist and swung it about and connected with Pearl's head during one of the dance movements. Unbelievable.

Sometimes Pearl's ability to annoy people was more amusing than harmful. One week we had the famous opera singer Leontyne Price on the show. Now, here was one fabulous lady. During the run-through in the rehearsal hall, she sang an aria. What a glorious experience to hear that incredible voice in close quarters. Powerful. We were all in awe. Well, Miss Price decided enough was enough, and as she hit a high note, she put things in perspective by placing her fingers on the top of her head, spinning around and around the room while performing umbrella turns and bringing us all back to our childhoods and to reality. She was fun, warm, and charming. However, one person who wasn't charmed was Pearl.

The next day, during the taping of the show, Pearl and Leontyne were to reminisce about how Leontyne had sung "I Love You Truly" at Louie and Pearl's wedding 18 years earlier. The idea was that Pearl would then encourage Leontyne to sing the song for the audience, which is what she did. I did notice how low-key Pearl had seemed when she and Leontyne had reminisced–totally out of character for Pearl. There was Pearl demurely telling the wedding story with her hands behind her back. (Pearl had beautiful hands and always used them when speaking.) As Miss Price began singing "I Love You Truly," to everyone's horror, Pearl brought out a tambourine she had been hiding behind her back and started to bang it to the beat of the song. So incredibly rude! Leontyne, no fool she, proceed to say, "Come on Pearl, join in!" And, of course, Pearl couldn't resist, so the solo became a duet. Then something amazing happened, and it happened fast. As Pearl sang, Leontyne ripped the tambourine out of Pearl's hand and went down into the audience leaving Pearl up on stage singing by herself as Leontyne passed the tambourine around the audience and took up a collection for Pearl. Great sense of humor, and great one-upmanship.

The bottom line was this: Pearl was exasperating to the point where she drove her producer, Bob Finkel, right over the edge. One night he was found passed out, drunk in Pearl's dressing room from frustration.

ABC gave Pearl video copies of all her shows. What did she do with them? She put them in her freezer for safekeeping. Of course, they were immediately destroyed. My impression was that Pearl did her best to overcome her rough upbringing on the streets of Newport News, Va. Sometimes she did inappropriate things that came across as self-promoting or selfish. Other times it was hard not to love her for her generosity of spirit. In fact, in 1988 she received the Presidential Medal of Freedom. Always, she was larger than life and always fascinating. And you know what? No matter how hard the production team worked to make her look good, ultimately when Pearl sat on a stool without scenery or an expensive wardrobe and without a guest star and just sang, you couldn't touch her. She was simply great.

Chapter 14

Cher

W hat was Cher like in the '70s? I was about to find out. Sandy called with the news that producer George Schlatter would like me to design the sets for the second season of Cher's television series. It was 1976, the year after she and Sonny had called it quits (or so we thought), and Cher had ventured out on her own.

The first season of her solo show had been reasonably successful, and the production team was strong, talented, and friendly. Bob Mackie was doing Cher's remarkable costumes, Anita Mann had signed on as choreographer, and Lee Miller was the producer (and would become a dear and important friend). As executive producer, George Schlatter brought an off-the-wall humor to the mix; he had recently produced the highly rated "Rowan and Martin's Laugh-In." Bob Kelly had established a high mark for the set designs that first season but had chosen not to do the second season. My call to replace Bob most likely came at the urging of Lee Miller, who had liked my work on "Pearl." In the television business, as in so many other businesses, it often came down to whom you knew.

My first day on the job, I went to check out my office and meet the production team. CBS had no space on its lot for the extensive "Cher" staff, so a suite of rooms near the CBS studios had been rented. The production company took all the rooms on an upper level of the building except for two rooms already occupied by a community health clinic. Security inside and outside the rented offices was non-existent–unlike at the

151

CBS studios, where guards had been posted after a stalker had showed up twice in Cher's dressing room.

So, unannounced, I walked into George Schlatter's office to say hello and get to know him better. George was bigger than life and had a career that matched his personality. In 1967, his groundbreaking "Laugh-In" had changed the face of television and epitomized his unique ability to conceive and produce exciting television shows. Up to now we had only a nodding acquaintance, and it was important for me to get closer to him. But before a word was uttered, I realized my timing was off. George was talking to a pathetic-looking girl. I assumed she was interviewing for a secretarial position, and I couldn't help feeling sorry for her. With her big nose, long, matted hair, bad skin, and crooked teeth she was clearly out of place in this glamorous environment. The poor girl had probably never been on a date in her life. But then it hit me: *This was Cher.*

Cher, born Cherilyn Sarkisian, might not have looked like much as a civilian, but when she got in front of a camera, everything changed. I never could figure it out. True, it helped that we used camera filters that softened Cher's skin and hid the many imperfections that makeup couldn't. But the truth is, Cher had a magic about her that made her unique. The cameras simply loved her.

Before we could start shooting, Cher went to New York for a skin peel. She reacted badly to it, and we had to postpone the taping of the first show by a week. Even then she still looked blotchy, and I wondered if she could pull it off. The day we went on camera, the shooting schedule stated that late that afternoon we would take a break. "Hiawatha washes her hair," was how the schedule jokingly put it, an inside reference to Cher's Native American ancestry (in fact, her ancestry is half Armenian and maybe a little bit of Cherokee, but maybe not). In those days her long, freshly washed hair was pure silk. I doubt that she washed it herself, but she did apply her own makeup. When she emerged from her dressing room three hours later and stood four feet away from me, she was flawless–truly beautiful in an exotic sort of way.

Having survived the Pearl Bailey series, I thought I could handle this new assignment fairly easily. Wrong. I had certainly gained some confidence but still didn't have any extensive experience to draw upon. And I was, as mentioned, the youngest set/production designer in the industry. I so wanted to be the best in the business but had not hit my stride. I had to work even harder than usual to meet the show's high standards as well as the standards I had set for myself.

Mackie's extraordinary talent also set a very high mark for me. I loved working with Bob. The high caliber of his professional output made me work even harder. Without fail, spending time with him was a pleasure. His wit, charm, and graciousness were much appreciated. I'm sure there were times when he didn't particularly care for some of the ideas I came up with, but he was always smiling and enthusiastic toward me. How Bob is able, to this day, to turn out in quantity and quality such fine, stylish designs is amazing to me.

My favorite part of the show was Cher's solo. Every week Bob and I would try something different. My first chance to shine with Cher's solo number did not begin auspiciously, since the star made clear her desire to keep the look simple. She wanted to wear blue jeans and sing "Send in the Clowns" in front of the famous Richard Avedon portrait of her that had appeared on the cover of *Time* magazine. How could I shine if

I had to adhere to this seemingly mundane approach to the number? Designed by Mackie, the dress she wore in that photograph was simply sensational, a rhinestone-studded, nearly nude sheath trimmed with bleached vulture feathers.

What to do to make the solo special? Well, I had the Avedon photograph reproduced and hand painted in the CBS scenic paint shop on a 15- by 20-foot piece of framed muslin. I then had just her figure painted on the backside of the muslin so only the figure was opaque. When the painting was lit from behind, Cher appeared just in silhouette. When the lights came up on the front of the painting, her other self appeared, all very stylish, chicly gowned, and glamorous. Quite the contrast between public and private image. In addition, I had the shop take three-quarter-inch Plexiglas and make what I believe was the first clear staircase ever used on television. When we shot the number, there was Cher in her blue jeans reclining on that clear staircase, looking as if she were floating on air.

Another time, I found some handsome blue-and-white patterned fabric and had yards of it hung flat about 15 feet above the stage and then draped it flat onto the floor like a photographer's backdrop. I gave the rest of the fabric to Bob, who made a marvelous outfit that had various parts of Cher's bare skin exposed. The result was this blue-and-white pattern with an arm here and a leg there, revealing a good part of Cher's thigh. Very sexy and exotic.

Of course, Bob Mackie's costumes for Cher were what made her solos truly special. What always amused me was that he could put her in a nude body stocking with three sequins strategically placed (I'm exaggerating a bit, but not much) and the CBS Standards and Practices lady who oversaw the propriety of what aired never said a word. But if Cher actually exposed some skin, as she did once in an Indian costume that was bare down both sides of her body, the lady told Cher that the costume was out. Well, guess how Cher dealt with that? She cried. And she was given permission to wear the costume.

Bob and his team of assistants really fussed over Cher's costumes. You never saw an unsightly seam or wrinkle. Everyone kept a close eye on those valuable outfits. One day, when Bob was unable to attend a fitting, an assistant covered for him in Cher's dressing room. A timid soul, the assistant fussed over the star's typically revealing costume, checking here and there for imperfections. At one point he saw a loose thread on her bikini brief and attempted to remove it. Well, it wasn't a loose thread. It was her tampon. Cher screamed with laughter. The poor assistant turned red with embarrassment–and disappeared for 24 hours.

One favorite design concept originated with a leopard coat rented by Bob and valued at $75,000 (in 1976 dollars). Not to be outdone, I went to the Burbank Studios, on the old Warner Bros. lot, and rented a private first-class railroad compartment complete with ormolu, inlaid wood, brass fixtures, bud vases–the works. When Cher sat in that opulent compartment with two dozen of the longest stemmed roses I had ever seen (provided by Bob Chechie, our wonderful set dresser), she looked like a million bucks. Swathed in all this luxury, she began singing the lyrics to "500 Miles": "Not a shirt on my back, not a penny to my name. Lord I can't go a-home this a-way." As Bob Mackie and I sat in the control booth grinning from ear to ear, so pleased with ourselves, George Schlatter came charging in and screamed, "What are you guys doing?"

"Who cares?" we responded. "Doesn't she look fabulous?!" The irony of the lyrics and the image made for an especially memorable moment on the show. In truth, I felt that despite Cher's talent as a vocalist, people just looked at her and paid little attention to the words. I still feel that way. Her beauty canceled out everything else. The bottom line was this: She never complained when we made her look terrific. On another occasion, the stage managers were having trouble getting Cher out of her dressing room. Now, when one is working in the studio, time is everything because time is money. We all worked hard to be prepared so that the taping of each part of the show would occur with the minimum number of interruptions. So, every minute Cher delayed had a financial consequence. It turned out she was having her nails painted. Big deal, one would think. In fact, it was. Her hands were key players in her performance. After Cher emerged from her dressing room and took up her position, she stood stone still in a simple black sheath with her hand upon her hip. As she sang, the only movement aside from her lips came from her fingers rolling over and over on her hip and flashing their red nails. Smart lady!

The pace of producing the show was a killer. I remember one Saturday receiving a script and being expected to get three of our stock sets ready for taping, *plus* design eight new sets, have the designs approved, drafted up, bid, built, and ready by Wednesday. Sounds impossible, and it nearly was. I felt as if I were bleeding all over the drafting table.

I survived. Well, almost. By the time we broke for the holiday my nerves were shot and I had developed colitis. Both Bob Mackie and I kept losing weight, with mine dropping from 150 to 134 pounds. My deteriorating health was no joke.

Doctors at Los Angeles County Hospital said I could never work like that again. It was just too intense. So I eased up on myself a bit. As I worked on future shows, I became better at actualizing my design concepts with less pressure on myself. Gradually, I developed a design vocabulary that made the work less intense and even better in quality. As a result, I never suffered another bout of colitis and, hey, I got some cheekbones out of it, at least for a while.

I wasn't the only one on our production floor to have problems. One day when I was sitting at my desk, I heard a gun go off. Was it Jerry Lewis running through the production offices again, shooting off blanks as he had been known to do? But then I heard someone crying. Looking for an excuse not to work, I decided to investigate. In the medical clinic that shared our floor, a secretary was sobbing into the phone. I asked, "Are you alright?" She gestured to the clinic's other room and said, "He's been shot!"

I froze. What to do? One part of me knew I should go in and try to help, whatever the consequences. The other part wanted to run. Needless to say, there really was no choice. I opened the door and saw a man slumped in the corner, his chest covered in blood. So much blood! To this day I remain horrified by my reaction, which was to think, "That blood doesn't look real. The red's too bright." But it *was* real. I was alone with the poor guy and decided to stop the bleeding as best I could.

Before I could finish taking off my shirt, thinking I would use it to staunch the blood flow, a woman arrived who clearly knew what to do. She asked me for a pair of scissors, presumably to cut away the victim's shirt and use it as a tourniquet. This gave me an excuse to get away. I ran to my

157

office, grabbed the pair of scissors, ran back, gave them to the woman, and then asked the secretary if anyone had called an ambulance (no 911 in those days). She said yes, and I ran downstairs to await the medics and guide them up to the room which, in fact, would be difficult for them to find. When the ambulance pulled up along with a police car, I yelled, "Up this way!" and started to go back into the building.

"Stay back," a policeman cautioned me. "The guy doing the shooting may still be in there." Too late now to worry about that, I thought. If the killer was still in the office, I'd probably be dead. I refused the officer's command and led the way to the clinic. When we got up to the crime scene, emergency services personnel took charge, and I returned to my office.

By this time, our production company was upset, especially our own secretary, who had apparently been asked by the gunman to help him locate the clinic. A nightmare for her, as she could identify the gunman and he could identify her. Would he return to silence her? Shockingly, the victim died, and the killer was never found. I continue to be appalled by my reaction to all that blood and can no longer stand to watch violent films.

And so, for me, the "Cher" show was a killer in more ways than I would have liked. The pressure stayed on, but not in the same way. One day I was called into Lee Miller's office and told there had just been a casting addition. The multi-talented Anthony Newley would be joining the show for the upcoming week. We already had the terrific Tina Turner on board, and I had spent the week's budget creating a glitzy finale set, which now had to be trashed. The new finale was to feature a gospel revival meeting, in a tent. Where was I to get the money for that? Coming from a family where one never asked one's parents for money above one's allowance, it never dawned on me to request additional funds to cover this change. In any case, there was no time to build an elaborate set.

Driving home that night, I recalled seeing the stagehands pulling the great drape that formed the studio cyclorama around on its track. A cyclorama, or "cyc" as we called it, was made of two layers of fabric. The back layer was white seamless muslin measuring 30 by 100 feet. In front of it, on a separate traveler track, was a white scrim, a seamless gauzelike material the same size as the muslin. This was the material that formed the background for much of the sets in those days. Now, remembering that the scrim draped beautifully as it was pulled on its track, I thought, "Ah, I can make a tent by pulling up the scrim and draping both the scrim and muslin in a tent-like fashion." I added a few tent poles made from inexpensive, cardboard Sono tubes. Bob Checchi, our innovative set decorator, scattered sawdust on the floor and added some rustic benches rented from a local prop house. The result: a revival tent. Everyone loved the look, and best of all, I won an Emmy Award for that episode. My first nomination was a win. What a high!

Another, different kind of high occurred one night when we were running late. Technical problems with the video machines had stopped us from taping for an hour or so. It was 1 a.m., and Cher and her guests, who happened to be the Muppets, were stuck, just standing around waiting until we could start taping again. Cher and Kermit began talking, and unfortunately for future generations, no cameras were running because the exchange between the two of them was priceless. That frog (a.k.a. Jim Henson) kept up with Cher every step of

159

the way, right down to her raw and raunchy language. He gave as good as he got–two great talents in an off-the-cuff moment. So unexpected and so funny.

Around this time, I was offered two television specials that fell in the middle of a break in our schedule, so I went to Lee Miller and asked if it was okay to take on these two shows. He approved, thank God, because Cher had been having secret meetings with Sonny about dropping the show and reuniting with him. Suddenly, we were all fired. I had never been fired in my life! The upside was that Cher's production company had to pay each of us for the remaining seven shows. But we were not allowed legally to accept any other work without the producer's permission, which they certainly were not going to give. Everyone who was fired had to sit out the rest of the time on his or her contract except me. I had already received permission to do the two specials, so I got paid for the rest of the Cher series and I was able to continue working, as well. Great!

What really made the hard work on Cher's show worth it was the Emmy Award I received. I was 100 percent sure I wouldn't win, as I was up against Ken Johnson. Ken had designed a fantastic special for John Denver, which featured a huge plastic dome in the middle of a snowfield high in the mountains. Inside the dome he created a summer environment for John that included blossoming trees, grass, and flowers. In one of many magical moments, a butterfly landed on Denver's hand. How could I top that?

Well, the day came for the awards to be announced, and to my amazement and incredible delight, I won. As I raced up to the podium to get my Emmy, I heard John's voice cheering above the rest. Not fully believing I had won my first time out, when I got to the podium, I grabbed the card that Jean Stapleton had just used to announce the winner to double check that my name was actually on it. What a wonderful moment for me. Even though my mentor and friend Jim Trittipo was gone, I got to thank him. I said that, in many ways, he was still winning Emmys. The win put me in a new league from which I was able, with Sandy Wernick's help, to build a career beyond my wildest dreams. Thank you Sandy, thank you Jim, and thank you Cher!

Chapter 15

I've Got Stories

One of the things I did while working was to never let on when things were not right. This meant that if something was messed up in the shop or if something wasn't right on stage, like when the candles started dripping hot wax down on people in the audience during the prepping of that Dick Clark show, I never let on that there was a potential or worse yet an unfixable problem. As the production designer, if I let on that the show was in any way shape or form in trouble, the problem would escalate and an atmosphere of worry and negativity would permeate the entire production. Interestingly the same situation carried over to my health. By this I mean, if I were suffering from a cold or another health issue that could affect my efficiency as a production designer, I would never let on that I was anything other than very healthy. One had to instill a sense of confidence that the job would be done in the usual, predictable, perfect way. A positive attitude on my part would usually produce a positive reaction in those I was dealing with. Clearly a negative attitude would produce a response that was unnecessary and unacceptable. That said, I tried always to be up and full of fun when working on a production. Sometimes I wasn't as "up" as I should have been but I did strive to make each show a positive experience.

A truly strange and wondrous business, this show business. Over the years there were some, shall we say, odd, interesting, and occasionally scary moments. In 1972, Charlie Chaplin was honored with a special Oscar for his lifetime achievements. Unfortunately, at this point Mr. Chaplin had managed to acquire a number of enemies who really hated him and had made threats against his life. While I never got involved in the politics of Hollywood, Mr. Chaplin certainly did. Consequently, his security on Oscar night was tight. But were the guards enough? We knew that if someone really wanted to harm him, a way might be found. That night, while standing in the wings, I watched as Mr. Chaplin entered from stage right and stood at the podium center stage to receive his special Oscar. I was a mere 35 feet from him, standing in the wings. To be safe, I made sure that the area beyond Mr. Chaplin was just the theatre's blank wood paneled wall. If someone were to point a gun, I would not be in the direct line of fire. Luckily, no one fired a shot during the 12-minute standing ovation (the longest in the history of the Academy Awards), but I wasn't taking any chances.

You can be in the line of fire even when there's no gun involved. This became clear to me in 1980 when I was installing my sets for the show "Jubilee!" at the MGM Grand Hotel in Las Vegas. The producer and director, Donn Arden, had decided to take a break. As he often did, he went out for dinner at 10 p.m. in the middle of the evening's rehearsal, had way too much to drink, and came back drunk, mean, and nasty. When Donn spoke under these conditions, his tongue would dart in and out of his mouth, very much like a snake. I've never seen this in any other human. Somehow it fit Arden's reptilian, diabolical nature. He had an other-worldly evilness about him that was married to his ability to charm. I eventually came to dread dealing with him.

Around midnight, while walking across the stage, I foolishly looked toward Donn's production table out in the audience and made eye contact with him. Now, this table was Donn's control center. Using a handheld microphone, he would direct his show in a voice so loud it carried out over the entire theatre and even into the dressing rooms. Suddenly I heard his menacing tones ricocheting off the theatre walls as he aimed his ire at me. He was screaming at me about something that didn't even remotely involve me. Infuriated and upset, I muttered an obscenity under my breath, walked off stage, and ran into my assistant Bob Rang and our lighting designer, John McLain. They had heard Donn's outburst and were looking at me with great sympathy. In an attempt to change the subject and lighten the mood, the guys reminded me that it was Halloween and there was a costume competition at a nearby hotel. Great! A distraction. We decided to enter the contest. But what to wear? John mentioned that down in the theatre basement there were costumes left over from "Hallelujah Hollywood," the show that had just closed in preparation for our own extravaganza. Perfect.

We three hightailed it down to the basement, found some "Hallelujah Hollywood!" costumes from the "Red Rock" number, and started to dress. And what costumes they were. These Bob Mackie creations consisted of red satin bell bottoms with appliquéd mirrors, harnesses that criss-crossed our chests, and shiny red helmets with three-foot-high red plumes on top. The pants were a bit too long; tall dancers we weren't. However, a paper stapler solved the hemming problem fast. The rest of the costumes fit perfectly. I sure was glad I had been going to the gym. We looked sensational, if I do say so myself.

Off we went in a terrific mood, having forgotten all about Donn's drunken outburst. We arrived at the hotel full of laughter, feeling a bit giddy and really great. After a celebratory drink, we entered the contest certain we would win. After all, we were in Bob Mackie creations, and we thought we looked *hot*. Well, we lost. It turned out one of the judges was none other than Bob Mackie himself, and conflict-of-interest issues no doubt entered the picture. We did, however, appear on the cover of that month's *Las Vegas* magazine.

Back at work the next day, when Donn was sober, I felt I was in the position to say to him, "Donn, I don't appreciate being yelled at in front of everyone. I need to tell you that if you ever do that again, I'm out of here." He said simply, "Okay."

Working under Donn Arden presented its challenges, but the show he created was nothing short of spectacular. "Jubilee!," which cost $10 million to produce in those days, was completely over the top. One of the people who was a co-costume designer with Bob Mackie was the immensely talented Pete Menefee who, in addition to designing the costumes for a large part of the show, was in charge of procuring the show's costume jewelry. Sketches in hand, he flew to Paris and made the rounds among the manufacturers and collected bids from them. Still busy checking out the various sample necklaces, armbands, and G-strings, he realized he was running late and had a plane to catch back to Los Angeles. In a rush, he quickly stuffed the jewelry samples into the pockets of his sports jacket and made his flight, which unfortunately was diverted to Washington, D.C., where the customs personnel were rigid. Pete was waved through, but at the last minute an agent picked up Pete's jacket, felt the weight of the jewels in the pockets, pulled out a G-string, and at the top of his voice yelled, "My God, diamonds!" Everyone converged to see this remarkable discovery. It wasn't until Pete explained what he was up to that the officer relented. He looked at the sketches, saw that he was holding a G-string that matched one of the drawings, and promptly dropped the piece of jewelry as if it were contaminated.

In 1977, I was busy installing scenery I had designed for Donn Arden's MGM production of "Hello, Hollywood, Hello!" in Reno, Nevada. At one acre, the stage was the largest in the United States. A fine set designer named Brian Bartholomew had designed the first half of the show with a huge opening number that included a full scale 737 jet with dancers on its wings and a "San Francisco" number with the famous earthquake scene. I had designed the second half of the show, which featured a wild space number, as well as a flooding sequence complete with three-story-high rock formations; every night, gallons and gallons of water cascaded over the faux rock– every night, that is, except for the first night after the show opened. During that performance, when the guys in the control booth pushed the button to trigger the torrent, nothing happened. It turned out that the flood system was inexplicably tied to the same system that provided water for the hotel's laundry system, and consequently it didn't work when the hotel was washing its sheets and towels. I loved the idea that we might have had hotel laundry cascading down over those enormous scenic rocks. My boss was Bill DeAngelis, a middle-aged, pleasant-looking man with a fondness for expensive jewelry, especially a watch made out of a $20 gold coin, and lots of gold chains. He was considered a dangerous man. This was confirmed, at least in my mind, when we started to have problems with the steel workers union, which was trying to gain control of the backstage crew. They were willing to do anything to intimidate Bill. Wrong move, as Bill was having no part of their plan.

One morning I arrived to discover Bill fuming. Overnight, someone had shredded a 120-foot-wide by 35-foot-tall white chiffon curtain that had thousands of small seed lights sewn into its fullness. It was an incredibly beautiful and expensive piece of scenery, to say the least, and now it was totally destroyed. Bill was certain the steelworkers were responsible. Another morning we discovered that 17 heavy lighting devices (or instruments, as they're called in the trade) that had been hung high above the audience to illuminate the dancers and singers, were no longer securely anchored. The "C" clamps that attached the instruments to the ceiling had been loosened, and now the slightest vibration could cause the instruments to crash down onto anyone unlucky enough to be seated below. On yet another day, 32 dancers were rehearsing on the stage when suddenly and mysteriously a trap door opened in the stage floor. Fortunately, no one fell through it, but then another trap door and another slowly opened. Frightening.

The day after discovering the shredded curtain, Bill said in a quiet but intense voice, "Ray, I wander through this theatre late at night, and I swear on my mother's grave if I ever find the son-of-a-bitch who's doing this *I will kill him.*" The culprit or culprits were never caught, but at the same time, the steelworkers never got a toehold on the MGM theatre. It was clear that Bill DeAngelis was no one to fool around with.

One day Bill said to a group of us, "Would you guys like to have dinner tonight?" No problem. However, after a very pleasant meal in the hotel, Bill had another suggestion: "How about all of us going for a ride?" An odd request, I thought, and one that unnerved me, but no one ever said "No" to Bill. And so, the six of us set off into the wilds outside Reno in Bill's big white Cadillac. We kept driving and driving, and as I looked back and saw the lights of Reno fading from view, my apprehension grew. Eventually, we were out in the middle of nowhere, surrounded by nothing but emptiness. No one knew we were out there. What had I gotten myself into? None of my companions had a clue where we were going either, and as I said, this man was quite possibly dangerous.

Suddenly, we arrived at a ranch-type house with a tall chain-link fence around it and saw a group of Asian men filing out of the front door and into a waiting tour bus. They all had big smiles on their faces. We had arrived at the notorious Mustang Ranch, a legal brothel. Great, I thought. Just what I need. I'm gay and two of the other guys are, too. What do we do now? Well, Bill clearly knew what he was doing. He was, in fact, aware of our orientation, and so we guessed there was no real problem. Or was there?

We decided we might as well enjoy this adventure, and that's exactly what we did. As a set designer, I was fascinated with the place. The interior was lit way too brightly, the furniture was a step above a cheap motel, and the paintings on black velvet did nothing to help. This famous brothel had no style or atmosphere at all. The ladies, however, were nicely dressed in evening lounge wear and were beautifully made up and coiffed.

It soon became clear that Bill had hired the girls to seduce us. As I had never before had an opportunity to sit around and chat with a bunch of ladies of the night, it was riveting. I loved it! At one point, one of the more attractive ladies suggested that we check out her Jacuzzi, to which we three gay guys told her we really weren't into that, to which she politely asked, "Well, what are you gentlemen into?"

One of our guys pointed to a handsome man in a gray suit down at the end of the bar and said, "That's what we're into." Damned if she didn't go down to the guy, talk to him and gesture to us, to which the guy looked in our direction and shook his head in the negative. No surprise there. In any case, I had a wonderful time getting to know the ladies. Bill had paid them to entertain us in whatever way they could.

Later, as we were leaving and passed that handsome guy at the end of the bar, I said, "You don't know what you missed!

It turned out that the Mustang Ranch sold souvenir T-shirts, so I bought one for everyone, including one for my John. I even had the ladies autograph John's shirt. On one, "Denice" wrote, "Dear John, you lucky son of a bitch!" Another, "Yvette" scribbled, "If you weren't the other way–Wow!" However, my favorite inscription, from "Connie," read, "Dear John, Do Cum Again!

In those days, John and I owned a house located behind the Hollywood Bowl. We could sit in our backyard and watch the concerts that took place there. It was great fun having dinner parties with a live concert and sometimes fireworks with dessert.

Every spring we enjoyed having 20 or so friends over for the Easter Sunrise Service that took place in the Hollywood

Bowl. The Easter following my trip to Nevada, John and I overslept and at 6:30 a.m. awoke to a bunch of friends banging on our door. Quickly, we threw on some clothes, started to set out chairs, got the food ready, and mixed the drinks, mostly Bloody Marys and Screwdrivers. Frantically busy though I was, I stopped in my tracks when suddenly I saw John wearing a T-shirt emblazoned, "Do Cum Again!" Some Easter!

My work often took me into some surprising situations. For instance, when I first started in the business in 1968, after working with Jim Trittipo, I spent a season as an assistant to Spencer Davis on the Dean Martin Show at NBC. The first show of that season featured Lena Horne, who was the epitome of elegance. Spencer, like Miss Horne, was classy. For her big number he had devised a beautiful, cylindrical cage about 14 feet tall and 8 feet in diameter. Its base was on casters and designed so that the unit could be split open by pulling two thin, almost invisible cables. The idea was that Miss Horne would be inside the cage and hidden among hundreds of clear and frosted balloons. As the cage was pulled open, the balloons would float away, revealing our star. It seemed like a simple and charming idea, except for two things. First, for some reason, during rehearsal the balloons began to pop loudly and, second, Miss Horne had a real aversion to popping balloons. In fact, every time a balloon burst, our elegantly gowned star would lose all her class and scream, "Oh, shit! Oh, fuck!" She was most apologetic but obviously could not help herself. Needless to say, the balloons were eliminated. No matter how wonderful some design ideas might be, they sometimes don't make the cut.

There's also the ever-present concern of knowing when to stop. By that, I mean, when one has a beautiful design

170

concept, one has to be on guard and know when to stop adding design elements to the look. I like to think that I'm known as an elegant designer who presents his ideas in simple, handsome ways. If you look at some of the photos of my sets in this book, I think you'll see what I mean. That's why at times I have stopped working with certain directors or producers who think more is better. Most times it's just the opposite. It took me a while to realize this as a designer and once I did, it became my mantra.

Later, for the "American Music Awards," I designed another set piece that didn't work. After countless designs for that show, I was eager to come up with something unique. And so, to create a podium unlike any other I had the shop create a clear, two foot-diameter Plexiglas tube, which they sealed on the bottom and filled with water. The tube, which would form the base of the podium, looked exactly like solid Plexiglas –at a fraction of the cost. Unfortunately, the first woman to stand behind the podium during rehearsals was the hapless victim of a strange phenomenon. Who would have thought the water in the tube would magnify the person standing behind it? The poor victim could have given the fat lady in a sideshow a run for her money. Her legs and hips were huge! And that was the end of the water, and my brilliant idea.

Sometimes a wrong can end up right or at the very least an okay situation. In 1973, I was hired to design The American Film Institute's Life Achievement Award for Fred Astaire. Over the years I did the same show honoring John Ford, James Cagney, Orson Wells, William Wyler, Bette Davis, Alfred Hitchcock and Jimmy Steward. In spite of the difficulty with the hotel's low ceiling, I came up with what I thought was a perfect solution for Fred's set. It was simply a series of cutout profile images of Mr. Astaire leaping and dancing across the stage in his signature white tie and black tails, very elegant and a look that captured the man at his best. No problem. Everyone loved my design and I was kind of pleased with it myself. That was until the TV director Marty Pasetta called me aside and announced that he had to have a camera stage center aimed at the head table where Mr. Astaire would be seated as well as to get shots of the audience around the room. This was a serious problem as there appeared to be no place to hide the camera.

When I did the television show "My Favorite Broadway: The leading Ladies" at Carnegie Hall, I faced a similar problem but was able to hide the camera in a huge 12' tall flower arrangement, but this challenge was more difficult. Where was I to hide that damn camera? It just so happened that the only available area was right in Mr. Astaire's crotch! Fortunately, the black camera in the center of Fred's black tuxedo didn't show when the various cameras shot that central figure but it certainly looked odd to the audience in the ballroom. Not a bad situation but a close call to having things go wrong and certainly not a very attractive solution to the problem. A close call that one!

One afternoon around 2004, I had some business to discuss with my agent Sandy, and since I was in the neighborhood I decided to drop by his office. When I arrived, I was shown to a conference room where five men and Sandy were sitting around talking. It was all very casual. Sandy and I spoke briefly, and just as I was about to leave, in walked Michael Jackson. He was thin, weighing about 135, and gave the appearance of being taller than his five feet, nine inches– so different from the little kid who used to appear with his brothers on the American Music Awards.

I recalled one time on that awards show when Michael was maybe 15 or 16 years old and he had great difficulty reading the cue cards. I wondered if the people shaping his life had neglected his education. Despite clearly being a very bright boy, he was having trouble reading. Another time, Dick Clark tried to lure Michael into appearing on the show by suggesting that the show would bestow a special honorary American Music Award on him. Michael agreed, but with the condition that he receive *two* awards. He knew how to grab center stage and stay there.

And now there he was in Sandy's conference room and once again commanding attention. As he worked the room, it became clear that he knew everyone; warm hugs were shared by all–that is, until he got to me. He stopped and said, "Do I know you?" I replied that we had worked together quite a bit, but there was no reason he should know me, to which he responded, "Well, you get a hug, too!" And with that we embraced each other. It was like hugging a skeleton. Fortunately, he didn't see the look of horror that must have flashed across my face.

Jackie Gleason was a bit of a surprise for me. In Miami, while working on one of his television specials, I noticed he had his own way of getting things worked out to his personal satisfaction. Every morning he'd get a stack of jokes, each on a separate sheet of typewriter paper, from his comic writers. Jackie would then head for the golf course, get into a golf cart and, along with a few of his cronies, hit the links. While driving over the course, he would test out the jokes on his golfing buddies. If he didn't get the laugh he wanted, he would simply toss the joke out onto the fairway. After a typical morning of golf, one could see a path of rejected jokes strewn across the course. I met June Taylor, with her famous June Taylor Dancers, on that show and loved her. Miss Taylor was a charming, yet forceful, lady–talented and fun, and someone I quickly came to admire.

Back in Los Angeles, in a show that Marty Pasetta was directing, the plan was to tape June's dancers doing a kick line while the credits were rolled. It turned out that the credits took longer than June had planned for her dancers to kick. Having run out of patience and concerned for her girls' safety, June dashed in front of the camera, thereby ruining the shot, and demanded that the taping be stopped. She was not going to let her girls get hurt. Marty was, shall we say, less than pleased, but he had met his match. June explained, categorically, that her girls could not kick that long, and that was that. No arguing with her. She was one of the few professionals I ever encountered who had the nerve to stand up to Marty and got away with it.

My friend Mort Solowitz had the enviable job of providing props and prizes for game shows such as "Let's Make a Deal" and "The Price Is Right" in the 1970s. These shows gave away cars, dishes, washing machines–you name it. Consequently, whenever I went to Mort's home for dinner, there was always a different, handsome set of china. Mort had an acquaintance who always wanted to know the manufacturer of the china and would peek at the bottom of the plate when he thought Mort was in the kitchen and not looking. This really annoyed Mort, so one night when I was there Mort went into the kitchen and secretly watched as this guest surreptitiously turned over one of the dinner plates. To the guest's surprise, and to the amusement of everyone at the party, a note was taped to the bottom of the plate: "IT'S NONE OF YOUR

174

FUCKING BUSINESS WHO MADE THIS PLATE."
Delicious.

In 1987 I had the privilege of designing an extravagant three-hour television special called "Happy Birthday Hollywood," which was taped at the Shrine Auditorium in Los Angeles and saluted Tinseltown and its many stars. One of my numerous sets consisted of a curved staircase on a large turntable and shiny black floor (a look I used frequently). The rehearsal went well, until a stage manager informed me that Ann Miller had a problem with the floor. At the time, she was 64 and revisiting her famous tap number from the 1948 movie "Easter Parade."

Now, the floor consisted of more than 150 four-by-eight-foot panels of shiny black Formica laminated on quarter-inch backing; it had taken hours to install. There was no way it could be switched out. I went to Miss Miller and asked her what the problem was. The floor was uneven, she said, "If you'll just show me where you have a concern, we'll take care of it," I told her. At that point she proceeded to tap her way across the stage gesturing gracefully as she sang out, "High" . . . "Low" . . . "High" . . . "Low," until she had drawn my attention to all the trouble spots. All the while she was followed by a conga line of carpenters hammering away on my special floor. What a delightful lady, and what a charming Hollywood moment.

As mentioned, one of my favorite producers was Bob Finkel. Bob was a master at handling people, especially stars. Once in the early '60s when he was producing "The Dinah Shore Show," he became irritated with Dinah because after each taping, when everyone was tired and ready to go home, she would call a meeting in the conference room. These

175

meetings could go on for hours. At the time, Dinah wore a lot of red, so one day Bob ordered up a number of large, bright-orange patent-leather armchairs. When she gathered everyone for her next marathon meeting, she found herself sitting in a chair that clashed with her dress. Being very color conscious, she grew fidgety. She simply couldn't stand all her red against that orange and called the meeting to a close in no time at all. Smart man, that Bob.

Part of my job was to coordinate the costume of the star or stars with my set and the lighting. Most times this was not difficult, but occasionally surprises occurred. Twice this happened on "The American Music Awards." The first time came when Stevie Wonder was on the show and I tried to find out what he was going to wear for his number. I approached him while he was getting ready to rehearse. Performers on that show typically wore whatever they wanted. When asked, Stevie told me he wasn't sure if he wanted to wear his red outfit or his gold one. I suggested the gold costume, but Stevie was leaning toward the red number. A rather long discussion ensued, during which I found myself thinking, "I can't believe I'm arguing with a blind man about the color of his costume." It turned out that Stevie liked the red look because it had a hat, and that's what he ended up wearing.

The second time came in 1980, when Elton John couldn't decide whether to wear yellow or pink. No matter how much I urged him to decide, he simply couldn't, or wouldn't, make up his mind. To be safe, I asked the lighting crew to use pink and amber accents on my all-white set. And guess what? Elton showed up wearing one pink shoe and one yellow shoe, pink pants and a yellow top. Never try to outguess a free spirit like Elton John.

In 1994 I turned 55 and wanted an answer to a long-standing question: Could I hack it as a sculptor? I had taken sculpture classes as an undergraduate at Hofstra College when I was in my early 20s and had decided it was not a realistic field to pursue. I was trying to be practical and sensible. But now that I had achieved professional success and financial security, "practical and sensible" didn't seem to matter so much. So I gave myself a wonderful birthday gift: a six-month sabbatical. I would devote my time to sculpting to see where it would lead me. I ended up with numerous exhibits in the United States and two one-man shows in Tokyo.

Encouragement to have a go at fine art had, in fact, come not long after I arrived in Los Angeles in the late '60s. Somehow, in the course of looking for "real" work, I had found time to produce a number of three-dimensional pieces that were displayed in a one-man show at the Kinsey Gallery on La Cienega Boulevard. My work consisted of wall pieces that utilized small electric lights set between a two-way mirror in front, and a regular mirror behind. The mirrors captured the light all the way to infinity. I sold a number of pieces to people like Fred Astaire, and ultimately, I also used this discovery to make a giant background unit for an Emmy Awards show. When combined with a mirrored ramp leading all the way to the podium, the reflective ramp created the visual impact of walking on a deep and scary chasm of light.

I was told that no one would tolerate such a frightening catwalk, to which I replied, "Are you kidding? Hold an Emmy up to a winner and the recipient would walk over hot coals!" And in truth we had no problems. The effect was spectacular.

In the '70s, when I was working at NBC, for lunch I typically would grab a quick bite from the food wagon out in

177

the drive-in area alongside the studio and then wander around checking out what was happening on the other stages. This one day I wandered into the studio across from our own and instead of the usual cameras and lighting focusing on the talent of the day, I saw Jerry Lewis playing football with the crew. When I asked a stagehand what was going on, he explained that Jerry had gotten annoyed at the producers and had decided to stop working and was playing with the crew instead to teach the producers a lesson. Because Jerry was a star of considerable magnitude, there was little the producers could do to get everyone back to work. Jerry knew this, and so to get even, he wasted four hours of valuable studio time just to drive the producers crazy. Needless to say, after that my respect for Jerry took a dive. Interesting, the difference between Dean and Jerry. When they went their separate ways, each took on his own operating style. I loved and respected Dean. Jerry, not so much.

As I've said, time is money. Every delay, everything that runs the clock in the studio costs the producers money. Consequently, every crew member is geared toward being super-efficient. Sometimes, though, there are unanticipated problems. In 1972, on a "Three Dog Night" special, we had a guest star who had just flown into LA and was late reporting to the stage. My set consisted of a square performance stage with the audience seated on all four sides. Giant mirrors in each corner made the audience appear to be much larger than it actually was. Everyone was on the set, including the audience, keyed up, and ready for the show to begin–everyone, that is, except our guest star, who shall remain nameless and who wouldn't leave the hair department. We waited and waited. Finally, word came that she couldn't make up her mind as to which Afro to wear. At last, she appeared on stage wearing *both* wigs–two huge, hairy puffs, one on each side of her head. She looked like Minnie Mouse on a bad hair day. Of course, no one said a word. The result of her indecision was strange and funny. For the producers, it was costly and not funny at all.

As mentioned earlier, when I took over the job as Art Director on "Cher" in 1976, I replaced Bob Kelly, who had filled that position the previous season. In addition to being a fine designer, Bob had a wicked sense of humor. Sharp and witty, he nearly always got the last laugh. At one legendary costume party in the 1960s, though, he met his match. After being invited to this particular high-end Hollywood party, he gave a lot of thought as to what his costume should be. Some exceptionally clever people would be attending this event. He decided to go as Judy Garland in her "Get Happy" costume from the 1950 movie "Summer Stock." Judy's iconic look in that unforgettable musical number included a black fedora, silver earrings, a short black tuxedo jacket, black mesh hose, and black high heels to show off her terrific legs. Bob's legs were one of his best features . . . enough said.

The competition was stiff and included some extraordinary outfits. Even so, Bob was a standout and received many compliments from the assembled guests. All went well until suddenly the room became very quiet and the guests around Bob parted to reveal Judy Garland herself. Bob had no choice but to stand there in his Judy outfit in a moment that seemed to go on forever. Judy simply walked by and said, out of the side of her mouth, "You better know how to sing!"

In August of 1999, a producer whose name I can no longer remember asked me to go to Saudi Arabia to design a set for the televised annual King Faisal International Prize Awards, which for 23 years had been honoring men who had contributed something important to the country and the world. What a strange land, and what an odd experience.

In Riyadh, I had my first meeting with one of the King's princes (there seemed to be thousands of them). The man's office was in a mid-rise office building guarded by six men in uniform, all wielding large, intimidating machine guns. Upstairs, the prince's office was designed to impress: gilded, French-style furniture, richly woven carpets, and plenty of bling, including a prominently displayed solid gold model of an entire town, given in gratitude by "the people" of that town. After some introductory small talk, the producers, lighting director, and I were invited to the prince's "palace" for lunch. To get there, we caravanned in high-end luxury cars through three or so miles of desert on a two-lane road. Every 30 feet or so, a carefully clipped, cone-shaped shrub stood at attention in the center island that separated the lanes. How much manpower did it take to keep those plants watered and perfectly pruned in that desert terrain? The thought was staggering.

The "palace" turned out to be a vast collection of rooms in a single-story building–nothing eye-catching on the outside, and all rather dull on the inside. During our time there, we heard women giggling and talking in other parts of the compound, but we never saw any of them. The 25'X60' living room where our meeting took place had walls upholstered in white brocade and a floor covered in light beige carpeting. A fireplace at one end of the room had many large gold objects displayed on its mantel. Within this cavernous space were three sitting areas, each centered by a round, wooden coffee table; oversized armchairs upholstered in soft, cream-colored brocade surrounded the tables and complemented the walls. On each table, a large candy-filled bowl was covered with cellophane. Did they have a problem with flies? I never found out. Oddly, the plastic was never removed by any of the many male servants.

Eventually, we were ushered into lunch and seated at a table that could easily have accommodated twenty-four people. Since there were just eight of us, we gathered at one end while five butlers stood at attention behind us. Each servant wore handsome green attire, part tuxedo and part military uniform. The help all spoke English, and after talking to them I discovered that they were indeed from the UK and had been brought over from England to Riyadh. While they looked great, it soon became clear their skills as waiters were less than stellar. They didn't have a clue as to how to serve a meal. Or could it have been that our host simply didn't care? The various courses arrived in a slapdash order, with some guests getting the meat course first, while others received a salad or a mystery appetizer. As we were winding down our conversation at the end of the meal, we Americans were offered toothpicks while the Saudis were each given a plastic hoop-like affair threaded with dental floss that enabled them to floss right there at the table. How interesting, as well as amusing, to see everyone cleaning his teeth in the company of others.

During my four day stay in Riyadh, the only time I saw even a glimpse of an Arab woman was when a group of them were driven in large, dark-windowed cars to special stores where only women shopped. No men were allowed inside these stores–not even to sweep the floors. When we boarded our plane for the flight home, we did, finally, mix with the opposite sex. The women were fully shrouded, head to toe, in black burqas. As soon as the plane took off and the seatbelt sign went out, these ladies made a mad dash for the restrooms and returned wearing Yves Saint Laurent and Christian Dior suits. Hidden behind large sunglasses, they were fully made up and covered in jewels. Quickly they stashed their burqas beneath their seats or in the overhead bins. Quite the transformation.

We were put up in a Western-type hotel where, despite strict laws prohibiting the consumption of alcoholic beverages, you could get a drink if you wanted one. Typically, the Saudis looked the other way as long as Muslims were not doing the drinking, and as long as the hotels stood to make money. Also, Westerners working in the country could make their own wine, beer, and spirits. Unfortunately, the stills made by foreigners had a tendency to explode. The problem became so acute that the American embassy finally published and distributed (at U.S. taxpayer expense?) a brochure on safe methods for still production. Crazy.

One afternoon, I decided to explore the hotel pool. It, too, turned out to be an all-male operation–no surprise there. Every man wore baggy, black hotel-issued bathing trunks that covered the wearer from well above his navel to below his knees. Quite honestly, it made me nervous to not know the customs, and I certainly did not want to get into trouble, so I quickly left. After I got back to the States, I found out that I had been in Saudi Arabia under the sponsorship of that one particular prince, and at his discretion I could have been forced to leave. Or, worse yet, he could have refused to allow me to leave. And by the way, the punishment for being gay was flogging, life imprisonment, or death, not necessarily in that order.

At one of several social gatherings during my stay, I met a number of Australians, Americans, and Britons. One man told me of walking with his wife to some evening event and being approached by the religious police, who demanded that he have "his" woman cover her hair. The man ignored them and continued walking with his wife. They were again stopped by the police and told to "have your woman cover her hair." Again they ignored the police. On the third confrontation, the man said to the police, "You should not be looking at my woman." Quickly, the police disappeared. All very odd, and more than a bit unsettling.

While the awards show was intended to honor men (and only men) who had done good things for the country, the prince who organized the event was himself less than honorable. The balance of my fee, which was considerable, went unpaid. However, as a result of my work in Saudi Arabia I was hired along with two other designers (one of whom was Elina Katsioula, who received the first scholarship I established at Yale) to develop a number of wedding themes. "Fire and Ice," "The Gardens of Versailles," "Lace and Roses," and "Winter Wonderland," were four of them. Saudi weddings are affairs attended exclusively by women, usually in large hotel ballrooms. The only man permitted at the party is the groom. The groom's male friends and male family members must meet in a separate entertainment area. The wedding themes we devised were easy, fun, and very appealing to Saudi women. We were paid handsomely for our ideas and, best of all, we did not have to travel to Saudi Arabia to execute them.

Chapter 16

The Academy Awards

W orking at the Dorothy Chandler Pavilion, where I designed the sets for 10 Academy Awards shows after learning the ropes as an assistant designer in 1969, was high pressure but thrilling. Roughly 100 workers were on hand to help execute my concepts, but I was the one who had to keep the crew productive and get the job done on time and on budget. Looking back, it was the producers of three of the shows–Howard W. Koch, William Friedkin, and Allan Carr–plus Madonna, who performed during the 1992 Oscars, who provided the most interesting experiences.

Howard W. Koch was a class act. He was an old-world gentleman who had produced such films as "The Manchurian Candidate," "On a Clear Day You Can See Forever," "Airplane!" and "The Odd Couple." He also served as President of the Academy of Motion Picture Arts and Sciences (the governing body of the Oscars) from 1977 to 1979. Regardless of his position of power within the Academy, he was kind and thoughtful. The only time I found myself at odds with him was when Mary Pickford appeared on the 49th Academy Awards in 1976.

Known in the early days of silent film as "America's Sweetheart," Mary Pickford had co-founded, with Charlie Chaplin and D. W. Griffith, United Artists, one of the earliest and most successful Hollywood studios. In her time, she was the wealthiest and most famous woman in America. She had also been one of the founders of the Academy Awards, and now the Academy had decided to honor her with a special Oscar.

At 84, Miss Pickford was infirm in mind and body, so it was decided that we would pre-tape her acceptance of the award at Pickfair, the 18-acre estate in Beverly Hills she shared first with Douglas Fairbanks and later with Charles "Buddy" Rogers, her husband of 42 years. The day of the taping, we were ushered into her elegant living room. The cameras and the sound and lighting equipment were set up, and then we were asked to leave the room. Wandering outside by the pool, I found the place rather sad. Half-heartedly cared for, Pickfair was well past its prime. It was hard to believe that the Hollywood elite had once been wined and dined in this famous home. By the time we were called back into the house, Buddy had carried Mary down the grand staircase and we found her sitting in an armchair, wearing a fur-collared, satin bed jacket. There wasn't a wrinkle on her face, but it looked to me as if she had on a very bad wig. She seemed frail and didn't relate to anyone, even Buddy.

Walter Mirisch, the president of the Board of Governors of the Academy, presented the Oscar to Mary. Dead silence. Off camera, Buddy urged, "Say 'Thank you,' Mary."

"Say thank you Mary," Mary dutifully responded. It was sad and disturbing, but eventually we got enough on tape to create an edited version that would run during the actual Awards ceremony.

The week after the pre-taping I got a call from Howard saying the decision had been made to have Mary at the Oscars after all, and could I work up a way to get her on stage. I thought, sure, I can set up a wagon unit with a chair for her to sit on, roll it on stage behind a drape, and on the introduction fly the drape. Easy. However, what I actually said to Howard was, "Yes, I can do that, but I won't. I think it's disrespectful to her and totally inappropriate." Now, I have never refused to fulfill a request from a producer before or since, but I felt strongly about this. Thank God, Howard understood and backed off. Miss Pickford died following a stroke three years later.

The next year, in 1977, William Friedkin asked me to design that year's Oscar show. As the director of "The French Connection" and "The Exorcist," he had an impressive reputation, but beyond the reputation I knew nothing about him. I did surmise that he came with incredible power. Our initial meeting went well enough, and I remember him as handsome, dark-haired, and clearly very bright. When we got down to the concept of the show, he went on and on about the Academy being "a magic circle of filmmakers," etc., etc. Sorry to say this, but what kept flashing through my mind was, "Bullshit, bullshit, bullshit." No matter. I had lots of time to develop a scenic approach. Probably two or so months.

A week later, Bill's assistant called and announced that Mr. Friedkin was leaving in a week's time for France, where he would be marrying the legendary actress Jeanne Moreau. Could he please see my designs for the show before his departure? Oh, my God, he wanted the designs in seven days! I went to work, and with the help of two assistants, turned out what I thought was an excellent set design in model form.

Nonetheless, the night before my deadline, I was uneasy. I knew it wasn't enough that *I* liked my design. Would Bill like it? I really had no notion as to what made Bill tick. How did he think? All night long I struggled to find just the right way to present my work to him. To add to the tension, I had received word the day before that Bill had fired costume designer Bob Mackie. No one ever fired Bob Mackie. He was just too good–the best in the business. Was it my turn next? I felt I was in deep trouble.

The day of the presentation, I arrived at Bill's office carrying the model, which was covered up, and found to my horror that five of Bill's buddies would be joining him for the presentation. Oh, boy, just what I needed: an audience. I tossed out my planned presentation, whipped off the cover of the model, and said, "I took to heart your words about the Academy being 'a magic circle of filmmakers'." The set was simple yet elegant, as well as unique, and it was full of handsome circles and curves. But the results were unnerving. I have never had a producer swear at me. In a loud, clear voice, Bill exclaimed, "Klausen, you're a fucking . . . *genius!*" Bill's buddies had leaned forward for the kill, until they heard the word "genius." To this day, when I think about it, I let out a sigh of relief. It turned out that Bill's pals had actually done me a favor by causing me to toss out my original presentation. It turned out that Bill hated long spiels. After he departed for France, I took off several days to collapse before organizing the drafting of the set.

One of the nominated songs that year was "Evergreen" from "A Star Is Born," with lyrics by Paul Williams. Barbra Streisand, the song's composer as well as the star of the film, was going to perform it. She let it be known through Bill that she wanted to be in copper tones; she had died her hair copper and had a suntan to match. On her own she hired Bob Mackie to design a beautiful gown also in copper tones. Because I had worked with Bob in the past on the "Cher" series, I was able to get a swatch of the dress fabric and had her microphone

187

painted copper, along with the first six feet of the mic cord. The rest of the cord was black and blended into the black floor, a trick I had developed over the years, in the days before cordless mics.

It would be an understatement to say that Streisand was a strong-willed performer. We knew she could be difficult, so we were all very concerned about keeping her happy. In truth, I found that if you knew your business, working with her was fine.

For her entrance I had come up with the idea of making a platform that would rise up through a trap door and come to a stop six feet above the stage floor, with Miss Streisand on top of it. She would literally be on a pedestal. For a backdrop, luminescent Plexiglas discs, ranging in size from 6 to 10 feet in diameter, would fly in from the sides and supply bursts of gold, silver, bronze, and copper. All very dramatic and beautiful.

At one point, just before construction of the "Evergreen" set was scheduled to begin, I got yet another phone call from Bill's assistant asking if I would please have a special model made of the set so that Bill could take it out to Barbra's Malibu home. I've never had a request like that before or since, and at that point in time I had designed hundreds of sets. Well, at the cost of about $2,000, I had the model made, and Bill took it to Miss Streisand's home for her approval. All went well, and the set was constructed.

Soon after, while we were setting up the show on the Dorothy Chandler stage, Bill's assistant called once again (*ugh*) and informed me that Bill and Miss Streisand were coming down to see the set. Fortunately, everything was in place, and I was able to demonstrate how her entrance would work. After the demonstration, Bill said, "Can you guarantee that it will work–that the platform will rise the way it's supposed to?"

Foolishly, I replied, "Yes, it will work every time, except maybe once in a million." Now, I have no idea what was going through their minds, but all I could envision was a pair of hands with long, copper-colored nails clawing their way out of the trap opening. After a long pause, I said, "I think I'll design another entrance," to which they said in unison, "Good!" and left the stage. So much for my great idea.

The evening of the show I knew exactly where Miss Streisand would be standing after she finished singing "Evergreen." It had been decided that she would go stage right and wait to hear who the winner was, television cameras at the ready. I made sure to stand right next to her, with her companion, Jon Peters, on her other side. Remembering her excitement eight years earlier when she had won her first Oscar for "Funny Girl," I really wanted to see what the years had done and how she would react to winning a second time, as it was generally assumed she and Paul Williams would win Best Song. And when they did, Paul was strangely nowhere to be found, nor was there any excitement on Barbra's part. There was simply a nod between her and Jon, and out she went once again to collect a shared Oscar (in 1969 she and Katharine Hepburn had both won Best Actress). I found this to be really sad. Barbra Streisand is one of the most gifted performers around, and yet the thrill appeared to be gone. I decided I would never want to trade my life for one so devoid of excitement.

Now, for excitement, all one had to do was spend some time in the same room with producer Allan Carr. In 1989, when Allan hired me to design the 61st Annual Academy Awards, I thought he looked like a big kid. He was overweight and had a boyish face. To camouflage his extra pounds he wore flamboyant caftans, or dashikis, and reportedly owned more than 1,000 of them. As is so often the case, this first impression came up short, since no one could match Allan's sheer nerve and remarkable drive. He was self-made and accustomed to getting his way.

My first meeting with Allan took place at his house in Beverly Hills. Like Allan himself, there was nothing ordinary about this house, which was actually a five bedroom, Tudor-style, stone and redwood retreat built in 1927. Ingrid Bergman bought it in the '40s and years later sold it to Kim Novak. Just like its former occupants, the place had great bones, with generously proportioned rooms that featured fine moldings and other attractive architectural details. For the most part, Allan had respected the provenance of the house and had refrained from giving it the "Carr touch." That is, with one exception: He had transformed the basement into an over-the-top disco, complete with Plexiglas grand piano. Noted decorator Stephen Rieman gave the space an Egyptian theme in golds, reds, and oranges, with Nubian statues and a mirrored ceiling. Tons of disco lights and the usual flashiness reflected Allan's dress style. Miss Bergman clearly never shook her booty down there.

One morning after breakfast, John said, "You know, I hate the way they announce the Oscar winners by saying, '. ... and the winner is . . .' . To me, all the nominees are winners."

At this point I had been nominated numerous times for Emmy awards (winning three times out of eight nominations), so I knew what John was talking about. The next time I met with Allan, I told him about John's comment. Before I knew it, Allan had scheduled a big news conference and announced that, from now on, the Academy Awards presenter would say, "And the Oscar goes to...." The Tony and Emmy awards quickly followed suit. Good going, Allan!

Unfortunately, Allan didn't always make the wisest decisions. This soon became apparent when one of his brilliant ideas turned out to be anything but. Tasked with improving the show's ratings, he decided to open the 61st Academy Awards with a spoof of Hollywood itself. He hired some of the cast and crew from "Beach Blanket Babylon," the long-running San Francisco musical revue that parodied a wide range of cultural and political figures. Over the years, the people who were parodied in that show changed to reflect current events, but the figure who set the show in motion was always Snow White, who met the various personages while traveling the world in search of Prince Charming.

To play Snow White, Allan cast a 22-year-old actress named Eileen Bowman; a hapless Lily Tomlin was given the role of Cinderella. The company behind "Beach Blanket Babylon" specialized in outrageous costumes and huge hats, and Lily would make her entrance out of a 20-foot-tall hat. This Academy Awards opening was to be unlike any previously seen, and it could have been great fun, except for one big problem: The Oscars audience was accustomed to elegant, sophisticated openings, and Allan's was not.

I felt strongly that in order for the opening to work, it would need to be set up: The audience had to be let in on the joke ahead of time and not have it sprung on them. At a meeting of the production team at Allan's home, I was nervously about to expound on my theory when Marvin

Hamlisch, who was Allan's good friend and the show's Musical Director, voiced my exact concerns. What transpired next was frightening. Allan tore into Marvin in a mean and violent manner, and all I could do was sit there in amazement and marvel at the close call I had just survived.

The big evening finally arrived, and Marvin and I were right. As the opening number unfolded, you could see the audience, mouths agape, staring in disbelief. This was not the elegant opening everyone had expected. It was a *disaster*. The reaction was so negative that the Academy held a special meeting the morning after the show to assess the damage Allan's opening number had done to the Academy's image. Allan went into hiding for a year; his career never fully recovered.

The Academy Awards show I designed in 1991 was a mixed bag. My sets were well received by both director and producer and featured more circular shapes, which were an outgrowth of some of the sculptural pieces I had just shown at a one-man exhibition in Tokyo. The look, I thought, was elegant, handsome, and very controlled.

Enter Madonna, one of the few stars I have ever strongly disliked. Anyone with a more favorable opinion just needs to take a good look at the documentary "Truth or Dare," which was videotaped on one of her tours. You will see a spoiled star adept at abusing those around her. One time she was on the "American Music Awards" and I was forced to take orders from her brother, who was in his early 20s and had no apparent design experience. Nonetheless, Madonna decided he would design her set. Truly an insulting situation, but, hey, my job was to solve problems, not create them.

Besides, I had done a great deal of work with the producer, Dick Clark, and I knew it was best to make as few waves as possible. But that didn't mean I had to like it.

The year before the 1991 Oscars, Madonna had appeared in "Dick Tracy," in which she sang "Sooner or Later," now a Best Song nominee. Madonna had been asked to perform it live for the show. Once again, we would be working together. Normally I would listen to the song and consider the performer and then design the set, which is exactly what I did. I came up with a scrim drop with an opening built into it. Scrim is a netting-type fabric that comes in exceptionally large sizes. You can paint designs on it, and, depending on the lighting, see through it.

Well, Madonna would have none of it. She was heard to say, "Never ask for things. Demand them!" And so she demanded to have an Austrian drape behind her, the kind that is gathered in swags every three feet or so in vertical lines. This posed two problems. First, it was the wrong look—totally—for the rest of the scenery I had designed for the show. Second, there was very little time to find the right fabric and to make such a drape, as it would need to be a minimum of 30 feet high and 80 feet wide. This was the first time any star had rejected a design of mine, and at this point I had designed hundreds of sets for more than a hundred productions. Reba McEntire, who is a dream to work with, graciously accepted the rejected scrim. No trouble from her.

Madonna "solved" the first problem by insisting on the Austrian drape. "It's not too late to get out of this show," I overheard her saying to her choreographer as she left the meeting she had with me. So much for my carefully designed thematic look, not to mention any chance for an Emmy win. I knew if she bailed out because I refused to cooperate, I would be in big trouble. So, no discussion there.

The second problem was solved when I found a drape the exact size I needed that could be rented from Scott Webley, owner of ShowBiz, one of my favorite rental houses. The only hitch was that the drape was white, and Madonna wanted to wear a white gown. Normally this would not have been a problem, as we would simply light the drape behind her in a suitable color to show off the star, but Madonna couldn't comprehend this. You would have thought she had never worked in the business. Ultimately what I did was hang the drape and then spend 45 minutes of valuable stage time lighting the damn fabric until Madonna picked out a pink she liked.

Ah, but my troubles weren't over. The star wanted to come up on an elevator from beneath the stage floor. Remember Barbra Streisand? Well, Madonna never thought to ask, "Will it work every time?" Her plan was to come up on her elevator, do some movements, and then walk down to a mic stand that was to be placed between her and the camera out in the center of the audience. Seemed simple enough. The only problem was the camera would not have a clear shot of our star, so I suggested putting the mic stand on its own little elevator and have it come up out of the stage floor as Madonna moved toward it. Again, she had trouble understanding how this would work, but after several lengthy discussions she finally got it.

Now, as exasperating as she can be, I have to admit that Madonna is a hard worker. My theory is this: She knows she is a mediocre talent, but one with great marketing skills, and so she compensates for the lack of real talent by working extra

194

hard. She does her homework and is one smart cookie. For two weeks she practiced her song in a rehearsal gown (a rental gown similar to the one that would be made specially for her Oscar performance). She was determined that her mic stand had to be an exact height, not a quarter of an inch off. Every once in a while, I would drop by the rehearsal hall and there she would be, gowned yet unkempt, a good half-inch of dark roots in her dyed blond hair. What a mess this is going to be, I thought, but I was wrong. The day of the telecast we had a perfect dress rehearsal. She had taken care of the roots and was all glam in her shimmering gown. Very Marilyn Monroe.

But on the night of the show, disaster struck. Because the mic stand was located inside the ramp over the orchestra, there was a problem pre-adjusting the stand to the exact height Madonna demanded. We had to open the ramp's trap door during a commercial, have the stagehand below raise the mic six inches, and wait for the sound guy to put an extra seven-inch extension onto the mic to make it exactly tall enough. Well, during the commercial, the audio man (fittingly named Mike) went out onto the ramp, flipped open the trap door, and gestured for the stand to be raised so he could attach the extension cord to the stand. Nothing happened. It turned out the stagehand whose job it was to operate the mic elevator was exhausted following a previous show and had fallen asleep. So now the little elevator didn't budge: no mic stand and therefore no sound, and no way for Madonna to be heard once she came up on her elevator. After her little movement, she would be walking toward a nonexistent mic stand.

Alerted to the problem, the control booth called down to the stage manager, who was in the basement along with Madonna and Steve, one of my favorite stagehands, and me.

195

Steve was very funny but sometimes lacked common sense. Of course, scattered around the basement were other performers and stage crew, as well.

When Madonna heard that her mic stand wasn't working, she freaked out and started swearing like a drunken sailor. "Shut up, Madonna!" Steve demanded of her. "Why should I?" came the star's response. "Because there are children around," responded Steve, as he gestured to the kids who were there to perform a number from "Toy Story." "Besides," he added, "you've got better things to do 'cause I'm sending you up on stage *now*." He began raising her in the elevator.

The night of the show, up high in the flies where Madonna's drape and Reba's drop were stored when not in use, a virtual gale arose when the crew started to lower both the drape and the drop. The drop was being used to stabilize the drape and stop the effects of the strong drafts typical in the Shrine Auditorium. Madonna's drape got hung up in the lights and wouldn't come down. During the commercial, I saw to my horror that Madonna was about to ascend on the elevator and land in front of the drop she had rejected. Miraculously, at the last possible moment, the Austrian drape freed itself and flew in just as Madonna was being introduced at a side podium. Also fortunate was that Mike, the audio man, had anticipated a potential problem and had pre-rigged a second mic stand to the exact height Madonna required.

So, there was Madonna coming up on an elevator a bit ahead of time thinking she didn't have a mic. If you have ever seen a recording of her performance, you'll have noticed she's vibrating like a jackhammer. As much as I dislike the lady, I did feel really sorry for her distress and in no way would have wished that on anybody.

After she had finished her shaky performance and exited the stage, Steve and I scurried up from the basement. Steve said to her as she exited the stage, "See, that wasn't so bad, was it?" He then turned toward me and said in a voice loud enough for Madonna to hear, "Look at it this way, Ray, if it hadn't worked out, she's so rich she could have hired a hit man to get you." As it was, I felt as if I *had* been hit. Some evening!

And so, I've had the immense pleasure of designing 10 Oscar shows, two of which, the 1982 and 1983 show, resulted in Emmy awards for me. I also had two not terribly great moments, thanks to two iconic characters, Snow White and Madonna.

Two and two. I guess it comes with the territory, but, hey, I'm not complaining.

Chapter 17

The Kennedy Center Honors

In 1978 I got a call from George Stevens, Jr., head producer for the American Film Institute. I liked working with George; he was a class act. Shows that emerged from his tutelage were extremely well produced, so it was good to get his call. Or was it?

It seems that George had conceived of a show to be called "The Kennedy Center Honors" that would be an annual tribute to five artists who had enhanced and inspired the country through their artistic contributions over the years. Exciting! I couldn't wait to be involved. The only problem was that George hadn't called to ask me to design the show. He had called because he had hired a fellow designer, Bob Kelly, to do the show and he didn't like the design Bob had come up with. The killer part of the phone call was that George wanted me to critique Bob's design, which, to put it mildly, would have been in very bad form.

At first, I tried to explain to George that it would be unethical as well as very uncomfortable for me to evaluate another designer's work. Besides, I knew Bob fairly well and it would constitute a form of betrayal. George wouldn't buy that, and so knowing that my further refusal could mean he would most likely not ask me to design any future American Film Institute tributes, I met reluctantly with him in his Beverly Hills Hotel suite and said, "The design is fine. It's quite workable." It wasn't the best work I'd ever seen but perfectly serviceable.

My tepid approval wasn't enough. George asked Bob to redesign the set. "You know what? I'm too old, too rich, and too ugly to redo the design," Bob said, in keeping with his acerbic personality. "Get someone else."

Having lost his designer, George now asked me to do the show, but I was no longer available. Had he asked me earlier I would have jumped at the chance. And so, very late in the game, he had to go with a third choice, a wonderful designer named Brian Bartholomew. Brian would have been an excellent choice had George asked him earlier, but poor Brian had no time at all to come up with a workable design concept, the result being a mediocre set and a very unhappy George. Next year, in plenty of time, he asked me to come up with a new design.

The year was now 1979 and the theatre was the newly built Kennedy Center Opera House, a wonderful venue with a super crew. I remember flying to Washington to check out the theatre and being thrilled at the size of the backstage area. We could easily put a full orchestra of 50 or so musicians on an air wagon and glide it from its storage space upstage down to the performance area with just four stagehands pushing it. Air wagons used forced air to float the entire orchestra and its platform above the stage flooring. I settled on a design that had an all-white step motif. The look was a good one, as it adapted well with the various looks from year to year. Even after I left the show in 1990, my basic approach was used for the next 20 years.

The 1979 American Film Institute honorees were truly great: Aaron Copeland, Ella Fitzgerald, Henry Fonda,

Tennessee Williams, and Martha Graham. I met Miss Graham during a rehearsal of one of her dance pieces that was to be performed in tribute to her. What a thrill! The only mishap occurred when I shook her hand and had not been forewarned of her crippling arthritis; her fingers were knotted balls of skin and bone, not like a hand at all. A horrifying surprise. I only hoped that my face did not reveal my shock, and that I hadn't upset her. She was most gracious and said she loved the set I had designed for her dance piece and that she hoped we could work together sometime. Now here was one of the very few regrets of my career. I figured Miss Graham, being in her 90's, wouldn't be doing any more work. Wrong! She went on to create new pieces for a number of years, and I missed my chance to design for this inspired, and inspiring, lady. I don't often misjudge a work situation, but I certainly did in this case.

I did the "Honors," as they came to be called, for 10 years. During that time some amusing things happened. To set the stage, one has to realize that politically it was an important show for CBS in that much politicking was done over the weekend of the Honors. The first opportunity for the network executives, the celebrities, and the politicians to schmooze came at the State Dinner on Saturday night. The second opportunity came on Sunday, at a cocktail party at the White House, followed by the awards themselves at the Kennedy Center Opera House. A supper in the Grand Hall of the Kennedy Center following the awards offered still another chance to rub elbows. Usually, the production staff was invited only to the supper after the show, but once I was invited to the State Dinner. My guess is there was a shortage of men that year. Whatever the reason, I ended up sitting next to a lady who was large on emeralds but short on personality. No matter. I had a great time.

After that, I was invited twice to the White House for the pre-show cocktail party. The first time I was totally in awe. I arrived via a cab with an invitation and was passed through a guard gate. Inside, I heard the Marine Band playing as I walked up a grand staircase. About 300 guests, all in formal attire, filled those grand rooms. Somehow, being inside the White House was like being on the set of an MGM movie. The place reeked of power, wealth, fame, and connections. But unlike in the movies, as far as I could tell, the jewels on the women were the real deal. We guests enjoyed the freedom to wander through the smaller rooms, many still imprinted with the taste and style of Jacqueline Kennedy. Finally, we congregated in a large, elegant ballroom all gold and white with handsome crystal chandeliers, where drinks and hors d'oeuvres were served. Then we moved on to a reception line at the end of which we met President and Mrs. Carter.

Scattered around the various White House rooms were handpicked male members of the various branches of the armed forces, all in dress uniform. I suspected they were carefully selected for looks, personality, and also for being single. Just as they would in an MGM blockbuster, they lent glamour to the scene. One of them, movie-star attractive as well as seductive, did a little more than that. He and I got talking, and he made a pass at me. Was I free to see him the next night? Unbelievable. Yes, I was tempted and nearly changed my flight back to Los Angeles. Instead, I walked to a house phone and asked the operator to place a collect call to my friend Bud Look, who that night was hosting John at a

Los Angeles dinner party. I had the great fun and perhaps the rare distinction of telling John and our friends that I had been cruised at the White House. Later, I found out that Bud did not believe that I had actually called from the White House. When he got his phone bill, he looked up the number and dialed it. After an operator answered by saying, "White House," Bud was flummoxed. "Can Amy come out and play?" he stammered.

An interesting side note: Bud may have inadvertently changed the history of our country. He was a studio makeup man and had been doing Richard Nixon's makeup over the years. When Nixon was preparing for the famous debate with John Kennedy during the 1960 election campaign, the decision was made not to bother having Nixon made up. At least partly because someone decided to dispense with Bud's services, Nixon looked pale, sweaty, and ill at ease. Next to him stood the youthful, tanned JFK. The rest is history. Nixon lost. I can't help wondering: If he hadn't, would there have been a Kennedy Center, or a Kennedy Center Honors? Such are the vagaries of fate. One will never know.

The second time I was invited to the White House (as a sort of reward, I believe, for the work I had been doing), my invitation requested my attendance plus a guest. I decided to ask my recently widowed mother to accompany me. As I've mentioned, my parents were immigrants from Denmark, so the very idea that a child of theirs would not only be invited to the White House but would also be in the position to take one of his immigrant parents inside to a private function, was an extraordinary moment for my mother and myself. Mom lived in Tampa at the time and was as strong and sharp-willed as ever. The day I phoned and invited her for that coming Sunday, she stalled. Either the idea of a trip to the halls of power in Washington, D.C. was just too fantastic, or she was too stunned to accept at first. And so, she said, "Raymond, you know I'm going to Albuquerque to visit your aunt this weekend. If I change my plans, my travel agent will kill me."

"Ma, it's the *White House*," I responded. "You'll get to meet President Carter. Think about it and call me back."

At 6:30 the next morning she called and said, "I stayed up late last night and baked a batch of cookies for the travel agent. That should hold him. I'm coming. What should I wear?" "Wear the gown I bought you in Marrakech," I suggested. We were set. After all the sacrifices she had made for me, this was a great way for me to say, "Thank you."

To my surprise, Mom fit in amazingly well at the White House. At one point, a press agent or reporter approached us and said, "And who have we here?" Mom jumped right in. "This is my son, Ray Klausen, who designed the sets for the Kennedy Center Honors," she responded readily. When the two had run the course on that subject and the lady from the press (or whatever she was) started to look around for others to interview, mom stopped her cold: "And he just escaped the MGM fire in Las Vegas." (See Chapter 26.) No dummy, mom. She would have made a great press agent.

Later, we and 300 or so guests went through the reception line, with Lillian Gish and Jennifer Jones behind us. We met and shook hands with President and Mrs. Carter. At the end of the line, we ran into Sandy who, as any good agent would, asked if we had had our picture taken with the President. I told him we had not, and asked how, exactly, such a thing could be arranged. Sandy explained that President

Carter's term would soon be up and the official White House photographer was looking for work in Los Angeles. Sandy suspected the photographer would take our picture to curry favor with him. So, my rather nervous mother and I were escorted through a series of rooms and back to the front of the reception line. "What if they remember us?" Mom asked. "There are so many people here I doubt they will," I responded, naively.Well, we navigated the line successfully, but behind us I heard Mrs. Carter say to the wife of the associate producer on our show, who was also being shepherded through the line a second time so she could get a photo with the president, "Haven't I seen you before?" That Christmas, my gift to mom was a photograph autographed by President Carter showing him shaking my mother's hand–a great memory of a wonderful moment.

Designing the sets for the Kennedy Center Honors put me in close proximity to many astonishingly talented individuals. One year, for example, the great choreographer Agnes de Mille was on the show as a presenter. By then she was in a wheelchair but still very much in control of her life and what went on around her. The plan was for her to be wheeled from the green room to stage right, where two honor guards would assist her to the podium. Well, the award recipient who proceeded Miss de Mille went on and on with an endless speech. Finally, the speaker left the spotlight and out went Miss de Mille, her bearing magnificent, her words intelligent and brief. Later, as she was wheeled back to the green room, I complimented her on her presentation, to which she said, "Yes, short and to the point!"

Another time, Audrey Hepburn was featured in the lineup. Clearly, she was on edge. After all, she was a film actress and did not have a lot of experience making speeches in front of other famous performers, producers, network affiliates, and the President of the United States. Backstage, she nervously paced back and forth, up and down in what I believe was a Givenchy gown, her huge skirt sweeping the stage as she left a trail of cigarette smoke–a real no-no anywhere in the theatre. But who was going to tell this elegant star she couldn't smoke? Finally, Rex Harrison, her co-star years earlier in the monumentally successful film version of "My Fair Lady," went out on stage to introduce her. Now, Rex was apparently aging a bit and was not his usual sharp self. To everyone's horror we heard him say, "And now, ladies and gentlemen, my very own fair lady, Katharine Hepburn!" Poor Audrey. She got through her speech just fine, but backstage as Rex was getting ready to return to his seat, one of the stage managers grabbed him by the shoulder and told him he wasn't going anywhere. He was to stay there until after the show and then do a pickup, which meant they would retake his introductory speech and then splice it into the final version of the show. Ah, the advantages of taped television over live TV.

There was another time when taping the show rather than going with a live telecast saved the day. The honoree was Leonard Bernstein, and his daughter sang as part of the tribute to him. Well, there was a closeup of Lenny that showed tears streaming down his cheeks. The joke in the control room, however, was that Lenny wasn't crying out of fatherly pride but from distress that she was singing so off key. The miracles of the editing room went into play, and by the time the show was aired, the audio guys had manipulated her voice so that she was now pitch perfect. Imagine what the great conductor and composer must have thought when he finally saw and heard the telecast.

In 1988, after ten years as the Production Designer for the Kennedy Center Honors, I quit the show. Nick Vanoff, who had become co-producer with George Stevens, Jr., had finally pushed me over the edge. Because he was in the throes of producing "City of Angels" on Broadway, he simply wasn't focused on the Kennedy Honors. He made my work difficult and rushed, and it became impossible to get him to make important scenic decisions that only he could make, such as how an appearance by the Russian Army Orchestra would be staged. It got so bad that at one point he ordered me to build some platforms for a Russian chorus–while we were doing the show! To prevent the audience from hearing all the hammering, I had the crew working away during periods of applause as performers entered and exited the stage. As a rule, I worked hard to be organized and efficient, and I always made clear, timely design decisions so that everything would run smoothly on stage and behind the scenes. And now here I was in front of the stage crew looking like a rank amateur, building the set during the show.

Time and nature have a funny way of sorting things out. George and Nick hired a designer friend of mine, a top-level guy, to take over. The next year the producers were unhappy with his work, and George asked me to return. Tempting. However, as fate would have it, I was scheduled to be in Tokyo with a one-man show of my sculpture and was not free to return to Washington. And that was the end of that.

With the template I created for the basic Kennedy Honors set used for a good twenty years after I left, I feel fortunate to have made a contribution to such a worthwhile undertaking. Hey, as far as I know, I'm the only one connected with the show who got propositioned by a Marine in the White House.

Chapter 18

There She Is . . .

From 1993 to 2000, I traveled in late summer to Atlantic City, N.J., to install the sets for the Miss America pageant. For the most part, it was a sweet deal as John, who was by then retired, would accompany me. Typically, the production company would rent us a pleasant duplex apartment and provide a rental car. Because I spent my days at the convention center, John had the car at his disposal, allowing him to play golf, food shop, and cook dinner for friends who were working on the show. All very agreeable. The show was pleasant enough to design and didn't make too many demands on me.

Typically, I would design a basic look for that year's pageant, using a theme that would carry over to the interview, ten individual talent spots, the swimsuit and formalwear categories, and then the final crowning moment. The setting up of the scenery, or load-in, as it was called, was no big deal, and the hours were short so that the producers could avoid paying overtime. The flip side of these short hours, though, was that everything took twice as long. The load-in dragged on for several days.

Also unfortunate was the day the convention center's fire alarm went off. The alarm turned out to be a false one, but I have to tell you that after what I had experienced during the great MGM fire in 1980 (more on this to come), any alarm was one too many. When the alarm sounded at the Atlantic City convention center, the huge doors leading out of the center lowered loudly, sealing off the arena from other parts of the complex. As the automatic doors began their clamorous descent, I had the spooky sensation of being trapped in a fire with no apparent means of escape—a sensation with which I was all too familiar.

Most days, though, work at the convention center wasn't nearly so exciting. The show itself was largely predictable. To my surprise and delight, however, I found the contestants to be refreshing. They were smart, kind to each other, and strangely not as competitive as one might imagine. The ladies were placed in three groups labeled "A," "B," and "C." The groups would rotate, taking turns performing in the swimsuit, talent, and interview categories from night to night prior to the final evening of the crowning. Everyone participated in the evening-wear competition together, and by the final night each contestant had been judged, thus weeding out all but the 10 finalists. These were then voted down to three and finally down to the ultimate winner. I had the opportunity to create glamorous sets, and in doing so tuned in to my feminine side, which I rather enjoyed as it provided a welcome change. For instance, one year I found a source that made over-scaled faux gemstones, some up to 10 inches across. From these I created dazzling brooch-type scenic pieces with backings made out of foamcore, wood, and metal. Some were as big as 14 feet in diameter. Strikingly beautiful and supportive to the ladies and the show.

One year I watched from backstage as the 10 finalists were announced. I was curious to see how the contestants who were not chosen to advance would react when their names weren't called. Most applauded politely and, in general, were supportive of the winners, which surprised me. One unsuccessful contestant, however, exclaimed loudly, "Thank God! Now I can go home and marry my boyfriend without my parents yelling at me!"

I suppose I should have felt that the contest was sexist, but at this point in history many of us were still oblivious to these concerns. At the time, I assumed the women were there for the college scholarships, as the Miss America organization gave out more scholarships than any other organization in the world. Of course, there were some curious moments. I remember one contestant whose talent was singing opera. Just before performing, she had taken a mint that turned her tongue green. Despite her beautiful voice, the judges were turned off, and she lost the talent portion of the contest. To this day, I wonder if she took the mint not realizing what the results would be, or if someone had "helped" her out–out of the competition.

I have to say that I enjoyed the talent spot, as many of the contestants were quite good. Some, however, got into trouble. One memorable moment came when a young lady from a state that will remain nameless played the flute. Many of the contestants had backup tapes or tracks of musical instruments to support their talent solos, and this flutist was no exception. Unfortunately, she couldn't stay in sync with her tape. She started out fine, then suddenly moved ahead of the track, then fell behind, then moved ahead again, then behind again, and again. Awful. After she took her bow, she made her exit stage left. Actually, she stomped off. A few seconds later we saw her flute fly through the air and across the stage. Ironic, considering that the piece she had played was "I've Got Rhythm." There was also the usual selection of ventriloquists and mediocre comics who seldom made it into the finals. But with every year there were always one or two remarkable singers and dancers whose talent spot represented years of hard study or God-given natural talent. It was a pleasure and privilege to see these ladies perform.

The temptation to place women on a pedestal, as the Miss America pageant has done since 1921, is as old as mankind itself. Every culture has its own idea about what constitutes female perfection, be it the Greeks and their Aphrodite, the Italians and their Botticelli Venus, or the ancient Egyptians and Nefertiti. In our own time, a hands-down favorite *femme ideale* of mine is the world-renowned Miss Piggy. I first met this exemplar of porcine perfection when the Muppets stole the show during an episode of the "Cher" series in 1975. But I didn't really get to know Miss Piggy until 1979, when I was asked to design the sets for the "John Denver and the Muppets Christmas Special." As was usual with Christmas specials, the show had to be taped months ahead of the holiday season, in late summer in sunny California. Fake snow (Styrofoam, actually) made this possible.

The set I created in the NBC studio featured a rented 30'X200' painted drop of snow-covered mountains originally made for the movie "Seven Brides for Seven Brothers." In this winter environment were lots of bare trees rented from Walter Allen's, a local nursery that served the studios. All I had to do was drive to the nursery, select the trees I wanted, and wait for the studio to pick them up and deliver them to the specified stage at the appointed time. Walter Allen's had a huge stock

211

that included every imaginable plant or tree, both real and artificial. The nursery staff would even decorate a Christmas tree per my specifications. One time in 1972, to create a perfectly proportioned tree, I had a 16-foot-tall pole mounted on a stand and then drilled to take the branches from three evergreens, all flameproofed as required by the local fire marshal. In addition to the branches, more than 200 steel armatures extended from the pole. At the ends of each armature, pressed-glass tumblers were fitted with votive candles, making it possible to have a tree lit with real candles. Such were the resources of studios in those days. That tree cost $5,000, equivalent to what I made back in my first year of teaching junior high school. Things had certainly changed for me.

For "John Denver and the Muppets," my wonderfully creative assistant Rebecca Hollar Barkley decorated the various sets and even rented a deer (live, not fake) to complete the outdoor picture. But it was our indoor living room set that was my favorite. With Rebecca's loving touch, we created a cozy room with a wood-burning fireplace and custom-made, over-stuffed furniture. There, the whole Muppet gang gathered around John Denver to sing Christmas carols–a sweet, lovely moment, but not easy to achieve. While John Denver could not have been more cooperative and charming, the Muppets posed a few problems. Some of the nicest characters in the business, the actors portraying them had to be hidden from sight. In our staged living room, they were under the sofa and chairs. To accommodate Miss Piggy, Fozzie Bear, Kermit and the rest of the gang, I had the floor of the set built four feet above the stage floor. The puppeteers sat under the living room set in this rather cramped space along with television monitors so they

212

could see how each character's actions looked. They would stick their arms up through various openings, as I had arranged for holes to be cut into each and every piece of furniture, including a special sofa. Thanks to these openings, three Muppets could sit cozily alongside John Denver as they discussed their hopes and wishes for the Christmas season. (When unoccupied, the sofa looked like an upholstered three-holer in an outhouse.)

Jim Henson, the Muppets' creator and owner, had a strict rule that children were not allowed onto the set. I never understood this until the first time the puppeteers took a break. Because they had been crammed into a tight space, the operators needed to have regular, timed breaks to stretch, and when these periods were called, the Muppets' bodies would shake violently and collapse as the puppeteers' hands were pulled away. It looked as if nerve gas had spread throughout the room. Shocking and unnerving (pun intended). Eventually, I got used to the sight, but a child might not have.

That year I also did a Muppet special called "The Muppets Go Hollywood," which served to stir up interest in the gang's forthcoming feature film, "The Muppet Movie." The show was staged inside Hollywood's Coconut Grove, the legendary nightclub that had seen better days. When I went to survey the site, I was greatly disappointed. The place was worn and tired. It was up to me to re-create the atmosphere that had once existed at this historic site. Aided by my ever-resourceful assistant Paul Galbraith, that's exactly what we did. Paul had been head of display for Bullock's, the elegant Los Angeles department store, and was a wizard with paper sculpture. He had already helped me with many television shows, including the opening looks each week on the Cher series and, for Bing

Crosby, the transformation of a summertime Sun Valley town into a winter wonderland. At the Coconut Grove, Paul added flamboyant period accents to the set, which included Art Deco styling around the stage proscenium and, around the room itself, palm trees complete with frolicking monkeys, just like in the old days.

The scene was reminiscent of the work of Dorothy Draper, the interior decorator famous in the '30s for her theatrical looks. I designed silkscreened, silvery gray tablecloths with a pattern that echoed Paul's work as well as the history of the room. Centered on each of the 60 tables was an Art Deco styled lamp created from a silver fluted column topped by a handsome shade. I was crazy about the look of these lamps, and the glamorous look they gave to the room.

In fact, those Art Deco lamps nearly caused a disaster. So that we could dim them on cue, we had them hot-wired, which meant their electrical wires were connected to the lighting director's control board. At the same time, we replaced the seriously decrepit flooring with an inexpensive silvery gray carpet that picked up the tones in the tablecloths. What made the carpet affordable was its lack of pile. That carpeting was so thin you could actually see the backing through the fibers. Hey, what do you expect for $3.50 a yard? But you know what? It looked great on camera with the atmospheric lighting, and it cleaned up that run-down room in a big way. It also hid the wires leading from the table lamps to the control board.

After everything was set up, I went off on a dinner break with John, who had driven down to visit me. I wasn't needed on the set for the focusing of the lighting, yet all through dinner I kept fidgeting. I just couldn't relax and enjoy the break. "What's the matter with you?" John asked more than once. "I don't know," I answered, "but something's wrong." When it comes to spotting trouble, my intuition has always been pretty good. We cut the meal short, headed back to the Coconut Grove, and arrived to find the fire marshal standing in the middle of the room looking at a section of the floor as a puff of smoke rose and curled up and around his head. It turned out that the crew, when installing the carpet, had put a staple through one of the wires leading to a table lamp–a potential disaster, because without the lamps much of my atmosphere would be lost. Moreover, I couldn't remove the lamps because we had cut holes in the tablecloths for the wiring.

One of the best things about working with the Muppets is that everyone loves them, and the fire inspector was no exception. We were allowed to keep the lamps as long as we traced every darn wire and made sure no staples were remotely near them. It also helped that my very sharp and respected assistant Keaton Walker had an excellent working relationship with the LA Fire Department; they valued his word and accepted that everything would be okay and safe.

We had another potential problem: Miss Piggy wanted to make her entrance on a litter. That might sound easy enough, but the litter had to house Frank Oz, her operator, who was a good six feet, two inches tall. In addition, a portable television monitor with batteries, etc., needed to be concealed. I designed an elaborate litter with ostrich plumes, decorative woodturnings, golden pillows, the works. The poor musclemen, four in all, who had to transport Miss Piggy got a real workout, but she looked great and seemed very happy lording it over everyone from her position of power. In fact, we were all happy. The evening went off without a hitch. My only regret is that I never got up the nerve to ask Ginger Rogers, who was a guest that evening, for a dance. And, of course, when I did summon up the nerve to ask Miss Piggy for a turn around the floor, she refused to leave her litter.

My next project with Jim Hensen was a special called "The Fantastic Miss Piggy Show," which we taped in Toronto in 1982. The whole show revolved around the divine swine and her ego (no surprise there). We had a large opening number as well as a closing number, with dancers all in pink (of course), plus a highly charged production number with George Hamilton as a jungle Inca chief, who threatened to barbecue our star. Needless to say, she managed to escape. It seemed her entire script was typed in capitals and italics. This time she was the show's prima donna, and if you think her personality was big normally, you should have seen her with her very own special.

At first, the plot had the Muppet public relations people leaking the rumor to the press that Miss Piggy had gone to a fat farm in a wild attempt to slim down so she could more easily win Kermit's heart. She was to appear all svelte and gorgeous, but then she was to become upset with Kermit during the special, and during a fit of pique (forgive me) she would pig out and quickly regain her voluptuous figure. For one reason or another, this concept was scrapped in favor of a more predictable television formula featuring various sketches and production numbers but a weak storyline. Too bad. I thought the original idea was great, if thin (sorry about that, Miss Piggy).

The guests on the show were John Ritter (a sweeter man one could never hope to meet) and the aforementioned

216

George Hamilton, complete with his usual deep tan and great self-deprecating sense of humor. One of Miss Piggy's big numbers was with George, playing the aforementioned Inca chief. I created a jungle setting complete with an enormous idol whose jaw opened (courtesy of a hidden forklift) to reveal George in his Inca costume and all his tanned glory, flashing his own jaw of perfect, overly white teeth. The scene, dubbed "The King and Queen of the Luau," was hokey, silly, and very funny, and it was ripe with all sorts of jokes at our star's expense. Let's put it this way: It was difficult for her to talk with an apple in her mouth.

However, my favorite moment happened one day off camera when I was walking past one of my sets, which was an over-the-top dressing room for our star. Over the top? Well, let's put it this way: Blushing-pink satin tufted with large buttons, covered the walls, and pink lights surrounded a heart-shaped mirror hung above a dressing table strewn with powder puffs and typical superstar accoutrements. Of course, flowers from adoring fans and admirers were everywhere. As I walked by, I suddenly heard a familiar voice.

"*Oh, Raymie Poo,*" Miss Piggy called sweetly. So, I went over for a chat. There she was, trying out her *chaise longue* (another pink tufted wonder), tossing her hair from side to side, taking in this pink wonderland, a tribute to her fame and beauty. We chatted for a while, both of us making sure the star was happy with her set. Great fun. When the time came for me to leave and check on the other sets, I said how pleased I was that she appeared to like her dressing room and that I would see her later. Wrong move. I should have waited to be formally dismissed. As I walked away, I heard a newly harsh voice coming from the dressing room.

"But don't you think I should have MORE FLOWERS?!!!" A riot. And yes, there was no discussion. She got more flowers.

The last time I worked with Miss Piggy and Kermit was when they were doing a presentation on the Academy Awards (the gang appeared on no fewer than five Oscar nights). Just try designing a see-through podium that hides two grown men of considerable size and talent–a complicated, but rewarding, challenge.

It was sad when we heard of the untimely death of Jim Henson in 1990, when he was just 53. I cannot say enough kind words about him. I truly miss Jim and, of course, Miss Piggy, who for me will always be on a pedestal, exactly where she belongs.

Chapter 19

Grande Dames

Miss Piggy wasn't the only grande dame with whom I worked. In 1985 I had the pleasure of meeting **Lana Turner** when she was a judge on a 1985 beauty contest in Hawaii. I had been hired to design the sets for the contest called "The Most Beautiful Girl in the World," and my John had come for the taping. Afterward, while circulating around the cast party, John had returned to me saying, "Come on, Ray. I want you to meet Lana Turner." Because of my policy of never pushing myself onto celebrities, I refused. John, however, could be very persuasive, and so I reluctantly agreed. Miss Turner could not have been nicer. In addition to being very gracious, she knew a great deal about my work and recited the names of many of the shows I had designed. "How do you know these things about me?" I asked. "I read the credits," she replied, with a sly smile. I still can't figure out if, in fact, she really knew about me or had somehow heard about some of the shows I had done. Kind of impressive, either way.

In 1974, Jack Haley, Jr., the producer of that year's Academy Awards, wanted to have **Susan Hayward** appear on the Oscars along with Charlton Heston as presenters of the Best Actress award. At the time, she was gravely ill and close to death from brain cancer. In fact, on the night of the 46th Annual Oscars she was so weak they had to lay her down in a dressing room backstage in order to get her into a red wig and a beautiful dark-gray sequined gown by Nolan Miller. Despite being painfully thin, she looked great on camera. Her performance that night required exactly the grit and determination exemplified by so many of the characters she had portrayed over the years. After winning Best Actress herself in 1958 (for "I Want to Live!") and being nominated four times, Miss Hayward was a pro when it came to the Academy Awards. One wonders how she felt about her final appearance on the show. Perhaps it's telling that when she died 11 months later, she was buried in that gray sequined gown. She was 57 years old.

Noteworthy, too, was **Olivia de Havilland**. In 1977 at the age of 61 she was one of the stars on the American Film Institute Tribute to **Bette Davis** for which I designed the sets. At one point during the rehearsal, I asked the director to have the stage manager find out what Miss de Havilland was wearing so I could coordinate the lighting with her outfit. When asked, she signaled into the wings, and her assistant brought out not only her light blue gown but also the shoes to match. After the show I mentioned to her what a great help it had been to see her gown during the rehearsal period, to which she replied, "But my dear, I was trained by the studios. That's what we did."

Equally well trained by the studios was **Gloria Swanson**. One morning in 1966 while I was at Yale, we were told that Miss Swanson, age 65, would be giving a talk at the Drama School Theatre at 10 a.m. We students poured into the theatre to see this film legend. I'll never forget my first glimpse of her. Barely five feet tall, she nevertheless had a huge presence. Dressed to perfection in a dark blue, beautifully tailored suit with white trim at the collar, she carried a red carnation that matched her red shoes and red lipstick. Quite simply, she looked sensational– the consummate star. After graciously accepting her standing ovation, she said, "You'll have to forgive my appearance, but this is the middle of the night for me." This remark triggered even greater, explosive, applause, accompanied by whoops and cheers. Miss Swanson then proceeded to discuss what it was like being a star for close to half a century, what the studio system was like in the early years, and how her life had evolved. Fascinating.

Stella Adler, the renowned actress and teacher, also visited Yale during my time there. As part of her visit, she attended one of the student productions held at our theatre, a close copy of a typical Broadway theatre. When she arrived, just before the curtain went up, I saw her walk down the side of the audience, work her way across the seated first row (no easy move), and then proceed up the center aisle grabbing more attention than the play that followed. She knew how to be a star.

At home one night in 1990 in our Manhattan apartment, John told me he had seen **Lauren Bacall** that afternoon at the deli counter inside Zabar's, an upscale market on the Upper West Side. As was the practice there, customers would take a number and wait to be called to make their selections. John was waiting patiently to request some cheese and watched as Betty's (Bacall's nickname) number came up. She was too busy chatting with a friend to notice. John tapped her lightly on the shoulder to alert her. She spun around and screamed at the top of her voice, *"Don't touch me! Nobody touches me!"*

"You know what?" John replied. "I know a lot of people in the business and I've heard you were a bitch, but I never believed them. I do now!"

Peggy Lee grabbed attention in another way. In 1990 she was booked on "Night of 100 Stars," for which I designed the sets. She was to appear with five other well-known singers, all of whom were no trouble at all. Not so Miss Lee. I was informed that she had some breathing issues and would need a special chair to sit on during her performance. As luck would have it, my friend Clay Anderson had worked years earlier for Miss Lee, and when contacted, he was able to tell me what kind of chair to provide. I knew she could be a bit difficult, so getting the right chair was a big deal.

During rehearsals, she seemed quite pleased with the chair, so I naturally gave Clay credit for helping us. Big mistake. Clay was a gracious, soft-spoken, fine man, but not according to Miss Lee. Seldom have I heard such a tirade of venom directed toward another person. It was upsetting as well as greatly annoying. Normally I do my job in the best, most professional and supportive way possible for every performer, but in this case, I saw red.

When we were staging the dress rehearsal, she showed up in a hideous helmet-type wig. Truly ugly. On camera there was little evidence she was sitting on a chair. She looked like a three-foot, six-inch silver midget. When she asked me how she looked, I thought of Clay and lied. "You look fabulous," I said. In fact, when she performed her song, she was hands down better than any of the other talented ladies on the stage, which included Olivia Newton John, Carol Channing, Marilyn McCoo, Crystal Gayle, and Gladys Knight. All I could think was, *talent rules.*

Katharine Hepburn was also featured in "The Night of 100 Stars." I remember hearing her being introduced to the famous film director Joe Mankiewicz. She didn't let on that she already knew Mankiewicz, having worked with him on "Suddenly, Last Summer" in 1959. Instead, she looked at Mankiewicz and blithely quipped, "You're not Joe Mankiewicz. You've lost your hair and gotten fat. I hope time has been kinder to me!" Only a grande dame could get away with that.

Like Miss Hepburn, **Betty Buckley** had a way with words. Following her Tony Award-winning Broadway performance as Grizabella in "Cats," she appeared at a Kennedy Center Honors tribute that I designed. She sang "Memory," her hit song, while dressed in a stunning gown. As she came off the stage, I said, "You were wonderful!" "Oh, thanks," she replied. "It's the first time I've sung it without my ears."

And then there was the fabulous **Sophia Loren**. She was a presenter at one of the Academy Awards shows I designed and caused me to break my hard and fast rule about pushing myself onto celebrities. In this instance I simply could not help myself.

When Miss Loren entered the theatre for a rehearsal, the plan was for her to come down a long, glamorous staircase and walk to a podium. Brazenly I approached her, introduced myself as the show's production designer, and asked her if she would like to see where her entrance was. This was a big no-no, as showing the talent what to do and where to go is the job of the stage manager. Quite truthfully, I didn't give a damn. I was under her spell. I took her hand, which was silken soft, walked her to the top of the stairs, and guided her down to the podium. She was gracious and charming. She was perfection. She was a *star*.

I noticed she had a lot of sun damage on her décolletage, and she was wearing an awful ankle bracelet, but who cared? The amazing thing is I was lucky no one berated me for what I had done. I had broken the rules and gotten away with it. I also got the most wonderful memory. Would I risk doing it again? You bet.

In the mid-1970s, John and I took a vacation in the Mexican resort town of Puerto Vallarta. One day we took a break from lying on the beach and went for a walk along the main oceanfront street, visiting the various tourist shops. Inside one store specializing in trinkets, we spotted a grossly overweight woman holding up a cheap-looking, gaudy, purple necklace. We watched the woman looking at herself in a mirror and found her oddly compelling. Even though she was a sight, we couldn't take our eyes off her. A mystery–that is until she left the store and the owner told us the lady was none other than **Ava Gardner**. We later found out that when not working she had a tendency to gain a great deal of weight, but when a film role came up, she would go on a crash diet and regain the figure her fans loved. Still, even when she was bloated, she had that special quality that made a star.

Sometimes my work would take an odd and, yes, funny twist. Among my favorite actresses, choreographers, and directors is the wonderful **Debbie Allen**. I first encountered Debbie when she performed with Gregory Hines in a huge production number on the Academy Awards show I designed in 1981. It was a complicated number with many set changes. She was sensational.

After that, I started to do sets for her when she directed musicals at the Kennedy Center as well as at venues on the West Coast. These shows were often intended as vehicles for young performers and were great training grounds for aspiring children–not always the easiest group to work with. I remember one time she found out that some of the older boys had conned a few of the younger ones into signing them in at the beginning of the rehearsal day so the older guys could be a little late. Well, Debbie, being the sharp, wise lady she is, found out. Believe me, there was trouble. One didn't mess with Debbie or try to put something over on her. Aside from being the consummate professional, she had strong maternal instincts and wanted the kids to know there was a right way and a wrong way to conduct oneself backstage.

Debbie had no tolerance for the wrong way. She gathered all the children into a rehearsal room and closed the door. Frankly, I'm surprised the door didn't explode off its hinges from the intensity of her berating of these young performers. She cared deeply that they learn to conduct themselves properly and honestly. Everyone was on time after that.

One year I was back on the East Coast putting together a show for Debbie when she called to inform me that she needed a special prop: a python. Not a real one, thank God, but one that not only looked real but was also flexible. The actor handling the serpent needed to move it in a way that would make the audience believe it was alive. I had the prop department create a python, but both Debbie and I were unsatisfied. It simply looked fake. Debbie was concerned, but I assured her that the fake-snake problem could be fixed.

What I did was call a prop shop in Los Angeles that carried a large assortment of rentable stuffed animals. I explained my problem and was told they had the perfect solution. I stressed that the snake had to be large, flexible, and realistic. No problem. Their only question was, "Do you want the snake with or without the chihuahua?" I got it without the serpent's last meal. No extra charge.

Lucille Ball was interesting. In the 1960s and '70s, when John was doing all the negative cutting on her shows that followed "I Love Lucy," she was always pleasant. One day while driving around the Desilu Studios in her customized pink golf cart, she saw John and stopped. She had heard that John had just returned from a vacation in Spain and asked how it had gone. John assured her that the trip had been wonderful and mentioned that she was a big hit in Spain at three o'clock every afternoon. "Three p.m.? What the hell is *that* about?" She ranted. "You forget, in Spain, three p.m. is siesta time," John said. "Of course," came Lucy's flippant reply as she quickly drove off. But in 1971, when I worked with her on "The Pearl Bailey Show," she seemed devoid of humor. Off camera Lucy was more glum than fun. Was she frustrated at not being able to recreate the success she had experienced during her "I Love Lucy" years? Who knows? Later, I encountered her again when she was a presenter on the Academy Awards. Her companion backstage during a fitting for her elaborate, heavily beaded gown, which had tipped the scales at about 40 pounds, was her toy poodle, Tinker. During the fitting, Tinker was sniffing around the hem of her long skirt. Dryly, Lucy said, "Get away, Tinker. If this dress falls on you, it'll kill you!" So thankfully her sense of humor remained at least somewhat intact.

In 1983, **Cyndi Lauper** was scheduled to be on "The American Music Awards" singing "When You Were Mine." She had strong ideas as to what sort of set I should provide for her number. I didn't mind her involvement, even if I found it

226

odd. Late one morning I called her (one never called recording artists until at least 11 a.m., as they tend to be night owls). Her phone was answered by a sophisticated-sounding lady with an English accent. I identified myself, and suddenly the voice changed into the Cyndi Lauper we all know and love. I never found out if I had awakened her and she had answered in her real voice, meaning that the voice we all recognized was her stage persona. Or did Cyndi simply put on a fake accent so she could screen her incoming calls and duck anyone she didn't want to talk to? A mystery.

For some reason, she wanted her set to be all about shoes. I forget her reasoning, but what I did was send her out with my fun assistant, Randy Blom, to buy up as many used shoes as they could find. Randy drove Cyndi all over Los Angeles to consignment houses and used-clothing stores. In the end, Randy's car was filled with more than 300 pairs of old, stinking shoes. (It took weeks for the stench to leave his Car.)

Cyndi then came to the ABC scenic shop, where I had three large, abstract plywood shapes constructed. She supervised the stapling of the used shoes onto the wooden cutouts. These shoe collages were built to stand upright on the stage while Cyndi performed her song. Don't ask what it was all about. All I know is that she was very happy and we all loved working with her. The evening of the show, when I dropped by her dressing room to wish her luck, she was busy having some wonderful colors added to her hair. When I complimented her on the look, she asked if I'd like a streak or two myself. Before I knew it, she had her hairdresser put a bright red stripe in my hair. I loved it, but like Elvis's hair color, mine didn't last. The next day it washed out. Darn it.

One day in 1979, while working on a show at Radio City Music Hall, I was directed by the producers to lower the grand curtain at exactly 10 a.m. and to make sure all crew working upstage of it remained absolutely quiet. No problem. Well, shortly after the appointed time, when the curtain had been lowered, I was backstage working–silently–with the crew when all of a sudden we heard the most wonderful sounds.

Quietly, I left the crew and went down into the audience, where I sat alone. There on the stage stood the source of that astonishing music. **Ella Fitzgerald** was running through her repertoire for a show that would take place later that week. She was singing for her sound crew, but as I sat there, I pretended she was singing just for me. Heaven!

Nell Carter was grand in every sense of the word. In 1986, after I had been asked to design her TV special, "Nell Carter: Never Too Old to Dream," the star invited me and John to attend a Christmas party at her Los Angeles house. Her home was warm and inviting and filled with tons of tempting food. We couldn't help noticing that the oversized Nell didn't take one bite. As we left the party, John said to our hostess, "Well, you'll be on camera in eight days." "Oh, yes, I've got to go on a diet!" Nell responded.

I was told that her beaded gown for the show cost twice as much as a similar gown would normally run. She was as large as her talent. She was also extremely nice.

The show required a nightclub set that would time-travel through the ages. Four different eras needed to be represented–not easy. A set like this uses a lot of real estate, meaning I would need four times the usual amount of scenery to create the different time periods and moods. I wasn't the only one facing some problems. The producer had his hands full with Nell and her outsized ego. One day during rehearsals she announced that for the opening number she would love to have a "big old diamond on a chain" around her neck (shades of Pearl Bailey?). When the producer told her there wasn't any money in the budget for that, Nell said, "Oh, honey, you don't need to buy me one. Just rent one and I'll feel wonderful." Well, the production company checked out the cost and discovered that renting was less expensive than buying, but still very costly. I remember saying to the producer, "It will be interesting to see who wins this one!"

Soon enough, on the first day of taping, I discovered who had won. There stood Nell looking terrific and happy with a "big old diamond" hanging around her neck and a guard in uniform glued to her side for the duration of the session. I couldn't help myself and later said to the producer, "I see who won this round." "See that uniformed guard?" the producer replied with a sly grin. "He's from central casting, and the diamond is fake." I figured there would be hell to pay when Nell found out, as surely she would, since it's almost impossible to keep such a secret in our business. But she never did. Two weeks later I saw Nell on a talk show telling everyone how she was able to get the producer to rent this fabulous and very expensive diamond for her. Everyone ended up happy.

In 1987, when I was doing the sets for the 14th annual American Music Awards, the very clothes-conscious **Diana Ross** was tapped to be the show's hostess. It was arranged by Dick Clark Productions that I would fly to Las Vegas to meet Miss Ross at her home to discuss colors, etc. Well, we really hit it off and ended up sitting on her living room rug talking for quite a while. She was bright, elegant, and fun. Suddenly,

I remembered I had a plane to catch. "Oh, I'll drive you to the airport," she said. "You don't have to do that," I answered. "I'll get a cab." "No," she insisted, "I actually have to go there to pick up my husband."

And just the two of us got into her Rolls-Royce. Miss Ross took the wheel, and we headed for the airport. The only problem was we got talking and laughing so much we missed the turnoff for the airport not once but twice. We were now very late. Realizing this, she said, "Do you think they'll let me park out front?" "Let's see you play the star," I said.

When we arrived at the airport curb, we saw three officials wave frantically that she could not park there. She paused long enough for them to realize who, exactly, she was. Then the rules magically changed (remember, these were the days before 9/11), and we left the car at the curb. As we walked to our gates, it was interesting to see how people lit up when they recognized her. Amazing to think what life would be like if those around you would make accommodations when things, like arriving late at the airport, went wrong. I wondered what it would be like to be treated that way for most of your life. As it was, I benefitted from her reflected glory and made it just in time for my flight.

"Wonder Woman" **Lynda Carter** was a dream to work with. I loved designing sets for beautiful women, and Lynda was drop-dead gorgeous. The four TV specials I designed for her (1980-82, and 1984) were a pleasure, as the star was easy going and a lot of fun. Like Cher, Miss Carter's costumes were designed by the fabulous Bob Mackie, and so she always looked great. This actress and vocalist had the most amazing body. She was perfection itself and appeared to be happy with my support for her and her shows. Conflicts were minimal, and seldom was I made to feel compromised.

However, for one of the shows the production team came up with the idea of covering the set entirely in graffiti– something I was opposed to, as I didn't feel we should be seen as endorsing the vandalism of property that belongs to others. Once, when I was doing a set for Diana Ross and she asked to have a set decorated with graffiti, I suggested that she might not want to be associated with the destruction of private property. Miss Ross backed right down. Now I faced the same problem, but the director and production team were insistent. What I ended up doing was taking a swatch of floral-printed fabric that Bob Mackey was using for Miss Carter's dress and blowing it up so that the flowers stood 12 to 14 feet tall and flowed over the street, across a car, and up the buildings that formed the set. The scene was as surreal as it was stunning.

For "Lynda Carter's Celebration," Miss Carter's 1981 TV special, I designed one of my best sets, one that earned an Emmy nomination. Sculptural in nature, it reflected my ongoing interest in the fine arts and my work in my own studio as a sculptor. This set was for the star's closing concert and consisted of a 25-piece orchestra with the audience seated on bleachers rising up and around it. The stage itself was made from clear Plexiglas and rested above the orchestra section, which was contained within a boxed area painted hot pink. Against this vibrant background the musicians in their tuxedos looked great. Working with this much Plexiglas had its challenges.

First, we had to be sure Miss Carter could gauge where the transparent stage floor ended so that she wouldn't fall into the orchestra. My solution: neon lights to outline the Plexiglas.

231

The bigger challenge came from Ron Samuels, Miss Carter's husband at the time, who was one of the show's producers. Ron did not like the idea that the musicians seated below the star would have an unobstructed view up his wife's skirt. But leave it to Bob Mackie. He designed a terrific pants suit for Miss Carter. Everyone was happy.

In 1998, I worked on a "Great Performances" show at Carnegie Hall called "My Favorite Broadway: The Leading Ladies." Hosted by **Julie Andrews**, the show boasted a stellar lineup that included **Nell Carter, Debra Monk, Linda Eder, Rosie O'Donnell, Liza Minnelli, and Elaine Stritch**. Elaine was a wonder to watch. We did have some problems with her during the rehearsal, when it became clear she was having trouble with the lyrics of her signature song, "Here's to the Ladies Who Lunch." She just couldn't seem to remember the words. It was too late to replace her. But even if she could have been replaced, no one wanted to, as she was the perfect choice to perform the show's final song. Unfortunately, no cue cards were available to help her through the number. The producers were stuck for a solution and stuck with her. There was nothing to do except hope for the best.

I was off stage right during most of the show, watching a television monitor along with Elaine. It was interesting to see her reaction to the various celebrities. If she liked someone's performance, she made a beeline to the green room to compliment the person. If she didn't think the performance was up to snuff, Elaine stayed at her post. One person she didn't budge for was Liza Minnelli. Liza was really off that night–in fact, so much so that the producers got Liza into a control booth two weeks later and had her dub herself when she was in better voice.

When the time came for Elaine to close the show, it was a sight to remember. No one in the business can milk a song and stretch it more than Elaine. As she sang, the pauses and stretches were unnerving. This was the woman who, when she took over a role in the Broadway musical "A Little Night Music," reportedly slowed down her performance so much that the show ended 10 minutes later than normal and got the stage crew into overtime. She was very popular with the crew.

As she was dragging out that final performance, it wasn't clear if she was just doing her normal milking of the number, or if in fact she couldn't remember the lyrics. As I watched with a certain fascination and borderline horror, I could see on another monitor the look on the gifted conductor Paul Gemignani's sweating face. His concern was clear. Well, Elaine made it through her signature song, and the audience adored her.

In 1977, I had the immense pleasure of working with **Bette Davis**, then 69, who was the honoree of that year's American Film Institute tribute. I had been asked to design the set, at the Beverly Hilton Hotel in Beverly Hills. John was included in the production team, compounding the pleasure. It was one of the few times John and I ever worked together. The experience was as fascinating as it was fun, due in large part to our star.

Several days before the taping of the tribute, John was asked to take a limo out to the Los Angeles airport to pick up **Celeste Holm**, who had appeared with Miss Davis in the 1950 classic "All About Eve." Later, John recalled that on the ride to the hotel Miss Holm had said, "I don't know why I'm here. Bette and I hate each other's guts." The evening of the big event, John and I were included in a small group of people who were to greet Miss Davis in a hotel suite prior to the show. Miss Holm wasn't there.

To prepare for the reception, I went through the hotel suite and stashed the cheap plastic flower arrangements in a nearby closet to up the quality of the venue to match our star. Unfortunately, there was no time to order up some handsome fresh arrangements. We had been told that Miss Davis would arrive at 6 p.m. sharp, and that she was always prompt. Well, 6 p.m. came, and John looked at his watch. "So much for promptness," he said. At that very moment the door exploded open and in walked this little Sherman tank of a woman. Barely five feet tall, she entered and proceeded to eat up all the oxygen in the room. She was the ultimate star. When asked by Perry Lafferty, the producer, if she'd like a drink, Bette said, "Oh, no. I've had two already." She made it clear she intended to stay in control.

Talking with Miss Davis was fascinating. At one point she discussed her work on "All About Eve," one of my favorite films. She told John and me that she had been nervous about how to play the scene in which she is preparing for the party she is giving in honor of her boyfriend, played by Gary Merrill (who in real life eventually became her actual husband). Miss Davis was playing the part of Margo Channing, a volatile stage star who is about to have an out-and-out fight with the honored guest. She told us that when she arrived on the set, Joe Mankiewicz, the director, said, "See this candy dish? The madder you get, the more you want a piece of that candy." This advice made for a remarkable moment in that memorable film and for a great performance by Miss Davis.

Later, just before her entrance at the AFI tribute, John dropped by a small holding area where Miss Davis was waiting in her green gown and asked if there was anything he could do for her. In a clipped voice she replied, "No, John. I'm happy as a clam." John later said he was sure she would walk at the slightest provocation, as she was clearly nervous. To avoid trouble, he made a beeline out the door, and out of her sight.

That evening I saw one of the most celebrated stars of all time graciously accept her American Film Institute award for Lifetime Achievement. It was a privilege and an honor to have been in the presence of possibly the grandest dame of them all.

Bing at the time of a Christmas special I designed for him in 1971 with Kathryn and their children Harry, Nathaniel, and Mary Frances who later acted under the name Mary Crosby and gained fame for being the one who shot J.R. on the TV series "Dallas."

Dick Clark, who hired me to design 27 "American Music Awards" shows.

(photo: Tom Gibis)

Pearl Bailey was an enigma. She could be so very kind to the crew and cast, but often her bigger-than-life personality colored her actions. One never knew whether things would be difficult or delightful.

Bob Mackie and Cher. No costume designer in the business has more talent than Bob. He brought out the best in me and helped me win my first Emmy Award.

Cher wanted a simple set for her song "Send in the Clowns." She was dressed down in just jeans, but I tried to make the setting unique. I thought she and the set looked sensational.

Cher performs on the Emmy Award winning set I designed for her in 1975.

My set for Debbie Allen and Gregory Hines' huge production number, part of the 1981 Academy Awards for which I won my second Emmy Award.

My set for the 1982 Academy Awards production number "For Your Eyes Only"

More than 40 dancers filled my set for a "Tribute to Irving Berlin" part of the 1982 Academy Awards. Choreographed by Walter Painter and featuring Bernadette Peters and Peter Allen, this huge production number resulted in my third Emmy Award.

My circus set for "Hello Hollywood, Hello!" which opened at the MGM Hotel in Reno in 1978 and ran for 13 years. It was the largest stage in the USA, and built for a huge, spectacular circus finale including six full scaled circus wagons decorated with beautiful topless dancers.

The living curtain for "Hello Hollywood, Hello" descended with 17 ladies gyrating on this Space Disco set. Very frightening, at least for me when I demonstrated it to Donn and the cast for the first time.

One of the many sets that made up the MGM "Jubilee!" show. My design for this set was derived from Pete Menefe's wonderful costume designs for the number.

239

My mother and I prior to meeting President Carter at the White House when I designed the Kennedy Center Honors. I bought her dress in Marakesh.

I designed the Kennedy Center Honors from 1979 to 1990 and I'm very proud of my contribution to that show. The producers must have liked my work because they used my sets up to 1998 even after I left the show.

240

In 1980, Bob Rang (r) one of the best assistants I ever had, and clearly one with an incredible sense of humor, and I got dressed in some Bob Mackie costumes from the old MGM Grand "Hallelujah Hollywood" show. We went to a Halloween party where we lost the costume contest because Bob was one of the judges.

Bob Finkel was a star in his own right and while he was behind the camera, he was charismatic, intelligent, and a great television producer.

The set I designed for Elton John when he appeared on the "American Music Awards," in 1980. Suspended on cables, he and his piano descended 15 feet down onto the stage.

241

Chapter 20

Time for Others

When AIDS struck in the 1980s, it was devastating. At first no one knew what was causing this plague. All we knew was that our friends far and wide were getting sick and dying. Theories abounded, but back then no one knew the real cause. It demoralized the gay community, leaving all of us feeling helpless. Of the more than 30 friends and acquaintances John and I lost, three stand out: Kent Davidson, Jack Kennedy (obviously not the President), and David Archer. All three were charming, intelligent men, kind, giving souls who had the misfortune to get ill before there was a treatment. I remember visiting Jack numerous times in the hospital before he died and facing the strange dilemma of not knowing if it was safe to hug the man. We had heard terrible stories of friends who got ill with AIDS and entered the hospital and the orderlies refusing to feed them. Food trays were left outside the hospital room doors, and the patient was left to fend for himself. Terrible.

When I went to visit Jack the first time, I simply didn't know what to do. Should I stay a safe distance away? And really, what distance was that? Finally, I just took a deep breath and went to Jack and hugged him. I just had to. When Jack eventually died, John, who at one point had been very close to Jack and served as his executor, honored Jack's request to be cremated and to have his ashes scattered in Griffith Park, a notorious gay cruising area. As Jack had said with a sly grin, "After all, I did spend a lot of time there."

And so, John and I gathered three of Jack's closest friends–Ed Handler, David Archer, and Jeff Leith, and we met at a local bar. When John arrived, he slammed the metal box containing Jack's ashes onto the bar and announced that he had brought Jack by for "one last drink." After numerous toasts, we realized that it was getting late and that the park was now closed.

"Not to worry," said one of the guys. "I cruise the park a lot, and I know a back way in."

So off we went. When we arrived at the park, we headed up an incline and looked for an appropriate resting place for Jack. Dusk was settling in, but fortunately we could still see. The first location was nixed by John as being too ugly, owing to the presence of a large utility pole that John felt would ruin the view for Jack. We climbed farther and finally settled on a grassy knoll. But then we found that the metal box was impossible to open. We decided it was too far and too late to go all the way down to the parking lot to retrieve a tire iron to use to pry open the box. Banging the box on a nearby rock finally did the trick, and we took turns scattering Jack with lots of laughter and tears. When David's turn came, a blast of wind erupted, and suddenly he was covered in ashes. To much laughter, he yelled, "Off, Jack!" (All too soon, David's turn would come when he, too, would succumb to AIDS.) After the wind died down and Jack's box was empty, we all walked arm in arm down the hill, feeling that Jack's sendoff had taken place exactly as he would have wanted.

The devastation of losing someone you loved deeply and the adjustments one had to make before and after he died were huge. It was such a sad period. I remember feeling something akin to guilt: How could John and I be experiencing such good fortune during a time of plague? I'm not sure how, or why, we were spared. To this day I continue to support organizations such as God's Love We Deliver, Project Angel Food, and the Ali Forney Center, and it never seems to be enough.

By the 1980s, I had pretty much total control over how I spent my time day to day, and that meant I could dedicate Tuesday afternoons to making deliveries to people with AIDS for Project Angel Food. Often, our clients were shut-ins, but sometimes they were just in need of a good, warm, well-balanced meal. When I started delivering food, I had a system: I would go by Project Angel Food's headquarters in Hollywood, where the meals were prepared and packed for distribution. There I would pick up about 10 meal packs plus the directions to each recipient and proceed to drive from place to place.

In the beginning, I occasionally wondered if the meals were really needed by some of the recipients, as now and then I would see a client clearly able to get around. Soon, though, I realized that by delivering a meal I was enabling him to not waste the energy that would have been expended on food shopping and cooking. Instead, he could go to the doctor, visit friends, and maybe even enjoy life a bit in the face of what was, in most cases, a death sentence.

Some of my clients were dealing with the early stages of dementia, a condition that occasionally came with AIDS. Others were desperately poor. Once when I was working on a show that had a lot of leftover prop greenery, I asked the producer if I could have the unwanted surplus when the show was over. The greenery had been purchased at Moskatels, the craft supply store in downtown LA. "Sure," the producer said, no doubt thinking I was a little nutty to want the stuff.

What I did was go back to Moskatels and exchange the fake foliage for 10 small, artificial Christmas trees, as well as some ornaments and diminutive electric lights. I then decorated the trees and gave them to my clients for the holidays. One recipient confessed a few weeks later that because he was so poor the tiny tree bulbs had been his only source of light when the rest of the lightbulbs in his home had burned out. When the lights on the little Christmas tree burned out, he was left in the dark. Needless to say, the week following our conversation, I arrived at his home with a bagful of assorted lightbulbs. His case was especially sad since he had the beginnings of dementia and could not really take care of himself. In those days, we didn't have a system in place to help people in that situation. It was yet another powerful reminder of how fortunate John and I were.

Most of my clients were lucid and appreciative of our efforts on their behalf, but not always. Some sections of Los Angeles were a bit on the rough side, and in those neighborhoods, appreciation was not foremost in people's minds. I was assigned to deliver in the east side of Hollywood, which had its share of drug dealers and gangs. I used to park

245

my car, take off my watch, and put it along with my wallet under the front seat. First, though, I would remove $10 or $20 from my wallet and put it in my pocket, just in case I got held up. Once when I saw two really tough-looking guys zeroing in on me, I just kept moving fast and tried to give the impression I knew where I was going– not easy, since I was searching for the address where my client lived. In any case, it worked; I did not get held up. I never told John about any of this, as I knew he would have been upset that I was compromising my safety. Eventually, I requested a safer route in West Hollywood, where there were many gay men with smart-looking apartments.

When we moved to New York City, I was determined to continue delivering food. I contacted God's Love We Deliver and arranged for a new route. The big difference between LA and Manhattan was that I now had to make my deliveries on foot, as driving and parking would have been too difficult. Pat Costello, the lady with whom I dealt at God's Love, was organized, smart, and kind. If I had a conflict with work and couldn't deliver, she never laid a guilt trip on me. On my first day, I wasn't sure how to go about carrying the food, so I took our collapsible, two-wheeled shopping cart. And because it was raining, I wore my Burberry raincoat. After picking up the food, which was waiting in thermal hampers at a designated church, I headed for the first stop on my list: a skid-row-type unit in a housing complex for the down and out. Well, this was an eye-opener. As I entered the elevator, a man in his late 20s got on with me. He wore an old T-shirt; a pack of smokes was rolled up into one sleeve. To my horror, track marks ran up both arms. And there I was with my dumb

246

shopping cart and smart raincoat looking like a suburban housewife.

Very politely, the man turned toward me and asked, "What floor do you want?" "The sixth floor, please," I said, relieved. Most likely, this was not going to be a mugging. And up we went. Piece of cake–or so I thought. Two clients were on that floor, and one of them wasn't home. Usually, this wasn't a problem. We were told in our orientation program to give away any leftover or unclaimed food to any needy person we happened to see. Well, before I saw *her*, she saw *me*.

"Hey! You from God's Love? Got any food?" an obnoxious woman bellowed at me. "We're not allowed to say," I replied, stupidly. "This son of a bitch won't say he's from God's Love!" she shouted to anyone within hearing distance. She went on to address me with words I hadn't heard since my Army days. I set off down the staircase, delivering my food to the various apartments on my list. She in turn followed me down every floor, needling me for free food. I ended up with an extra meal and had the supreme pleasure of giving it to someone else in need. I learned the territory fast, and never again made myself a target.

Yes, most of my clients were appreciative, friendly people who were, sadly, just plain unlucky. I remember one pleasant, well-educated man who lived near our apartment building. He was still able to move around fairly easily so, to get to know him better, I decided to find an opportunity to ask him out for a cup of coffee. To be honest, he was very attractive. One day, as I was delivering to him, an equally good-looking younger man was leaving his apartment. "Ah, ha!" I thought. "This guy is gay and into young men." Wrong. It turned out my client's name was John Doyle (not the theatre director), and the young man was his son, who was visiting from out of town. John was straight and highly intelligent, and just as I was about to ask him out for coffee, he invited me in. Soon we realized we had many interests in common, and I started to look forward to my deliveries to him–so much so that I wound up reworking my route so that John would be my last delivery of the day and we could enjoy talking for an hour or so about everything from the latest news to life itself. What a pleasure.

John Doyle, it turned out, didn't have AIDS. He was suffering from cancer of the lungs, and through him I discovered that God's Love was now including clients who were in need of help even if they didn't have AIDS. Roughly 10 months after I first met him, John ended up in a hospital on the lower West Side. I would visit him in the hospital and then call his sister who lived out of town and report on John's condition. At one point, he was having great difficulty breathing and, as he struggled to talk, I feared my presence at his bedside was making matters worse.

"John, I can see you're having trouble talking, so I'll be on my way and you can rest," I told him. On my way out, I stopped by the nurses' station and informed the head nurse that John was in difficulty. Then I went home.

Well, I can sometimes be so stupid. I should have asked John if he wanted me to stay or go. Two hours after I left, he died. Another lesson learned the hard way. A short time later, his sister called and invited me to John's wake in Greenwich, Connecticut. While there, I was amazed at the number of people who came up to me and commented that John had mentioned how important our friendship had been to him. That meant a great deal to me. For years thereafter I made a

248

Christmas donation to God's Love We Deliver in John's memory.

In 2002 I became involved with the Ali Forney Center, an organization that works to get supervised housing for gay kids who have been kicked out of their homes. In fact, I had no trouble understanding these kids. While it appeared to others that I had led an idyllic life, the fact is I have always carried memories of a father who had never been warm or loving. While John and I did not flaunt our sexual orientation, we likewise never hid the life, or the bed, we shared. One night during a dinner party when my parents were guests at our house, the subject of Anita Bryant and her antigay stance came up. I expressed in no uncertain terms my contempt for her and the hurt she had caused to gay men and women. I said I thought Bryant was truly evil.

This was more than my father could swallow. After the company left, he announced that he would have my mother pack and that they would leave the house the next morning and return immediately to their home in Florida. I was devastated. All that time I had thought he had finally understood and accepted our lifestyle. Instead, my father walked out of our house the next morning and out of my life forever. This continues to haunt me. I had spent my life trying to prove to him that I was worthy of his love and respect, and I had failed. Or maybe he failed in his role as a father. In any case, I never saw him again. He died several years later, a bitter man who had become abusive to my mother. Sad to say, I was relieved that he was gone. I will never get over the hatred that Anita Bryant spread. Organizations such as the Ali Forney Center that strive to counteract the damage she and others like her have done to so many people, will always have my support and gratitude.

Carl Siciliano, the founder of the Ali Forney Center, began by volunteering in monasteries that operated soup kitchens, and serving in shelters run by the Catholic Worker movement. Eventually, he set up a 24-hour drop-in center for homeless young people. In 1997, a teenager in his care, Ali Forney, was shot and killed near a housing project on 135th Street and Fifth Avenue in Harlem. His murder was never solved. Carl was so moved that he formed the Ali Forney Center to house LGBTQ young people.

To raise much-needed cash, the Center stages various events, including plays and musicals. At first, I was just doing the stage decors for these fundraising events, but after joining the organization's Board, my involvement deepened. I became increasingly aware of the crucial role fundraising played in the organization's success or failure. What could I do to help the bottom line? The solution I came up with–a one-night performance by the spectacular Bea Arthur–is a story in itself which you will learn more about later.

Another way I tried to give back to others was by lecturing at colleges and universities. At Temple University in Japan, Wagner College, Yale Drama School, the Costume Institute in New York, St. Bonaventure University in Bonaventure, N.Y., Stockton University in Galloway, N.J., and Florida University in Tallahassee (where I was honored with an Eminent Scholar chair), I found enthusiastic audiences who responded to my stories about my experiences over the years. I enjoyed lecturing but knew I could never be tied down to the job of teaching on a regular basis. Higher education came into my life again, when I retired and no longer needed the extensive library of theatre arts reference books I had assembled over my 50 years in the business. With a bit of research, I found the College of the Desert, in Palm Springs, California, which gladly accepted my gift of 800 volumes on everything from period architecture to theatre history. My library was put to good use.

Always, I left myself open for opportunities to help out. It made sense: Over the years I had learned that helping others worked both ways. My mother used to say, "The more you give to others, the more you get back." Getting back isn't the reason one gives, but there does appear to be a blessing that comes back in return. I cherished the many friends I had made by volunteering at God's Love, Angel Food, and the Ali Forney Center.

Often, opportunities to help our friends appeared unexpectedly. One day in 1988, for instance, I got a call from Bob Shanks, a producer friend. Would I be interested in designing a children's show in London? The timing could not have been better, as we were having a strike that included my union, United Scenic Artists, and no one was working. A nice fee was settled on, and I was to buy myself a first class ticket to London. We agreed that I would be reimbursed for the ticket upon arrival. Just two days later, I had settled into my London hotel and met the people involved with the show; all went well. At one point during our initial meeting, a secretary asked me for my air ticket, left the room, and returned with the cost of the round-trip ticket in one-hundred-dollar bills. At that moment, I had an idea

While I was busy in London, my dear friend Billy Erigo, who had once worked for John and me around our Hancock Park house in Los Angeles, was in an LA hospital dying of AIDS. He was destitute. He was also proud and would accept help from no one. So, when I left that meeting in London, I took the return portion of my air ticket and called the airport. How much would I save, I asked, if I turned in my first-class ticket and rebooked myself into economy class? About $1,000 was the answer. When I arrived back in Los Angeles, I went to see Billy in the hospital and asked him a question: If I was in serious trouble and he could help me simply by being a bit uncomfortable for 10 hours, would he do it? "Of course," he said. I explained what I had done and proceeded to lay 10 one-hundred-dollar bills on his chest. We laughed and had a bit of a cry. I was so happy to be able to help him in a way he would accept.

Chapter 21

Bea Arthur

In 2002, I had the privilege of designing the set for Bea Arthur's one-woman Broadway show, "Just Between Friends." The show did more than entertain the scores of fans who adored this actress and comedienne, so famous for her pathbreaking television role as the liberated "Maude," for which she won an Emmy award in 1977, and the acerbic Dorothy Zbornak of "The Golden Girls," for which she garnered an additional Emmy in 1988. My encounter with Bea would eventually lead to her helping scores of teenagers who had been kicked out of their homes for being gay. It's a story of Bea's remarkable generosity of spirit and how it resulted in life-saving support for homeless young people. It's a story that needs to be told.

My future relationship with this outstanding actress and human being began inauspiciously enough. Bea's 2002 Broadway show at the Booth Theatre had a limited run and therefore a limited budget for sets–just $10,000, which was ridiculously small. Consequently, I kept the look simple. To form the wings of the stage and to frame the star, I used a series of apricot velour drapes recycled from a Miss America pageant I had designed in 2000. After the pageant, I had arranged to have the drapes sold to a drapery company called Show Biz, whose owner, Scott Webley, gave me a deal on the rental price so that the drapes could be repurposed for Bea's show at the Booth. I carpeted the Booth's stage floor in beige and added a circular area rug in apricot to pick up the tones in the drapes and center the acting space. Here, eight times a week for eight weeks, all eyes were drawn to the star as she sang and told stories about her life and career. Our relationship during the course of the production was strictly businesslike; I never got to really know her.

While on tour in the Midwest prior to her Broadway appearance, Bea had injured her foot. An inexpensive but comfortable upholstered armchair (again, in apricot tones) provided a place for our star to take a load off her feet. To avoid wearing a shoe on the injured foot, she decided to perform barefoot, and so the rugs were a big hit with her. For an accent, I brought in an elegant Art Nouveau plant stand that I had used when designing the 1999 Broadway staging of Noel Coward's "Waiting in the Wings"; the producers had given me the stand after the play closed. A stunning arrangement of silk flowers in apricots and beiges crowned the stand and cost nothing, thanks to floral designer Joseph Macchia, who lent us the arrangement in exchange for credit in the program. The only other scenic element was a flat black border, hung high in front of the cyclorama. Created from black Duvetyne, an inexpensive velvet-like fabric, this border gave the illusion that the flat white drop at the back of the stage was curved, making the space look as if it was embracing our star. In short, Bea's set was simple but elegant, and supportive of her. It was also on budget, which was not lost on our producer, the savvy Daryl Roth. Mark Waldrop, a good friend, was the show's excellent director. All in all, we put together a fine production for a highly engaging performer.

For the show's two-month run, Bea was ably assisted by composer Billy Goldenberg, her remarkable accompanist, and Matt Berman, her gifted sound and lighting director, two people whom she loved and who had worked with her for years. Both were also long-time friends of mine, with whom I had worked on various shows over the years. By now you will have surmised that show business is a very small community with lots of talented people who connect and reconnect from show to show.

Three years after "Bea Arthur: Just Between Friends" had closed, I invited Billy for dinner. He had an interesting request: "Ray, Bea is coming to New York the day of your dinner party. Could I bring her along? I don't want her to be alone on her first night here." The opportunity to get to know a "Golden Girl" was as irresistible as it was exciting.

With pleasure, I told Billy, "Yes, of course. Please bring her." At that point, the question became, what to cook for dinner? John, who, as you are aware by now, was the cook in our house, had just returned from a business trip with our good friend Dawna O'Brien and all he knew was that we were having a dinner party for four, one of whom would remain a surprise. My suggestion: Why not prepare a leg of lamb? Bea always opened "Just Between Friends" with a description of the best way to cook a leg of lamb, so at least I knew she liked lamb. Now, how else to make her comfortable?

That Tuesday night, Billy Goldenberg and Bea arrived and we were off and running–well, kind of, as Bea, it turned out, was rather shy–surprising, considering her forceful stage persona as well as her past, which included a stint as a truck driver for the Marines during the Second World War. In fact, she was not at all what I had expected. John, once he recovered from having Bea Arthur in the house, asked if she would like a drink.

"We like vodka," Bea replied. And did she ever. After John produced three different vodkas, she chose the one with which she was unfamiliar–and quickly became acquainted with it. As the party progressed, Bea became less shy and more outgoing. In short, she was great fun, reminiscing about her eventful past and telling jokes. She was particularly good at ribald, off-color stories.

Toward the end of the evening, Billy said to Bea, "How about telling everyone the Voodoo Dick story?" "Oh, I couldn't possibly do that," she replied. "I've had way too much to drink." Without missing much more than a beat, she launched into a hilarious, bawdy story that everyone loved. It was a terrific evening. Here is the joke Bea told at the dinner party.

"There was a traveling salesman who was married to a nymphomaniac who would go wild whenever the salesman went out of town. In desperation, he went to a porn shop and explained his problem to the owner who went into the back room and brought out an old box, blew off the dust, and opened it to reveal a life-sized cock and balls. The salesman said, "What am I supposed to do with that?" The owner said, "Watch this. Voodoo Dick, the keyhole!" and the cock and balls flew out of the box, over to the keyhole, and started screwing the keyhole. After a while, the owner said, "Voodoo Dick, the box!" and the cock and balls flew into the box. The owner closed the lid, and the salesman said, "SOLD!" He then brought it home to his wife and showed her the new toy. A few days later, the salesman went out of town and after a day or two, his wife got horny and decided to take the cock and balls out. She then said, "Voodoo Dick the pussy!" and the cock and balls started servicing the wife. Well, she had the best time, but after climaxing a number of times, she decided that she had had enough but couldn't remember how to turn it off. In desperation, she decided to try to drive to the hospital and needless to say she was driving erratically. She was all over the road when a motorcycle cop pulled her over and said, "OK lady what's going on?" She explained the situation to the cop, and he replied, "VOODOO DICK, MY ASS!"

It was great fun to have a Golden Girl tell such a story in my home!

A few weeks later, I was trying to figure out how to raise some much-needed money for the Ali Forney Center. When I mentioned this to Billy and Matt, we came up with an idea. Why not ask Bea to perform her one-woman show as a fundraiser? Billy and Matt approached her, and once she understood the purpose of the Ali Forney Center, she readily agreed. I found a venue (Symphony Space, on the Upper West Side) for the one-night-only performance, set a date of December 5, 2005, and I became a producer overnight. This was a new adventure for me, and what a challenge it was. It was up to me to solicit the donations that would cover Bea's airfare, housing, and car and driver. With the help of others, everything came together. Bea's only complaint was that she thought her donated hotel suite was too large! She also had to figure out what to wear. Because she hated winter, she had given away all her cold-weather clothes when she moved full-time to California. What to do? "I'll go over to Angie's [Angela Lansbury's] and borrow something warm," she announced. No problem.

All in all, the fundraiser was a great success, realizing $40,000 for the Center in a single night. But that was just the beginning. After much work, I was able to organize the event so that it would be fun and easy for Bea. In fact, she later told me she had had such a good time she was going to "leave something for the Ali Forney Center in my will." That's nice, I thought. Little did I know she had terminal lung cancer at the time, and four years later, in 2009, she left $300,000 to the center.

So, in the long run, Bea's one-night stand provided the start-up funds for what is now known as the Ali Forney Center's Bea Arthur Residence. The city turned over a long-abandoned building to the center and, along with generous funding from the New York City Council, in partnership with the Cooper Square Committee, they undertook the renovation to transform the building into an 18-bed, long-term housing facility for homeless LGBTQ teenagers. Other organizations joined in donating the necessary furnishings.

What a great start for more much-needed housing. By 2020, the center had beds for 156 homeless youths, making it by far the largest charity of its kind in the country. At the time of this writing, in 2021, a 21-bed site in Astoria and a 36-bed site in East Harlem are in the works, but given the slowness of city bureaucracy, it will be several years before either site opens its doors.

Many people, myself included, have Bea to thank for sharing her remarkable talent, her caring and giving nature, and her love of people.

For more information on the Ali Forney Center, please call (212) 206-0574.

Chapter 22

When Things Go Wrong/ Part 1

O kay, so when working on anywhere from three to nine shows at a time, not everything can go perfectly. When things go wrong it sure makes life interesting. On my first Academy Awards show, in 1982, I was out to impress everyone. Howard W. Koch, the producer that year, had decided to do a big musical tribute to Irving Berlin. Originally, he had wanted Alice Faye to sing the finale song, "There's No Business Like Show Business," but negotiations broke down so Howard settled on Bernadette Peters and Peter Allen to carry the production. I had 10 flymen (guys who pull the ropes that lower and raise the scenery from high above the stage through a system of pulleys) operating the set. Not a smart idea, as it was easy for the flying scenery to get messed up, which is exactly what happened. When the drop behind her didn't fly out, there stood Miss Peters in the middle of a song medley all alone and without the cast and scenic support to help us build to the number's conclusion. I quickly contacted the director's booth, asked for a musical cue, and on it had the drop fly out–to great applause. The finale came to its conclusion without anyone the wiser. A close call.

On another Oscars show, in 1980, director Marty Pasetta insisted on having "dancing waters"–twin fountains that would flank the star–for a number that had Melissa

Manchester singing a nominated song. Now, dancing waters required a complicated setup of two 20-foot-diameter pools containing about two inches of water, with a fountain positioned in the center of each pool. I told Marty that the setup would take a *very* long time and was iffy at best. Well, Marty knew no fear, and we moved forward with his idea. The dress rehearsal was a disaster and I wanted dearly to have the effect cut, but not Marty! He had arranged for an award, a commercial, and another award to gain as much time as possible to get the damn ponds in place.

The night of the show, I watched on a TV monitor as the crew worked frantically. Suddenly, Miss Manchester was in place, the number was being introduced, and the pond, stage-left, was up and running–but not the stage-right fountain. The crew was clearly having a problem. Well, there was no turning back. We were in trouble.

Luckily, the first video shot was of Miss Manchester with the camera looking at her and into the stage-left fountain that was bubbling away. A very pretty image. Meanwhile the crew was still setting up the fountain on the right. As the camera panned around the set, the crew finished and raced off stage, and the stage-right fountain began to function beautifully.

Ah, but not so fast. To my horror, there stood Miss Manchester, elegantly gowned and singing alongside dancing waters–with a great big two-by-four lying decoratively at her feet. It seems the crew had failed to pick up that piece in their haste to exit the stage. This may not sound so bad to you, but to me that ugly two-by-four was a disaster. I have always been a bit of a perfectionist, and so while I may never become a drunk because of stress I did go home that night and demolish an entire box of cookies.

In hindsight, it does seem that the Academy Awards hosted its share of mishaps and near-mishaps. In 1974 my set involved a huge, multi-level platform on a 60-foot turntable with numerous pieces of scenery designed to fly in to meet the various levels of the platform when it turned. Complicated, but the rehearsal went well. Everything worked fine–that is, until we went live on the air and the time came for the turntable to make its first move. *Nothing happened.* Fortunately, one of the electricians discovered there was no juice to power the table. The power plug had been accidentally yanked out of its socket. The electrician reinserted the plug, and we were back in business. Phew.

In 1974, streaking was all the rage. You remember– that's when someone would take off all his clothes and run through an event at an inappropriate time. (Is there ever an appropriate time to streak? And have you ever wondered why it's always a man? Maybe women have more sense.) Now, David Niven, who was that year's host of the Academy Awards, was good at thinking ahead. He asked the writers to come up with three different lines that he could have on hand to use if a streaker should happen to infiltrate the show while he was on camera. Well, as luck would have it, a man named Robert Opel, who had some kind of credentials and wore a sweat suit, managed to get backstage. He then cut a hole in the cyc (or cyclorama, the show's very expensive cloth backdrop), stripped off his clothes, and streaked across the stage. The director had given specific instructions to the camera crew that, if this were to happen, the camera should be aimed anywhere but at the streaker. So what happened? All the cameras ended up aiming directly at the streaker–no doubt just what the streaker wanted. David Niven, well prepared, chose his favorite of the three lines that had been supplied to him: "Some people will do anything to show their shortcomings." Clever.

In September of 1980, I was getting ready to present my set design for the Kennedy Center Honors to director George Stevens, Jr., who originated the honors. I asked my terrific assistant Rebecca Barkley to put the model in my car. What neither Rebecca nor I realized was that the car was parked in the sun, and the model was held together with a lot of rubber cement. After a couple of hours in the midday heat, the model melted. Fortunately, I had planned carefully, budgeting some extra time just in case. When I arrived for the meeting at the Beverly Hilton Hotel, I had 15 minutes to spare.

Quickly, I fanned the model and was able to slap it together so that it was somewhat presentable. That was until I was carrying it into the hotel elevator, the doors of which closed faster than anticipated and took a chunk out of the model's side. As the doors closed on the model I yelled, "No!" and pulled the model free, only to have the elevator doors close on the model again. All in all, those damn doors took three bites out of the model. So now I had a model that was no longer presentable. It was a wreck. What to do? I told everyone at the presentation exactly what had happened and got them laughing so hard that my design was approved enthusiastically.

You have to realize that my job came with an amazing gift: I could design and build almost anything I wanted, within limits. Of course, there were budgets and time limitations and always the needs of the celebrities and the scripts, but often I could go wild with my own crazy ideas. In 1980, I got the plum job of designing a Bea Arthur special, with guest stars Rock Hudson, Melba Moore, and Wayland Flowers.

When I got the script, I saw that there was a big opening production number with a series of musical cameos featuring our star and her guests. I had long harbored the desire to have some set pieces that would move around the stage as if by magic, without any visible means of powering them. Here was the perfect opportunity. What I did was design four units with steps, platforms, and walls all in white that the actors could perform on while the units themselves moved independently around the stage. Concealed inside each unit was a golf cart and a driver, whose job was to steer the units around the white stage floor in various predetermined patterns. The units each had a small, gauze-covered window for the driver to look through. It seemed like a really good idea–I thought it was quite special, just like our star.

I should point out that this opening number was taped at CBS in Television City, Los Angeles, on a stage that was unique at the time. It had a two-foot-deep lighting trough around three sides of the stage. This allowed the cyclorama to be lit in such a way that the white stage floor would blend in with the cyc to create a look of flawless infinity. Perfect.

That is, until disaster almost struck. What I didn't realize was that the driver of the unit Bea was riding on couldn't see well. At one point, for no apparent reason, he drove his unit in the wrong direction and headed for the lighting trough. He was about to drive into it when he heard everyone scream, "*Stop!*" Poor Bea was helpless in her slinky black sequined gown, a terrific-looking dress but one she could hardly walk in– not great, either, for making an emergency escape.

Lucky for me, after we calmed everyone down, the driver was shown where and when to drive, and the opening number went off without a hitch. I got my moment of magic, but we were seconds away from my set going very wrong.

One of my favorite celebrities was Helen Reddy of "I Am Woman" fame. I designed her summer television series in 1973, and she was just terrific. Wonderfully talented, she was also one of the best lip-syncers in the business. That's where a performer matches his or her lip movements with a pre-recorded soundtrack of the performer's voice. Helen gave even Julie Andrews a run for her money in that department.

After doing Helen's show, I was approached by her then-husband and manager, Jeff Wald, who called me into his office and asked me to do Helen's new act at the MGM Grand Hotel in Las Vegas. This was a first for her, and very important for her career. Now, Jeff was a man who could be quite volatile. There was a story going around about Jeff getting angry at a producer, jumping on the man's desk and stomping his feet to make a point. Fortunately, Jeff and I got along.

As part of our discussion about Helen's act, Jeff strongly suggested that I go up to Lake Tahoe to see her performance. "Feel free to bring your girlfriend," he suggested. "I don't have a girlfriend," I replied, "but I'd like to bring my partner, John." Jeff readily agreed. The trip to Tahoe was great fun, Helen's act was excellent, and Jeff was the perfect host.

After seeing Helen's show, John and I went backstage and Jeff asked if John and I had "hit the slopes," to which John confided, "No. I won't let Ray do that 'cause if he were to break an arm, we'd be out of business for a long time." "Oh, I know what you mean," Jeff responded. "I won't let Helen get into any drafts."

The next day, the four of us went out on two snowmobiles, with Helen and me on the back hanging on for dear life as we bounced and skidded all over the place. So much for protecting us!

Now for the part "When things go wrong." For Helen's Las Vegas show I designed a handsome drop that consisted of a beautiful geometric pattern painted on a 40- by 60-foot drop of black velour, selected so that the black unpainted areas would be extra dark. Thousands of small white lightbulbs were worked into the design. Stunning. There was one problem: The scenic artists who painted the drop had laid the paint on too thickly. The paint cracked. There wasn't an area larger than, say, four inches square, that was smooth. Disaster!

Soon after I discovered this huge problem, I saw Jeff storming down the theatre aisle, glaring at the drop. Thinking quickly, I said to him, "I bet you're really pleased." "Why should I be pleased?" Jeff asked, heatedly. "Because Helen has the first batik drop ever in a Vegas act," I told him shamelessly. And you know what? That drop actually looked handsome. Jeff spent the day dragging his buddies down to see "Helen's new batik drop."

In 1973, I was hired by producers and director Marty Pasetta to design Elvis Presley's last television special, "Elvis: Aloha from Hawaii." It was the first live via satellite concert by a solo artist, and it took place in a Honolulu arena on January 14th. Because the show was to be televised worldwide, I was told to incorporate Elvis's name into the drop, using the various spellings of "Elvis" familiar in different regions of the world where the show would be aired.

265

The black velour drop also featured Elvis's image, which we took the liberty of slimming down. Wrong thing to do. When Elvis arrived for rehearsals the day of the show, he looked a bit bloated, so much so that during the rehearsal he split his pants. Strangely, and thankfully, no one commented that the image didn't come close to resembling our star.

At one point, Marty wanted to pre-tape a brief scene on the beach to set the Hawaiian mood. He asked me to provide a sandcastle along the shore. Of course, it couldn't be just any sandcastle, so I went and bought $300 worth of seashells and recruited my assistant's two young daughters. Together we built a castle encrusted with exotic shells that appeared for a matter of seconds on the show. Who cared? Certainly, I didn't, as I got to briefly enjoy the sun and air.

The rehearsal was fascinating. Elvis arrived with an entourage of about a dozen male assistants, all of whom wore gold chains around their necks with the initials "TCB," for "Taking Care of Business." Each man was ranked as to his status: The "TCB" on the chains of the lesser personnel were plain silver, while the few "chosen ones" had diamonds on their platinum initials. Most of Elvis's men arrived with their girlfriends, who sat throughout the rehearsal decked out in flashy outfits, towering hairdos, and lots of sparkling jewels on their arms, fingers, around their necks and in their ears. Some even wore tiaras. The diamond status carried over to the ladies. All was flashiness and status points, which unfortunately got into my area when Marty asked me to create an impressive green room where the VIPs and network executives could watch the concert performed live.

I was shown a large, ugly storeroom filled with junk. The 40- by 50-foot space had a high ceiling and a soiled cement floor full of cracks. Not an ideal environment, but when I objected to the room, I was told that, of course, I would work my usual magic and make the space special–a room that supported the grand occasion and the VIPs who would be using it.

And so I went to work and had the room cleared out. By the evening of the big event, this ugly storeroom had its floor covered in miles of lush green wall-to-wall carpet. I rented lots of attractive white wicker furniture along with several bar and food stations, plus large television monitors and enough tropical plants and orchids to open a sizable floral shop. Everyone seemed thrilled. That is, except me. I kept saying, "But guys, it's still a *storeroom!*"

That evening the VIPs and their elegantly dressed lady friends, many in colorful mumus, watched the show and drank champagne when a rat the size of a small dog ran across the storeroom floor. The screams were delicious.

One of my big three-hour specials for producer Alexander A. Cohen was called "Night of 100 Stars III." Alex and his wife, Hildy Parks, a savvy and strong-willed lady and the writer on the show, concocted a salute to some of the great movie stars including Esther Williams, Alice Faye, Arlene Dahl, and Luise Rainer. I designed a pretty off-white gazebo, and costume designer Alvin Colt put all the ladies in ecru Victorian gowns. All very classy, until Ginger Rogers showed up at the dress rehearsal wearing a bright yellow dress that ruined the look of the number. I made a beeline to the producer's desk to complain, but Hildy beat me to it. I heard Hildy scream, "If she stays in that dress, she's off the show!" Miss Rogers claimed there weren't any ecru gowns that fit her. Well, Alvin quickly got her one, and so the look of that part of

267

the show was saved. But when the time came for the curtain calls, there was Ginger, like a beam of light in her damned yellow dress. In 1976, the year of America's bicentennial, the Academy Awards reflected the country's patriotic mood. It was decided that the show should end with a star leading the audience in singing "God Bless America." So, who did the producer and director choose to lead this all-American moment? None other than the English-born Elizabeth Taylor. I remember standing in the wings 20 feet away from her when she was introduced by Gene Kelly. Resplendent in a tight red gown, she was halfway into the song when she forgot the lyrics. How embarrassing, I thought, to flub those famous words in front of millions of viewers. Not to our Liz! When she came off stage and walked past me, she was laughing hysterically. Amazing to be that self-confident.

Back when I was working as an assistant art director on "The Dean Martin Show" at NBC, I went out to the scene shop to check on some work being done for the show. NBC housed the carpentry, drapery, electric, special effects, and paint shops, so the building was huge. It was comparable to about two city blocks in length. At any one time, many shows would be in production, including "Rowan and Martin's Laugh-In" and "The Red Skelton Hour," plus the usual number of television specials. This was the era when much of America tuned in together to watch the major entertainers of the day.

I was walking through the paint shop when I saw an artist spraying the outsides of seven upright pianos bright red for some show. As a joke, I said, "Don't forget to paint the insides," and then walked on. I got about a block and a half away when I thought, I wonder if he knows I'm kidding? My doubt grew with every step. I rushed back just in time to see the guy with his spray gun poised and ready to paint the piano's insides. I never made that sort of joke again. Things go wrong often enough without my instigating them.

In 2009, I was asked to design the set for a fundraiser staged on behalf of Friends in Deed, a crisis intervention center for those suffering from life-threatening physical illness. It was to be a one-night-only performance of the fun play "Legends," originally written for Mary Martin and Carol Channing. It was to star the fabulous drag queens Charles Busch and John Epperson (Lypsinka), along with the very funny Whoopi Goldberg. Being a benefit, there was hardly any money for the set, but I did manage to borrow some drapes and furniture and create a rather handsome room for these three special ladies.

The rehearsals were a riot–despite Whoopi's absence. Whoopi's stand-in for the rehearsals, Lisa Estridge, was amazingly good. All systems were "Go" that evening when it was announced that Whoopi wouldn't be joining us at all. She was sick and could not do the show. While things appeared to be going wrong, in fact they were quite right. Lisa Estridge repeated the fine performance we had witnessed during rehearsals. And, of course, the super talented Charles Busch and the remarkable John Epperson were *fabulous!* Professional beyond words and really great. The evening provided a perfect example of how gifted actors can make the best of an off situation. The show must go on, and it did, with an excellent time having been had by all. It was a very special experience.

My all-time favorite tale about something going wrong in front of a camera involved a Christmas show I did for John Davidson who, by the way, is one terrific guy. The premise was this: even though John and his family lived in California's San Fernando Valley, which was dry and dead-looking when we were taping in the summer, John would give his two children a white Christmas. We had discovered a foam used by fire fighters that looked a great deal like snow. As Production Designer, I had fake icicles made up to hang on the eaves, and we frosted the windows. Inside, we decorated the house for Christmas even though the holiday was months away. The scene looked amazing, especially in the helicopter shot. Imagine seeing all that golden, dried terrain of the San Fernando Valley surrounding that patch of snow–totally unreal and pure magic. That year, John Davidson gave his children a magic Christmas, and he gave one to the television audience, as well. We were all very happy with the look of the show.

About two hours from wrapping the taping, I got a call from the producers of the Bing Crosby Christmas Special I was working on simultaneously on the other side of Los Angeles. I was needed back at the ABC studio. Sally Struthers had accidentally wounded one of the dancers with a prop spear. Why my presence was required I have no idea, but off I went, leaving my very smart assistant Bob Rang in charge of what was left to shoot for the Davidson special.

All Bob had to do was supervise the arrival shot of the Lennon sisters in a sleigh pulled by two rented white horses. The runners on the sleigh had been fitted with casters, which were hidden by the fake foam snow. It should make for a charming arrival for the sisters. No problem, or so I thought. That evening I called Bob just to make sure everything had gone according to plan. "Well, not exactly," said Bob. "We had a problem." "What could possibly go wrong?" I replied. "Well," said Bob, when the sleigh pulled up, the horse closest

270

to the camera kept getting a huge erection." "Oh, my God. What did you do?" Bob, ever resourceful, explained, "You know that can of spray snow we were using? Well, it has other

It's a miracle the horse didn't bolt all the way to Pasadena. Ah, when things go wrong.

Chapter 23

When Things Go Wrong/ Part II

Backstage, while fascinating and exciting, can also be dangerous. When I first took on "Jubilee!" at the MGM Grand in Las Vegas, for example, I worried about the safety of the cast and how I could create an exciting show and yet a safe one for those who worked backstage. "Hallelujah Hollywood!," the show that preceded "Jubilee!," had endured its share of accidents. A reporter who had wanted to interview the cast and had been denied the opportunity, decided to sneak backstage after the show. He crawled under the curtain right after it came down. What the reporter didn't realize was that the elevator behind the curtain had been lowered; when he fell into the hole he was seriously hurt. Another time, one of the men on the crew was flirting with one of the showgirls and wasn't watching where he was going. Again, the elevator had been lowered–this time by a good 30 feet. The crewman survived his fall into the elevator shaft but ended up with a bad limp. For years afterward he used a cane. MGM management smartly had put him in charge of safety backstage. Good move on their part. I, in turn, was determined to make my show as exciting as possible, but safe. To my relief, no serious accidents occurred in the 34 years that "Jubilee!" ran.

One of the most embarrassing experiences I ever had occurred while preparing the set for MGM's "Hello Hollywood Hello," which opened in Reno in 1978. Part of my job was to design the huge circus finale, which posed an interesting challenge: how to present the topless ladies who would be riding on the six large circus wagons. My plan was to show the director, Donn Arden, my ideas for the wagons in the form of scale models. One thought I had was that Barbie-type dolls could possibly represent the ladies.

So early one Tuesday morning, at an hour when I assumed customers would be few, I went to the Hollywood Toy Store on Hollywood Boulevard just as it was opening and headed for the doll section. I found the type of doll I thought would serve nicely, but I had to be sure. After looking around to confirm that the store was still empty, I quickly grabbed a doll and pulled up her little sweater to check out her breasts. Would this doll look good and sexy on my model wagons?

I never got to fully analyze the relevant anatomy because a woman with two small children suddenly came around the corner, saw this middle-aged man peaking at a doll's breasts, and screamed, "*Pervert!*" I had to buy 17 of those damn dolls and never did use them, opting instead for cardboard cutouts.

In 1978 I also designed the sets for a Natalie Cole television special. As usual, I was on the lookout for a unique design approach. Around that time, on a trip to New York City, I was wandering through Bloomingdale's and saw large rattan paddle fans used decoratively as wall sconces and chandeliers, as well as ceiling fans. Why not try this as a thematic approach for Miss Cole's special? I located a source for a wide selection of fans and ordered 750 of them. As the date of the taping approached, there was still no sign of the shipment. It turned out the fans had been shipped accidentally to Alaska, of all places–just what they need in that frigid climate.

When the re-ordered fans finally arrived, they looked great. I used them in many ways, as they were now the design theme for the show. But I had two problems: The first was that while the largest fans, reserved for the ceiling above the orchestra, looked great on the drawing board, they didn't look so good to the naked eye. In fact, when viewed on the television monitor, they looked like giant potato chips. I never said a word about it, and no one commented on the silliness of the look.

The other problem wasn't quite so silly. I had created a wall with a rosette of the fans as a backdrop for Miss Cole, to be used when she made a short introductory speech. No problem. It looked great–at least it did when it was moved onto the stage the day before the scheduled taping. The next morning, I discovered that someone had stolen a third of the fans. Just ripped them off the wall. As luck would have it, the fire marshal had required that all the fans be flame-proofed, and the flame proofing had a tendency to cause a rash on the hands of anyone who handled it. All we had to do was look at the hands of the members of the crew to see who had swiped the fans. Fortunately, I had enough spare fans to complete the wall at no cost to the production company.

In 1976 I was asked to design a television show for Olympic gold medal skater Dorothy Hamill. Ultimately, I did three TV specials for her. Dorothy was beautiful and easy to work with, if a bit cold. But, hey, wouldn't you be if most of your life was spent on ice?

The shows were especially challenging, with immense problems for the set designer. The simple fact is that ice rinks are typically huge, but TV budgets are not. Vast areas needed scenery, and the arena seats had to be covered, usually with a large cyclorama or, at times, a black drape. Not easy. There was also the cold itself. Working on ice rinks can be brutal. I would always end up with the skin on my hands cracked and bleeding. On one of the specials, in Plattsburgh, N.Y., my hands were in such bad shape that I couldn't hold a pencil on the flight home after the show.

While the ice was tough on the hands, it was also a great canvas. The wonderful thing about ice is this: You can paint it. For the special we did in Toronto, we painted the ice with blue latex paint for the opening scene, then overnight added pink on top of the blue. To create an all-black look for the final group of scenes, I had the ice painted black and had a 30-foot-tall black drape hung around the perimeter of the rink. For one number, Dorothy skated in and around a dozen white snowflakes that my immensely gifted assistant Paul Galbraith had made. With frosty white foamcore snowflakes, ranging in size from four to eight feet in diameter, floating in this black environment, the scene was stunning.

The different ice colors lent variety to the show and were a big help–except when it came to the finale, a medley of songs made famous by our guest star, Gene Kelly. For "An American in Paris," I used the all-black environment and re-created the base of the Eiffel Tower. Measuring 40 feet square at the base and 35 feet high, the all-wood tower had thousands of tiny white lights and looked simply terrific. Well, we almost didn't get to use it. At 6 a.m. I got a call from my assistant Bob Rang, who told me that the tower had fallen like a house of cards; the shop hadn't used enough glue, nor the correct nails. First one side fell down, then the next, and the rest followed. It was a disaster, as the taping was delayed and the shop had to spend the rest of the day rebuilding the set. We lost a lot of valuable time, but luckily no one got hurt, and no one blamed me. Of course, I felt badly that my set was causing the taping delay, but it was never my responsibility to make sure the shop used enough glue or the right nails. The studio had built the tower and ended up paying for the overtime and additional materials.

Well, our problems didn't stop there. After the Eiffel Tower was restored and the "American in Paris" number almost complete, we had a rain effect for "Singin' in the Rain," the last song in the show's finale. That's when I discovered that if you add water to painted ice the shine is terrific, but guess what? The water that creates that shine also eventually melts the ice. We taped the scene, and it was great, but we knew it could be even better. When we took a second pass at taping the number, we saw huge areas of previous colors breaking the surface of our beautiful black ice. To our horror, large pink sores erupted on the ice, followed by blue ones under the pink. It was fascinating as well as ugly and made the second take totally unusable. Fortunately, the first take was more than acceptable. Once again, I had somehow lucked out when things went wrong.

In 1972 I worked on an American Film Institute tribute to John Ford. Later I would do tributes to Bette Davis, Lillian Gish, Fred Astaire, Orson Welles, Henry Fonda, Alfred Hitchcock, and others. This first of many AFI tributes was immensely important, as we all wanted the show to become an annual event. (Now that the AFI film tributes are still running after 47 years, it's safe to say we succeeded.) Well, the problem I faced in that ballroom of the Beverly Hilton, from where the early AFI tributes were broadcast, was two-fold. First, the ceiling was low, and second, the podium got in the way of the projected film clips. The only way to get rid of the podium when not in use was to have stagehands carry it off (unacceptable) or to have it telescope through a trapdoor in the thrust stage floor we built–a difficult bit of engineering that the CBS shop solved at considerable expense.

Because President Nixon was going to be attending, the FBI conducted a security sweep during the crew's meal break a few hours before the taping of the show. During the sweep I decided to check the set one last time, just to be sure everything was as it should be. A good thing, too: When I entered the ballroom, the Secret Service men were about to dismantle the podium as part of their inspection. Now, as mentioned, the podium was a complicated piece of engineering. If taken apart, it could never have been reassembled in time for the show. We would not have been able to stage the show as rehearsed. Fortunately, I was able to talk the men through what the podium was and how it worked and managed to convince them that they didn't need to take it apart. Close call, that one.

A note: When the band played "The Yellow Rose of Texas," we saw Nixon banging his spoon on the table like a child. I remember saying to our producer, Carolyn Raskin, "I think this country is in trouble."

One summer, after visiting friends on Fire Island, John and I decided to splurge. When the time came to head home to New York, instead of battling crowds on the Long Island Railroad, we arranged to take a seaplane. We had little luggage, which was a good thing, because we had to hold our bags above our heads and wade out to the plane.

The plane was a cute little thing, and the pilot was cheery and friendly. We taxied across the bay and took off over

277

Long Island. From the start I was a bit apprehensive. What would we do if the plane failed? I felt better when I saw the many small lakes scattered across the land below. This plane could float, after all. But panic quickly returned when we flew over Queens County and the lakes became fewer and fewer. Again I wondered, what would we do if, for some bizarre reason, the plane developed mechanical difficulties? Well, I bet you can guess from the title of this chapter what happened next. *The engine stopped dead.* The only sound, apart from the air rushing past, came from me: *"Oh, my God!"* I yelled. *"What's happened?"*

The pilot turned around merrily and said, "Oh, I guess I should have told you. My mother is down in the hospital below, and I always signal her by cutting the engine for a few seconds." Well, he almost cut me, too, and permanently. It's a miracle I didn't have a heart attack and end up in a hospital bed next to his mother. Needless to say, we never splurged like that again

Ah, but my adventures with airplanes were not over. At one point I did a fair amount of work for Kenny Rogers, including his national tour and a talk show pilot. Kenny was terrific and fun to work with. One day his manager, Ken Kragen, called and said Kenny wanted to meet with me. Great! Going to meet him was always an adventure. Typically on these occasions, I would be asked to fly to a city where he was appearing, go to the concert hall, watch him perform, and stand in a pre-arranged spot when he sang his last song. As Kenny left the arena, he and his musicians and I would be swept up by his people and taken out to one of Kenny's planes (he owned two). Usually this was done in a caravan of three matching Jeeps. On the flight back to Atlanta, everyone would be talking and having a drink or two, while I would read.

We'd land and be driven to Kenny's handsome Georgia home on a sizable piece of property, which included the largest (at that time) privately owned barn in the United States. I would be put up in the "bunk house," which was equivalent to a suite of rooms in a top Las Vegas hotel. The next morning, I would awake to find a large tray of pastries of every kind–at least 30 types–just for me. I would then go down to the main house and meet Kenny, to hear what was on his mind

In this case, Kenny needed help with something personal. He had just started to raise horses professionally, and because he was not yet established, he needed a way to present his horses and gain recognition at horse conventions. We discussed what we thought might work. Instead of creating an ordinary display or exhibit at the convention center, why not build something different? I suggested a conference office and screening room off of a handsome circular room, say 15 feet in diameter. The room would have a 360-degree photo mural of Kenny's ranch. In this way potential clients would see how large and impressive his facilities were.

Kenny liked the idea and said he would get back to me. As he usually did when the time came for me to return to Los Angeles, he picked up the phone, said a few words into it, and 20 minutes later a helicopter landed in his front yard, and off I went to the Atlanta airport. During this particular flight I spotted Stone Mountain and the huge bas relief carved into its face. I had just seen this Confederate memorial featured in *National Geographic* and marveled at its size–more than an acre and a half across. I commented about it, and the pilot asked if I'd like a closer look. He then gave me a bird's-eye view of this controversial landmark, completed in 1972. Unforgettable.

Once again, I was nervous about flying, especially with a pilot who looked to be in his 60s. What would I do if something happened to him? What if he had a heart attack? I asked as tactfully as possible, "How do you make this thing go up? Go down? Left? Right?" I pictured the pilot suddenly being unable to fly and the helicopter, while on autopilot, flying us to the center of the airport and hovering in place until it ran out of gas and....

Several years later, something did go wrong. That same pilot flew the helicopter into a building and was killed instantly. I was deeply sorry to hear the news, as he was an extremely nice man, but I have to say I was glad that something hadn't gone wrong when I was with him.

Back in LA, I completed my design for Kenny only to be informed that his foreman had told him there was no point to moving forward with the convention display since no horses were available for sale. The whole project was dropped. In hindsight, I had the pleasure of trips to Atlanta but none of the bother of dealing with the bidding, supervision of construction, or installation of my design. And I was paid handsomely for my time. All (or almost all) of this was fun, and nothing went wrong.

I once had a wonderful collection of models of shows I had done, mostly of Broadway and off-Broadway productions. After John died, I had no desire to stay in our apartment, so I put all our furniture into storage. Only the models remained–on a high shelf–when I rented the place to a couple with two young children. The mother specifically requested that I leave the models; she hoped her children would be inspired by the creativity the models represented. One day, when I was speaking to her on the phone, she announced that the models were falling apart, so the family had thrown them out. Just like that, the history of my work was gone except for a few models the renters hadn't gotten around to destroying. I'm not sure how I feel about this. While the models were of incredible value to me, they are in fact gone, and like good friends who are no longer with me, there is just no way to replace them. They are lost. I tend to look forward.

One day, when I was in my 60's, I experienced a different kind of loss. One moment I was with a friend, Terry Lorden, on the East Side of Manhattan, and the next thing I knew I was in a hospital bed. John was sitting near me, looking very concerned. I asked, "Have I had a stroke?" Everything was so terribly strange. I had no idea where I was or what was going on and had no memory of the preceding eight hours.

It turned out I had suffered a case of Transient Global Amnesia (TGA), described as a sudden, temporary loss of memory. Typically, one may not remember information or experiences from the recent past or know where one is or how he or she got there. That was certainly the case with me. No one knows what causes TGA. Fortunately, Terry had been with me and had rushed me to a hospital on the West Side so John could visit me easily if I were to be there for any length of time.

I cannot begin to describe how strange it is to lose one's mind. It was as if someone had poured the contents out of my head. Within a matter of hours, my brain slowly refilled with the same old contents. Nothing was lost, except for the hours between the time I was walking on the street and the moment I found myself in the hospital. Those eight or so hours are lost to me forever, but it was wonderful to become whole again.

While Transient Global Amnesia is rare and almost never strikes the same person twice, my brother had the same experience years later. Because we all knew what I had experienced and that the condition was temporary, his family was not nearly as upset as John and my friend Terry had been. Of course, when things really go wrong, a lawsuit is often involved. After designing more than 400 productions, I feel lucky that no one tried to nail me more than just a few times.

The first suit came from Perry Como. In 1971 I was doing the "Perry Como Winter Show" at CBS with the divine Mitzi Gaynor, and on the last day of taping we discovered that the director's assistant had made a mistake in the timing of the show. We were three minutes short. What to do? It was decided that Perry would do one more song, but what would we use for a set?

The song Perry had just performed had him on a large hexagonal platform I had designed. The platform was so wide it had to be made in two pieces so that it could fit through the massive load-in doors that led into the studio. Once inside, the two pieces were locked together, and the standby scenic artist taped over the seam and touched up the large snowflake pattern on top of the platform. The overall set looked appropriately Christmassy, with large, stylized icicles hanging around the platform. Now, for the unanticipated final song I needed to change the look a bit.

Time was running short. Quickly, I had pivot points and pull cables installed on both halves of the hexagonal platform so that on camera we could pull the base apart and rearrange the platform into a new shape. Not brilliant, but a solution. The stage manager explained to Perry that all he had to do was step away from the center of the platform onto one of the two sections that formed the hexagon and ride it to its new position. Very simple. Perry appeared to understand what was needed. Wrong!

As the cameras were rolling, Perry stepped off onto one of the moving sections, but to our surprise he returned to the place where he had been originally standing–to an area where there was no longer a platform. He fell the two and a half feet down to the cement stage floor. Apparently, when he moved off the center mark and out of the spotlight, he assumed there had been a lighting error. Why wasn't the spotlight following him? As a joke, he tried to return to the spotlight, popping back onto that center mark. Alas, there was no platform beneath him.

After much fussing, Perry was taken to his dressing room. We waited. A half hour later, an ambulance arrived, and Perry was gone. Gone, as it turned out, back to his home in Florida. Everything was put on hold. God, so close to finishing this damn show. Now what?

Six months later, we set up the whole look again. Perry did his number, and the show was finally finished. And so was Perry. He sued the network, and they never allowed him to perform there again. As part of Perry's lawsuit, his lawyers called me and tried to get me to testify on Perry's behalf, but I wouldn't. "If you look at the tape," I explained, "you can clearly see that Perry was fooling around and not doing what he had been instructed to do." I never heard from them again. Perry won somewhere around $500,000, and I understand that was pretty much what the suit had cost him in legal fees.

Another lawsuit in which I was involved also occurred at CBS. During the taping of a talk show I had designed the set for, the host was giving away compact discs to the audience. The audience bleachers started at six feet above the studio floor so the audience could see over the cameras on the floor in front of them. When the host started to give away the CDs, he threw them out to the audience and people rushed forward to grab them. The forward rush caused the front railing to break and six people, including a pregnant woman, fell to the concrete below.

Needless to say, the lawyers were on the phone to me fairly fast. When questioned, I simply said, "If you look at the set-design drawings, you will see a note on each one that says the designer–me–is not a structural engineer, and that all construction of this set is the responsibility of the construction company," which was CBS. I was off the hook. I never heard from them again.

So we end up right back where we started, at the 1982 Academy Awards. You'll recall that things didn't go quite right when Bernadette Peters was left stranded in the middle of a song medley when the drop behind her didn't fly. Still more trouble came my way as a result of that show. As part of the show's tribute to Irving Berlin, Miss Peters had been asked to sing "What'll I Do?" I wanted a setting as special as she was. I did my usual research and found an old theatrical setting created by an artist in the 1920s. I adapted his style and created a great-looking drop, kind of like Art Nouveau Visits Venice.

Well, a few weeks after the show was over, Howard Koch, the producer of the Academy Awards that year, called and said that the widow of the artist who had influenced my design was suing the Academy for $10,000. I was appalled, as

284

I knew other designers had done variations of my work in the past, and I would never even think to sue them. Howard said not to worry, that it was a nuisance lawsuit. He added that it was easier for the Academy to simply pay the woman the ten grand. Easier, maybe, but I wish there could be a way to make things go wrong a little less often.

Chapter 24

Fire!

The date was November 20, 1980, and we were just 13 days from the scheduled opening of "Jubilee!," the new MGM production at the Las Vegas MGM Grand Hotel and Casino. Two years earlier I had been chosen by the legendary director Donn Arden to design the sets for the show. With more than 135 dancers and singers, all with sumptuous costumes designed by Bob Mackie and Pete Menefee, "Jubilee!" was to be, quite simply, fabulous. The jewelry had been custom made in Paris, and the feathers came from all over the world. My job as Production Designer was to create the scenery for an extravaganza bigger and better than anything ever seen in Las Vegas.

Previously, I had designed half of "Hello Hollywood Hello!" for the MGM Grand in Reno, and to date it had been the most difficult of all the shows I had worked on. I had made a pact with myself that if I were ever to work on such a show again, I would make them pay through the nose for the hell I had gone through. Well, one day I got a call saying that Donn, along with Bill De Angelis, the producer of "Jubilee!," wanted to talk to me. It turned out they had liked my work on the Reno show and wanted me to design "Jubilee!" in its entirety. I was conflicted. As noted earlier, Donn was a notorious drinker, and while he was a brilliant director, to say he wasn't a nice man would be an understatement. In Reno, I had vowed to think twice before ever working with Donn Arden again.

Yet there I was being offered "Jubilee!", the show of a lifetime. Imagine having endless design possibilities and no scenic budget. I could create almost anything I had ever envisioned. And so, I had Bill De Angelis talk to Sandy Wernick, who negotiated a handsome fee for me. I countered by saying that I would do the show if they paid me an additional $50,000 above the fee initially negotiated. In 1978 that was a substantial amount of money. To my surprise, Bill went for it, and I was on my way to designing the most exciting show of my life. Ultimately, it would also be the most dangerous.

Among the sets–the best designs I had done to date– was "The Sinking of the Titanic" with a dock scene complete with embarking passengers, as well as an elegant grand salon. A huge 40-foot-long model of the ship stuck out of the water and sank each night in front of the audience. Another set, "Samson and Delilah," included a 27' tall, three-ton idol of an ancient bull's head mounted on top of a 29' tall temple. Each night, when Samson pulled down the temple, it sank with him through the stage floor, all 56 feet of it.

To design the sets, MGM rented a three-bedroom house in Hollywood for me and my nine assistants. Here we drafted and made models in every room in the house except the bathroom. As mentioned, there was no budget, so I had carte blanche. The only exception came when I designed a black velour curtain measuring in fullness approximately 110' wide by 35' tall. The curtain was to be covered in 70,000 rhinestones, affixed at the rate of one every four inches. When Bill De Angelis got the bid for making it, he said, "No way, Ray. It's too expensive," to which I replied, "What if I can find the original source for the rhinestones, eliminate the middleman, and get the cost down?"

Back then we couldn't rely on the Internet for help, so one of my assistants spent a week tracking down the manufacturer of exactly the right rhinestones–multifaceted "gems" with the high lead content necessary for extreme brilliance. It turned out they came from a small company in Czechoslovakia. The price was much lower than the original bid, and I got my curtain. But here we were, less than two weeks before opening night, and my sets were not going to be ready. Bill De Angelis would not be happy and, as noted earlier, he was one guy you didn't want to make unhappy. Needless to say, it would not go well to tell Bill that "Jubilee!" could not go on because my sets weren't ready.

I was beside myself with worry. While not a churchgoing man at that time, I nevertheless sent up a prayer asking for help. During this last phase of getting the show set up, I was housed in a very nice room on the 14th floor of the twin-towered, 26-story MGM Grand. (As in many hotels, there wasn't a 13th floor, so technically I was on the 13th floor–not a good sign.)

After working to the point of collapse, I went to bed dreading what I was about to face with Bill and his cronies. All night long I kept getting calls from the crew, which worked in shifts in a frantic attempt to meet our deadline. There were three scaffolds and four teams of workers, and consequently some of the phone calls concerned teams fighting for the scaffolds. The night was not restful, but it was nothing compared to what I was about to face.

Shortly after 7 a.m. on November 21, 1980, I awoke and sleepily noticed smoke on the ceiling. "There's been a party in this room," was my initial thought. But, of course, there had been no party. In fact, a fire that had begun 13 floors beneath me (in a refrigerated pastry display case in a restaurant kitchen) had sent thick smoke through the ventilation system. Since I heard no alarms and no one was yelling "Fire!", I figured the problem, whatever it was, must be under control. As I dressed and prepared to leave for work, a nagging doubt persisted: "What if this really is an emergency? What should I take with me?" I grabbed my phone book, my work notes, and, of all things, a favorite ski jacket lined in possum that John had recently given me.

When I opened the door to the 14th floor corridor, I saw people fleeing their rooms, carrying hastily packed bags, some with clothing protruding from tops and sides. The men were mostly stoic, while a few of the women whimpered quietly. Still, no alarms sounded, and no one yelled, "Fire!" The scene consisted solely of people looking frantically for a way out.

What to do? Without a second thought I went down the hallway to a fire exit only to discover a stairwell filled with dense, black smoke. If I had tried to put my arm into the stairwell, I would not have seen my hand. At another stairwell, the story was the same. Determined to find a way out, I returned to my room. Luckily, I had taken my key. (Others, it turned out, had failed to take their keys and could not return to their rooms. They succumbed to toxic smoke that filled the corridors.)

From my little balcony I saw that the roof of the two-story casino below was burning on the edges, and the fire was coming toward my tower. I estimated that if I didn't find a way out, I would be dead in about 90 minutes. I grabbed a damp face towel from the bathroom, then raced back to the emergency exit, thinking I would cover my nose and mouth with the towel and try my luck on the stairs. Just as I was about to take a deep breath and go down that stairwell, I remembered that in the Reno MGM hotel a chorus guy was having an affair with another dancer. His room was on the 22nd floor. Instead of walking all the way down the hall to the elevator to go two floors down to the 20th floor, he simply took the fire escape stairwell–only to be trapped one night when the door closed and locked behind him. His only way out had been to walk down the 22 floors to the lobby and then take the elevator up to the 20th floor. Remembering this, I quickly realized that I would be stuck in that smoke-filled stairwell. (Later, I learned that many of the 85 victims of the MGM fire were discovered in stairwells, behind locked doors.) A close call.

So back to my room. I returned to the balcony and stuffed wet towels under the door to the hallway. Once again, I looked down onto the casino roof where three men were shouting, "Stay in your rooms! The fire is contained!" To which I yelled back, "Bullshit!" (Actually, I used a stronger term.) I could clearly see the far edges of the casino roof burning and heading for my tower. The question was, what now?

Among the many things I've learned in business and in life are these: Stay calm, and figure out rational, technical ways to solve difficult problems. I looked over the situation and made a decision–not one I particularly liked, but one that seemed my only option. I would have to climb down. Below my balcony were other balconies, one on each floor. Using my bed sheets, I made a long rope (good knots–thank you, Boy Scouts), put it through the top railing on my balcony, and tied the two ends together to form a loop. I would have to take the descent one balcony at a time, then unknot and re-knot the rope at each landing.

I swung my leg over the balcony, held tight to the rope, and said to myself, "You're not going to like this, but here goes." With great relief I made it to the balcony below. I've gone to the gym and exercised faithfully for most of my life, so I was strong and the climb was easy. Untying the knot at the end of the rope was not. In fact, I couldn't get the knot untied! The clock was ticking. Looking over my shoulder I saw a couple on whose balcony I was standing and asked them, "Do you mind if I borrow your sheets? I'm sure the hotel will replace them." In a daze they nodded their consent and I stripped their bed of two queen-sized sheets. This time I didn't tie the rope into a loop. Instead, I gathered both ends and held them as tightly as I could. In their late 50s or early 60s, the couple were clearly out of shape and unable to attempt an escape. "My husband has a heart condition," the wife explained. I left them on their balcony hugging and crying. I was on my way.

On each new balcony, I would land, then pull one end of my sheet-rope to get ready for the next floor. By the time I reached the sixth floor I had grown cocky. Carelessly I was about to release my hold on the rope when suddenly I slipped and ended up swinging wildly in the air. Luckily, I had not let go completely and so was able to safely land on the balcony. Seized by panic, I knew I had to calm down. Staying calm wasn't so easy, since I knew that my escape off the casino roof had to be completed soon, before the roof collapsed. The sounds of the people trapped in their rooms, screaming for help was so terrifying and echoed what was taking place in my frightened soul. Years later, when I saw the movie "Titanic," the sound of the doomed passengers as the boat was sinking duplicated the sounds I heard that day of the MGM fire. It is a sound I hope never to hear again.

After standing on the balcony and forcing myself to calm down, I continued my descent. Finally, I landed on the casino roof and thought, "I'm almost safe!" But then I caught a glimpse of my least favorite color combination: red and yellow. It was the housedress of a very large lady who was standing on that last balcony, staring, mesmerized, at the oncoming fire. The clock was ticking. "I don't have time to save you, lady," were the words that went through my mind. But my better half realized if she were my mother, I would want someone to save her. I decided to try. She weighed a good 300 pounds. Even though the balcony was a mere foot above the roofline, I simply could not lift her over the rail. I jumped over the balcony railing, went into her room, grabbed an ottoman, and made her stand on it so that I could get better leverage. To my surprise I was able to lift her like a feather. As I grabbed her under her butt, I remember thinking, "This is not a nice way to handle a lady." Unfortunately, she was barefooted. "Lady, you're going to cut and burn your feet," I said, "but we're not stopping to get your shoes!"

To my horror, the roof was beginning to bubble from the inferno underneath, and broken glass lay everywhere. People were breaking their windows in the hope of getting some air. I later learned that two people, who were hanging out of their windows, were decapitated by falling glass. I ran toward three men standing in the middle of the roof, handed the lady over to them, and said, "She's all yours. How do I get down from here?" They pointed toward a ladder, and I ran to it and took it to safety. I thought seriously of kissing the ground.

By now, the marquee of the hotel was engulfed in flames. Parts of it were falling to the ground. As I ran past, I stopped and grabbed a piece that was still warm, thinking, "This will make a great souvenir." But who would want a souvenir of this nightmare? I threw it back violently and proceeded to the theatre, adjacent to the casino.

Inside the theatre I ran up to one of my favorite stagehands and asked if everyone had gotten out alright. "Who are you?" he replied. I didn't realize my face and hands were black from the smoke, and I had lost my glasses. I was totally unrecognizable. In fact, I looked as though I had been rolled in a coal furnace. Later, I found out we had lost one member of our group, a lady dresser who had tried to escape by going down in one of the elevators. A big lesson from the MGM fire: Never, ever enter an elevator during a fire! Elevators are heat sensitive and will descend into the heart of the fire–exactly what happened to our colleague. Awful!

Across the street at the Barbary Coast hotel and casino, I approached a lady in the lounge. Chatting away on the phone and chewing gum, she seemed oblivious to what was going on at the building nearby. "And Gladys," I heard her say, "you should have seen what I won at craps. I just . . ." She took one look at me and said, "Gladys, I godda go. Can I help you?" She was clearly shocked by my appearance. "A cup of coffee, please," I replied, and off she went, returning in short order with my coffee.

I had always phoned my mother every weekend at her home in Florida– her phone number was easily memorized. But, poof, it was gone. However, I did remember my own phone number, so I decided to look for a telephone and call John. In those days we had a deal: Always call home before 8 a.m. That was the hour at which phone rates went up. My watch said 8:05. When John answered, I was greeted with, "You're late!" to which I said, looking at a nearby television flashing the image of the smoldering hotel, "Turn on the TV." Soon I heard John utter, "Holy shit." Then the strangest thing happened: I suddenly heard this tiny child's voice come out of me and say, "I lost . . . my . . . fur. . . coat!" It was the first sign of the rollercoaster of emotions–from exhilaration to depression and back again–that would overtake me for days to come.

Fortunately, my assistant Bob Rang picked me up and drove me to his apartment. It took three passes in the shower to get the soot and grease out of my hair and off my face. I was then able to arrange a flight that same day back to my home in Los Angeles.

Three days later I returned to Las Vegas to get my possessions out of my hotel room. Structurally, the building was still sound; most of the fire damage had occurred in the casino and restaurants. A hotel escort walked me up to my room. On our climb up the stairwells, I saw floor numbers spray-painted crudely on the walls, to help identify each floor. When we emerged onto the 14th floor and began our walk down the hall, we saw that all the rooms had been broken into by the fire department. It was haunting. Once substantial doors had been smashed into submission, affording a peek inside rooms hastily abandoned. I could see that people had left jewelry and other personal items sitting on dressers, desks, and nightstands. When I arrived at my own room, everything was just as I had left it, but anything I touched left a greasy black residue on my hands. The air was utterly, thoroughly contaminated. What would my chances have been if I had stayed in this room?

After clearing out my possessions, I went down to look at what was left of the casino. The sight was the eeriest I had ever seen, but one with a certain haunting beauty. Everywhere I turned, shafts of light, from openings in the destroyed roof above, played over drifts of silvery ash. All that remained of the casino's gaming tables were the metal decorative trimmings that had adorned the tabletops and table legs, skeletons of a former life. I stepped out of the casino's shell and was stopped by a kind, understanding reporter who, with a cameraman, tried to interview me. Here it was three days after the fire and still I couldn't speak coherently about it. I just couldn't handle the emotions that swept over me and I broke into uncontrollable sobs. Emotionally I was spent and operating on empty.

The fire's after-effects continued. In New York two weeks later, I had some free time and decided to do a little window shopping on Fifth Avenue. Suddenly I saw a cloud of smoke pass between me and a store window. Just 15 feet from me a car was on fire. I knew it made no sense, but nonetheless I took off down the street, running two blocks to get away from that fire. I simply could not get my legs to stop.

A short time later, John and I moved into a fabulously elegant period home in Hancock Park, Los Angeles. When I attempted to slide down the banister of the entry's curved grand staircase (something I had always wanted to do), I came up short. As I swung my leg over the banister, both legs began shaking violently. I realized I was mimicking the exact movement required to climb down the balconies at the MGM

Grand. Another souvenir of the fire was a cough that persisted for 20 years.

But hey, I survived. And so did the show. It took eight and a half months to rebuild "Jubilee!" which finally opened July 31, 1981. Before the fire, the immensely valuable costumes had been locked up by the insurance agents in a storeroom high enough off the ground to prevent water damage. But when the agents finally unlocked the storeroom, they found that the costumes had been destroyed by mildew. All of them had to be replaced. The feathers, in particular, presented a challenge. In some cases, the world supply had been used up, so substitutes had to be found. But the show did go on and ran for 34 years. I wrote 96 thank you notes to the crew–I certainly had much to be thankful for.

In 2020, "Jubilee!," which closed in 2016, remained the longest-running show in Las Vegas history. In addition to the 85 people who died in the fire, more than 700 were injured. It remains the deadliest disaster in Nevada history.

While I have never personally sued anyone for anything, I did participate in a class-action suit. Three days after the fire, MGM contacted me and said they would pay me $500 for my discomfort as a result of the fire. Was that okay? I refused to agree to the $500 deal. Several years later, as part of the class-action suit against MGM, I was awarded $20,000, which provided John and me with a very nice swimming pool. It seemed an interesting exchange: water for fire.

And I did hold on to one souvenir: my room key, which I framed and mounted above a note that said, **Remember: You've Had Harder Days.**

While I was grateful for the extra time to get my sets ready and especially for any assistance I might have received when escaping the fire, never again did I ask God for help on a show.

Chapter 25

The Tony Awards

In 1985 I was in New York on a survey for an ABC affiliates show at Radio City Music Hall. I was getting to know the television business in New York but knew little of the Broadway theatre world. What I did know was this: If I wanted to spread my wings and explore the challenges of designing for Broadway, I was going to have to meet a different set of people. In fact, the two worlds were starkly different. Whereas television shows tended to develop on a fairly fast track, Broadway shows can take years to materialize. Funded and run by a centralized management system, television productions often come to fruition more or less as planned and within a reasonable timeframe. Broadway productions, on the other hand, depended on well-connected producers who could raise money from investors, or "backers," then find and hire the talent, secure a theatre (not easy during the busy season), and finally try out the show in previews. The Broadway world was complex; finding a door into that world wasn't going to be easy.

My big break (although at the time I did not recognize it as such) came quite suddenly and unexpectedly and took the form of a little dog. I was walking with a lady friend down Sixth Avenue, having just left a meeting at Radio City Music Hall. Without warning, my friend screamed, "Duchess!" I was confused–until I realized she was referring to a King Charles Spaniel on the end of a leash held by a man who turned out to be the legendary producer Alexander H. Cohen. With him was his wife, the actress and writer Hildy Parks.

My friend introduced me to the two of them, and we had a nice chat. After shaking hands, we went our separate ways. Barely three hours later I got a phone call from Alex. How he found me is a puzzle to this day. I was staying at a hotel, and really very few people knew where I was.

Alex was larger than life and a very decisive man. Without wasting much time on small talk, he asked me to meet him in his posh office above Shubert Alley. Once I arrived, he got straight to the point. "How would you like to design this year's Tony Awards?" Maybe I should sign up Duchess as my new press agent, I thought.

Renowned for producing hits in London as well as New York, Alex was involved in many projects, not the least of which was the Tony Awards, founded in 1946 and named for thespian Antoinette Perry. What the Oscars are to film and the Grammys are to music, the Tonys are to theatre, and Alex had been producing them ever since they were first broadcast live on television in 1967. For a set designer eager to break into theatre, the Tonys were a great introduction to Broadway.

In the 1980s the Tony Awards always had a theme, or setting, which was usually the brainchild of Hildy Parks, an interesting woman, to say the least. Smart and assertive, she started out as an actress and was cast in one of Alex's Broadway shows. The story goes that one day, Alex was watching a rehearsal of that show when he saw Hildy on stage making a cup of coffee, studying her lines, and doing the Saturday *New York Times* crossword puzzle (in ink!)–all at the same time. Alex said to himself, "I want one of those."

They were married shortly thereafter. Hildy was soon involved in many of Alex's shows, especially the television specials, including three "Night of 100 Stars," the Tonys, and three Emmy Awards shows, as well as specials for Liza Minnelli, Placido Domingo, and Marlene Dietrich, to name just a few.

Hildy had decided that the setting for the 1986 Tonys would be a big cocktail party in a New York living room and the "guests"–some of the biggest names on Broadway–would present the awards. Bea Arthur, Helen Hayes, Jack Lemmon, Lee Remick, Nell Carter, and Debbie Allen would all be on hand. Finding inspiration for the set wasn't difficult. All I had to do was visit Hildy and Alex at their gorgeous apartment, one of the largest I had ever seen, located directly across the street from the Museum of Modern Art. The apartment's elegant living room became the visual jumping-off point for the "party" set.

In those days, the Tony Awards always used a theatre that had an up-and-running show in it. I never understood the reason for this. Perhaps it was a way to save money, or maybe all the theaters were in use. Whatever. In this case, our venue was the Minskoff Theatre, and it had a show in it. At 12:01a.m. Sunday, we got the green light to bring in our set, allowing us just 21 hours to get ready before the show went live that night. The idea was the matinee show at the Minskoff would be cancelled and the set would be loaded in, lighted, and ready to go for rehearsals at 10 a.m. that morning. We were to spend the day rehearsing, setting up the lighting cues and camera shots. Difficult but not impossible, provided you knew what you were doing and if everything went as planned. That year, my first as the show's set designer, this is not what happened.

We loaded in the set, which had a staircase I had designed for the penthouse-like setting. I had a Manhattan skyline drop approximately 30 feet high by 100 feet wide shipped in from Hollywood. A company that specialized in plants for movies and television created two large artificial dogwood trees in full bloom. True to the schedule, we were ready to rehearse, and by the end of the rehearsal day we had all the lighting cues set and were ready to do the show live. At least, we thought we were ready.

It turned out that thanks to a technical glitch we had lost all the lighting cues for each phase of the show. Without the lighting cues there would be no lights–and no show. What happened next was hair-raising. Alan Edelman, our superb lighting designer, began resetting the lighting cues one by one. As it happened, Alan was hypoglycemic and had to eat on a fixed schedule, so for the next two hours I sat in the production truck feeding Alan information about each scene, along with small amounts of food. Everyone else ate a leisurely meal and got into their gowns and tuxedos. No tux or food for me, just whatever food I could grab to feed Alan. I had been working since midnight, and I was a mess. At one point, Alex poked his head into the truck and said, "Is everything okay?" "Yeah," I replied. "Everything is under control."

Remember, my policy was to never let anyone know of *any* problem, because such knowledge invariably led to chaos and spread like wildfire, thereby sabotaging the show. So, there we were, unshaven, badly dressed, and barely putting the show together on time. To Alex's eyes I must have looked like I had been dragged up and down Shubert Alley, a wreck but clearly a hard worker who delivered the goods. We got the last

301

lighting cue installed two minutes before airtime; the show came off just fine. Alex must have been impressed, because he asked me to design the Tonys the next year as well as a huge three-hour special called "Happy Birthday Hollywood." Best of all, in 1994 he asked me to design the sets for "Comedy Tonight," my first Broadway show.

Alex was to become a pivotal person in my career. He was quite the character in life and, as it turned out, in death. The night after he was cremated, in April of 2000, they lowered the lights on Broadway to honor him. His two sons, Chris and Gerry, along with Hildy, took his ashes and put them in their pockets. Each pocket had a small hole, and the trio proceeded to quietly and secretly scatter Alex's ashes throughout the various lobbies of the theatres in which Alex had produced his many Broadway shows.

One would think that designing my first Tony Awards would have been the highlight of that time for me. In fact, seeing Lee Remick who, as mentioned, was part of the cast, was a bigger thrill. Before we tackled the load-in on that fateful day, I wanted to observe how the rehearsals evolved. Remember, I was very green to the Broadway scene.

So, one day I checked out the schedule and went over to the rehearsal studio that afternoon. The studio was a long, narrow room, maybe 80'X20' in size. There the performers gathered around a grand piano at the far end of the room, while I settled in quietly at the other end. What fun watching performers like Bea Arthur, Nell Carter, Jack Lemmon, Bernadette Peters, Chita Rivera, and Lee Remick rehearsing. Suddenly, Miss Remick looked my way and started walking toward me. I can't begin to describe how fantastic she looked– all that blond hair, a large canary yellow sweater with a big scooped neckline, and tight-fitting slacks. Why was she coming my way? I was the only person at that end of the room.

Well, I soon discovered that she had a large handbag sitting on the floor next to my chair, and when she got to it, without a word, she leaned over to rummage through it. Of course, she had a reason to come over, but as she reached down into her bag, I suddenly found myself looking down her scoop-necked sweater and directly at her breasts. No bra, which was more than a little unusual in those days. An amazing sight. Wow, not what I had expected to see at a rehearsal. No, not at all. Silently and without a nod or a smile, she retrieved what she was looking for, then went back to the other end of the room.

A short time later my assistant, Randy Blom, came by, took a seat next to me, and asked, "Anything interesting happening?" I told him what I had just seen. Randy gave me that doubting look he sometimes had, and that was it–or so I thought. A few minutes later, Miss Remick looked our way, walked back to our end of the room, and again reached into her bag. Randy and I were now both looking down her sweater. She went back to the rehearsal, and as she did, I looked over at Randy. He was vibrating as I said to him, "Don't you ever doubt me again!"

Looking back, it's clear I was really dense. It's more than likely that Miss Remick's movements were intentional. Otherwise, why on earth would she expose herself in such a way not once but twice? Whatever. The moment was truly amusing– and an eye-popping introduction to Broadway.

Over the next 18 years I used my work on the Tonys as a stepping stone to land nine Broadway shows and numerous

Off Broadway productions. The curtain was rising on my own Broadway act, and I could not have been happier.

Chapter 26

Broadway Bound

In 1994, nine years after my lucky encounter with Duchess the dog and designing my first Tony Awards show, I got another call from Alexander H. Cohen. Would I be interested in designing a new Broadway show? The show was to be called "Comedy Tonight," and I was in heaven. Finally, a Broadway show!

My assistant on "Comedy Tonight," at the Lunt-Fontanne Theatre, was Leigh Rand, a friend since my Yale days. I was in excellent hands, as Leigh was smart and knew the Broadway scene. She was like the sister I never had. But a few problems with the show hinted that Alex's heart wasn't really in it. The first clue was the absence of lobby cards–those 14"X22" posters that typically advertise Broadway shows. Then there was the mediocre material. The first act in a three-act, vaudeville-style evening starred Mort Sahl, the satirist; the second act featured Michael Davis, an amazing juggler; and the third showcased the fantastically funny actress and singer Dorothy Loudon.

My favorite story about Miss Loudon concerned a musical she was in that didn't quite make it to Broadway. One day during rehearsals for the ill-fated show's Boston tryouts, the producer came running down the aisle screaming,

"Everyone, leave the theater *now!*" Rather than beat a hasty retreat, Dorothy stood mid stage with her hands on her hips. "Why?" she asked, defiantly. "There's a bomb in the theatre!" the producer yelled back. "You mean there are two?" was Dorothy's succinct reply.

"Comedy Tonight" was heading in that direction. To shore up the show, a fourth act was added featuring comedienne and television host Joy Behar (before her fame on TV's "The View"). I had designed a basic set that could be rearranged into a fresh look for the original three acts, but not for the fourth. The budget was so small that adding another set change was out of the question. In fact, a whole new set for the fourth act probably wouldn't have made any difference. While the show improved greatly with Joy's performance, it wasn't enough to save the day. "Comedy Tonight" closed after eight performances.

No matter. This was my first Broadway show, and I was wildly excited about my first opening night. I planned to be fashionably late and arrived about 45 minutes after the party began. But the party was a bust. The venue, one step up from a cafeteria, was cheap, and hardly anyone was there. The producers, Alex included, were savvy enough to abandon the sinking ship. The show wouldn't continue, but fortunately my career did. I went on to design nine Broadway shows in fifteen years.

Around this time, I met the producer Chase Mishkin, who in 1998 would be one of the producers of "The Herbal Bed" by contemporary British playwright Peter Whelan, who set the piece in 1613. Chase knew little about me, so I needed to convince her that I was the right designer for the job. She agreed to allow me to present my concept for the show in the form of a scale model, with no obligation on her part. Alas, "The Herbal Bed" went to another designer, the terrifically talented David Jenkins, with whom Chase had worked previously. Small world, this theatre business. David was married to Leigh Rand, my assistant on "Comedy Tonight," and the three of us had gone to Yale together.

Creating that scale model was well worth the effort. When Chase, along with Alex Cohen, decided to produce Noel Coward's "Waiting in the Wings" about a feud between residents in a retirement home for British actresses, he brought me in to design the sets. This time I was in the right place at the right time. The show opened at the Walter Kerr Theatre on December 16, 1999, and ran until May 26, 2000. It was directed by Michael Langham, with the excellent Ken Billington as Lighting Designer and Alvin Colt doing the costumes. You might recall that Alvin was the costume designer on "Li'l Abner," the show Mrs. Dwyer took my class to see when I was in high school. Now, years later, he was someone I enjoyed working with, as well as a good friend. Overall, "Waiting in the Wings" was a wonderful experience and a big boost for me professionally. I worked hard, with no help from the yet-to-be-available Internet; all my research was done the old-fashioned way, with trips to various libraries. At Yale, Donald Oenslager had taught us that a set has to "smell right." Using some fine design books featuring English interiors that I had previously purchased at Foyles Bookshop in London, I captured the "scent" of a classic British manor house which, like its occupants, had seen better days.

First, I worked up a ground plan, which was tricky, as there were seven different entrances (doorways) within a limited backstage space. I asked Leigh Rand to make a half-inch scale model, which I presented to the director and producers, who signed off on the design. Leigh then drafted up the set and we solicited bids from three shops. The selection of a shop to create a Broadway set was quite different from my experience in Hollywood. For my work in television, I would go from shop to shop to describe the set and eventually collect the bids, but in New York we would set up a meeting and then invite representatives from three or four shops. During this meeting we would describe the show, present the model, and hand out blueprints. This was, in my opinion, a far better system, because everyone had exactly the same information from which to work up their bid. Once the bids came in, I could question a shop as to why their bid was higher (or lower) than the other shops. In addition, I could review the winning bid and see if there were any misunderstandings or perhaps a way to cut costs without hurting the look of the set. It was a lot of work, but I enjoyed the challenge of seeing how efficient I could be. From that point on, my job was to supervise the building of the set and answer any questions the scenic artists or shop construction team might have.

After the construction of the set, we were ready to move on to the next phase. My ever resourceful and organized prop man, Mike Pilipski, gathered the set's furnishings and, with permission from Chase and Alex, we dressed the set right there in the scene shop. That is, we presented the entire set for the director exactly as it would be seen by the audience, right down to the teacups on the tables and the pictures on the walls. The only missing element was the ceiling piece, which would have been too difficult to hang. I wanted everything to be as perfect as possible.

On schedule we arrived in Boston at the Colonial Theatre for the pre-Broadway tryouts. Minor glitches were easily fixed. For instance, the teacups didn't seem right. They weren't quite English enough, so Mike went out and bought some appropriate decals with flowers to dress them up. It also turned out that the piano on the set was in terrible shape–and sounded it. Actress Patricia Conolly, who would be playing the piano during the show, asked that it be replaced, and it was.

Since the show was about residents in a retirement home, the cast, with few exceptions, was on the elderly side. How best to make them comfortable? I worried especially about the actors who didn't have starring roles and therefore were assigned dressing rooms on the second and third floors of the theatre. To expect a 75 year-old in need of a rest to climb those steps wasn't just inconsiderate–it was dangerous. I approached Chase and told her that in the past, especially when designing the Academy Awards, I had created attractive and comfortable green rooms, lounge areas shared by the entire cast. (Origins of the term remain obscure. According to one theory, "green room" was coined in 1599, when the backstage lounge area of London's Blackfriars Theatre was painted green.)

I proposed that we build two green rooms, one on either side of the stage set so that the actors would have a place to relax, maybe read a bit, enjoy a cup of tea or coffee, and even chat quietly with each other. Chase understood immediately and approved the idea. I furnished the two rooms economically, without sacrificing comfort. We were in business, and the actors now had a pleasant area on either side of the stage where they could take it easy while "waiting in the wings."

309

It was a privilege working with the show's remarkable cast which included Dana Ivy, Elizabeth Wilson, Barnard Hughes, and his wife, Helen Stenborg. But before this stellar cast was selected, I asked Alex if it would be possible for me to sit in on some of the auditions; this part of the business was new to me. He readily agreed. Frankly, I found the audition process painful. The actors were mostly at the end of their careers, and opportunities for them on Broadway were slim indeed. During the auditions, a feeling of desperation pervaded the air. I recall one actor saying sadly, "If you can't use me in this part, I could do the part of so-and-so." Needless to say, I didn't hang around and left the room after just four auditions. Wonderful actors, including three-time Tony nominee Rosemary Murphy, landed a role, but at a low salary. It became clear to me that age and experience did not equate to respectable remuneration. Recalling my one attempt to act while in college, I was glad I had chosen the career that I had. Unlike actors, set designers typically get more in demand as they age; while logging in the years and fine-tuning their craft, they make the necessary connections that lead to more and better jobs.

The story was different for our stars Rosemary Harris and Lauren Bacall. Auditions for these two were simply not required. Miss Harris was a dream: Polite and prepared, she was the ultimate professional. One day I asked Mike, our prop man, how things were going in rehearsals, and he said the only problem he was having was with the chair Rosemary was using on stage. To accentuate the domineering personality of the character she was portraying, the chair needed to be made progressively higher, Miss Harris insisted. And so, Mike was constantly raising the height of Miss Harris's chair as her character evolved and became more and more overbearing. Her entire attention was directed at creating the best possible performance. What a pro. Everyone adored working with Miss Harris.

Lauren Bacall was another matter. From the get-go she requested that everyone call her "Miss Bacall." (For some reason, a few of us were permitted to refer to her as "Betty," and a good thing, too, as I was determined to never call her "Miss Bacall.") I found her to be disrespectful of others and at times unprofessional. During our tryouts in Boston, she was poorly prepared and didn't know her lines. Seated in the back row of the orchestra, I could hear her being prompted from the wings–terrible for the audience, and worse for the other actors. Betty ignored our costume designer Alvin Colt's suggestions for her wardrobe and wore whatever suited her fancy. She insisted that her prop purse contain an expensive Dunhill lighter, even though the purse was never opened.

I think the most telling story about Betty is this: During the middle of the run, on February 17, 2000, the company moved from the Walter Kerr Theatre down the street to the Eugene O'Neil Theatre (a move, by the way, that cost a whopping $200,000). Our new venue had space for only a single green room. My initial fear had now become a reality: Weary actors using the side of the stage without access to that single green room would be forced between scenes to climb steep flights of stairs to their tiny dressing rooms.

Randolph, our savvy stage manager, approached Betty and explained the problem, then asked if the actors could use the small anteroom outside Betty's dressing room during the show. She agreed, but not without conditions: Only certain actors were to be granted access. Unbelievable. A show with an actor who wasn't a team player was, in my experience, unusual. When it does happen, it is often not in the actor's best interest. There was a story of such an actor (not Betty), who annoyed the cast to the point where someone in wardrobe decided to get even. Every week, the actor's costume was taken in an eighth of an inch, until the actor went berserk wondering why she was gaining weight.

Most often actors, especially the big names, couldn't be more gracious. For instance, I did two shows with James Earl Jones, who was wonderful. One of those shows was "On Golden Pond," which opened at the Cort Theatre on March 22, 2005, and ran until June 26, 2005. The other was "Cat on a Hot Tin Roof," which opened on March 7, 2008, at the Broadhurst Theatre, and closed August 4, 2010. A consummate professional, Mr. Jones took his work seriously and expected that others would, too. My friend Terry Lorden once told me about a "Great White Hope" matinee he had attended in 1970 during which a group of teenagers in the audience became increasingly rowdy as the performance progressed. Suddenly the great actor stopped, broke out of his role, walked down to the edge of the stage, and said in that booming voice of his, "*Shut the fuck up!*" The audience froze, and all was quiet from then on. Yet one night in his dressing room, Mr. Jones told me he deeply regretted his outburst on that long ago occasion. He had interrupted the pace of the show and had caused his fellow actors to struggle needlessly in a quest to regain the rhythm of the play.

Directors can be as unpredictable as actors. For instance, Lenny Foglia, who directed "On Golden Pond," was a hard man to admire. We went around and around, trying to nail the set's ground plan, which was okay with me, as I never minded working hard to make a show the best it could possibly be. The problem for me was the director's habit of bad-mouthing my fellow members of the creative team; very unpleasant and not productive. I was pretty sure he did the same to me when I wasn't in the room. In any case, we finally agreed on the layout of the set, and I was happy with the results.

The show required a summer home on a lake, and so the key scenic element was a large drop featuring that body of water, which I commissioned from Global Scenic Services, a fine theatre shop with many talented craftspeople. Lucky for me that Brian Nason, an excellent lighting designer, was part of our show's production team. Brian accompanied me to the Global Scenic Services shop in Bridgeport, Connecticut, where we were able to arrange for our drop to be painted in a manner that supported the various looks and moods, depending on the time of day and season. The set also featured a subtle impression of a lakeside cottage, rather than a literal three-dimensional building. I loved to set up the skeleton of the location and let the audience fill in the details. Written by Ernest Thompson, "On Golden Pond" starred Leslie Uggams in addition to James Earl Jones, who had returned to Broadway after an 18 year absence. Following its brief Broadway run, the show toured successfully, with a cast that included Tom Bosley and Michael Learned.

"Cat on a Hot Tin Roof," the second show I worked on that starred James Earl Jones, was directed by the multi-talented Debbie Allen. I had worked with Debbie on a number of shows, most of them at the Kennedy Center in Washington, so when I heard she was going to direct "Cat" featuring an all-Black cast, I waited for the phone to ring with an invitation to

313

join her on Broadway. The call never came. Undeterred, I made an appointment to see her, then went to the Picture Collection at the 42nd Street and Fifth Avenue branch of the New York Public Library, where I researched the show and photocopied scores of helpful images. With that extra effort I got the job. An important lesson in how to advance one's career.

The set came together fairly easily, and I had my usual enjoyable time working with Debbie. The only problem for me involved the location of a small dressing table that Debbie wanted down stage right. I tried to explain that the table would block the audience's view of some of the upstage action. No matter. Debbie was adamant. She was going to have that darn table no matter what. So I had the shop make a dressing table out of clear Plexiglas so that the audience could see through it. Debbie was happy, and so was I. Problem solved.

Musicals land on Broadway by way of many different routes. Not infrequently they come from out of town, following successful runs in smaller venues. "Big River," for which I served as Scenic Designer in 2001, is one such example. Based on Mark Twain's *The Adventures of Huckleberry Finn*, the show was a revival, but one with a twist: Many of the actors were either deaf or hard of hearing. Initially produced in 2001 at the Deaf West Theatre in North Hollywood, it moved in 2002 to a larger Los Angeles venue, the Mark Taper Forum. From there it transferred in 2003 to Broadway, where the show was produced by the Roundabout Theatre Company and Deaf West, in association with the Mark Taper Forum. Roger Miller did the music, William Hauptman supplied the script, and Jeff Calhoun directed. Initially it was to be a small production, and I offered my services for free. I did this show for the fun of it, and fun it certainly was.

The set was based on a simple idea: Mark Twain takes his book and throws it up in the air. Scattered in the wind, the pages blow up to form the set and magically tell the story. I created about 15 different tricks that the set could do to support the show. Jeff loved them and came up with a number of additional tricks on his own. Rain, for example, was just a pipe with holes drilled into it and a hose attached to a sink backstage. A raft appeared and disappeared as if by magic, and a lean-to popped out of the floor.

On opening night, I was sadly disappointed when, at the conclusion of the final act, hardly any noise came from the audience. No clapping, no nothing. What I didn't realize was that many of the patrons were, like the actors, deaf and voiced their appreciation with wild hand gestures. What *none* of us realized was that the show would be a huge success. When "Big River" moved on to the Mark Taper Forum and eventually on to Broadway, the set was greatly enlarged, but the concept remained largely intact. There, the show played to enthusiastic audiences and eventually went on two tours, one national and the other in Japan.

"Brooklyn the Musical," which opened on October 21, 2004 at the Plymouth Theatre (later renamed the Gerald Schoenfeld), had its challenges. It was produced and directed by Jeff Calhoun, with whom I had worked on "Big River." I liked and respected Jeff greatly. That said, he turned out to be difficult on this show. Perhaps it was the pressure from wearing two hats: He served as both director and producer. Whatever the cause, we were at odds on this production. Unlike most directors, he tended to change his mind over and

315

over again and worry things to death. To be supportive, I decided to do my usual research. This time, the public library wouldn't suffice. To study the location, I had to hop on the subway and check out one of Brooklyn's roughest neighborhoods.

Because I had a production meeting to attend later that afternoon, I was dressed nicely, in a sports jacket and decent shoes. Wandering the grim streets, I snapped photos of graffitied walls, crumbled chain-link fences, and garbage-choked curbsides. Eventually I needed a restroom. Where in this depressed and nearly deserted area was I supposed to find one? I saw no signs of a bar or store that might have restroom facilities. Finally, I spotted a small Baptist church. In front of it, a man sat on a folding beach chair.

"Excuse me," I said to him. "Do you know where I could find a public toilet?" Clearly puzzled, he looked me up and down.

"Man, what are you doing here?" he replied. "Use the toilet inside this door and then you just keep movin' on." His message was clear: Get the hell out before you run into trouble. And that's what I did, but not before I had taken many useful photos. That afternoon, I took my film to a one-hour developing shop, then at 3p.m. walked into my meeting at the theatre with an armload of valuable research.

I must have designed that set nine times. Jeff simply could not make up his mind. It came as no surprise when Jeff called yet another meeting to plot the way forward, only this meeting was one too many; I had a conflict involving a meeting for another potential show. In my place I sent my assistant Tobin Ost to Jeff's meeting to cover for me. During that meeting Tobin, talented and eager, made a suggestion that

316

Jeff loved, and suddenly the basic design of the set was no longer mine. To his credit, Tobin was concerned about what had happened, and we continued to work well together.

Despite the disappointment, "Brooklyn the Musical" allowed me to witness for the first time the creation of a new musical. The show was written by Mark Schoenfeld and Barri McPherson, and while we had numerous workshops to test the material in New York and everyone worked incredibly hard to make the show a hit, it somehow never quite clicked. The cast of five little-known actors included Karen Olivo and Eden Espinosa, who both went on to do great things. Karen eventually won a Tony for Best Featured Actress in the 2009 revival of "West Side Story," and Eden ended up creating the lead part of the green-skinned Elphaba in "Wicked." We knew these ladies were special. The strange thing is this: We could see their greatness in our show, but their performances simply weren't enough to save "Brooklyn the Musical." From this experience I learned that creating a new Broadway show that would last long enough to become a hit wasn't easy. Broadway was one difficult challenge.

In 2008, I had the immense pleasure of being asked to design the Broadway set for "Liza's at the Palace." You might recall that the greatest performance I ever saw, and the one that cemented my determination to break into the performing arts, was "Judy Garland at Carnegie Hall" in 1961. Here I was, 47 years later, designing sets for Judy's daughter. Interesting how things come around. Liza was in great form, and I had a wonderful time.

The thing I remember most about my first meeting with Liza is her eyes. They are astounding—huge and intelligent. I recall saying to her, "Those eyes! They're amazing!" and

317

thinking, "God, that was pretty lame, Ray. She's probably heard that all her life." The production meetings for Liza's show were often held in her Manhattan apartment, on East 69th Street. Right away I noticed a handsome crystal vase on a prominent table. In the vase were three dozen roses–very limp and very dead. Those roses stayed there from meeting to meeting. Also eye-catching was the abundant memorabilia from her father, the famous film director Vincente Minnelli. I could see nothing representing her even more famous mother. And yet on stage she was her mother's daughter: energetic, magical, and a truly great performer.

One day I went to Liza with a model of her set for the show and asked her to sign it so that "Broadway Cares" could auction it to raise money to fight AIDS. "No," she said. "I want it as I have so little memorabilia of my own." How odd, I thought. I built a second model for her, and she was happy to sign the original model so we could raise some money.

For the first act of "Liza's at the Palace" I used two black fabric drapes that traveled open to reveal our star. When opened, the drapes formed a dynamic large triangular shape on the cyclorama that framed Liza in silhouette. This drop set then flew out and revealed the band. For the second act I devised a look that paid tribute to Liza's godmother Kay Thompson, the multi-talented vocalist, actor, and author. When people hear her name today, they usually think of Miss Thompson's delightful performance with Fred Astaire and Audrey Hepburn in the 1957 film "Funny Face," or her series of books about Eloise, *enfant terrible* of Manhattan's Plaza Hotel. What they often don't know is that in the 1940s and '50s Miss Thompson was a major cabaret star. To evoke her heyday, I had a large sign with "Ciro's" emblazoned in neon across it, in reference to the renowned Hollywood hangout where Miss Thompson had performed her legendary act.

I also modified the music stands by changing their facade from the first act to the second act, and helped to alter the lighting to give the set a fresh look.

The joy of "Liza's at the Palace" came from seeing Liza at the top of her game and in being a part of the team that supported her and the four talented male dancers and crack orchestra that performed with her. I'd like to think that my set made a big difference to the show, but the fact is that Liza could have performed in front of a simple drape and still wowed the audience. They loved her. "Liza's at the Palace" won the 2008 Tony for "Best Special Theatrical Event."

My final Broadway show was a live dance revue called "Burn the Floor," directed by Jason Gilkison. It opened at the Longacre Theatre on August 2, 2009 and ran until January 10, 2010. "Burn the Floor" had toured the world and arrived on Broadway with very little input from me. Nonetheless, I had a terrific time watching from backstage as the various dancers came off stage from doing a high-energy number, rested, then revved up to return to the stage for their next dance. When backstage, some of the dancers actually did relax, while others kept the beat going, building up their rhythm and energy before heading back to the footlights.

I went to New York to live a dream that had been with me since Mrs. Dwyer took me to see my first Broadway show when I was just 16. It was a risky move but ultimately a rewarding one. Along the way came some memorable adventures, remarkable new friends, and fresh creative challenges. It was a wonderful time.

Chapter 27

At Home

The places I've lived have always played an important part in how I presented myself to the world and particularly to the people with whom I've worked. No matter where it is, "home" has provided a base where I can entertain my friends and colleagues and enjoy the success I achieved over the years.

When I arrived in Los Angeles in 1968, I moved in with John Harrington, into the modest Studio City house he had owned and lived in since the 1950s. The place was perfectly comfortable, but as my career grew, so did my annoyance that our friends were always coming to "John's house," not "John and Ray's house." So, I started a campaign for us to own a house together. With that in mind, we began house shopping. Not finding anything we liked, we ended up buying a lot in the hills of Studio City. We would build a house together. Or so we thought.

In all the excitement I had failed to let one of the realtors know of our change in plans. His name was Randy Henderson, and one day I ran into him in the supermarket. "Ray, I just found the perfect house for you and John," he said. I'd like to think I was acting out of courtesy by not informing Randy that we had abandoned the idea of buying a house, but in fact it was more a case of not having the nerve to let him down. "Show it to me," I said. And he did.

That evening, when John got home from work, I said, "You're going to kill me." "Probably," John agreed. "Today I looked at a house for sale and I think we ought to buy it," I blurted. Now, John had a temper, and when he exploded it was not a pretty sight. But his outbursts typically lasted only a few minutes and were over as quickly as they had begun. After he had vented, we moved on. "Okay," he said, "tell me about it."

Built in 1949, the house was located in the Hollywood Hills, at 6901 Oporto Drive, and while it had some architectural drawbacks–no front entry hall, for one, and bedrooms accessible only through a hall off the kitchen, for another–it had some considerable assets. The front terrace overlooked all of Hollywood, for example. Even better, though, was the backyard with its spectacular view of the Hollywood Bowl. Without ever leaving home, we would be able to enjoy all the concerts for free.

And so, in 1971, we purchased our first house for $85,000. (In 2020, it was still standing and assessed at $3,611,700.) That was a lot of money back then but a smart investment for my career, as we had wonderful parties there that impressed producers and directors. The house was a dream to entertain in. At my mother's urging, my father built a handsome bar incorporating beveled tavern mirrors John and I had found on a trip to London. To complement the bar, we put in parquet floors and a marvelous mantelpiece found on another trip to Europe. In the backyard, overlooking the Hollywood Bowl, we often had sit-down dinners for 24, with Royal Copenhagen china and electric table lights with shades that matched the blue-and-white china pattern. And somehow, we seemed to have those dinner parties on nights when there were fireworks at the end of a performance. On some

321

evenings, the Hollywood Bowl Orchestra or a symphony orchestra managed by the Los Angeles Philharmonic Association provided the entertainment. On other evenings, we heard the Grateful Dead, Frank Zappa, Joe Cocker, or Rod Stewart, who made his debut at the Bowl in the early '70s. Often, if the concert was a rock concert, we would notice two or three policemen patrolling the ridge of the Bowl on foot, hoping to keep out trespassers. To our delight, there was nothing they could do about us freeloaders who lived above the Bowl. As the concert would start up and the lights began to dim, you could see the flicker of matches as countless joints were lit. On more than one occasion I heard a policeman say, "Boy, they sure are lighting up tonight!" At that point, the faint aroma of marijuana would waft up our way.

One weekend, on a visit to a friend at his home in Laguna Beach, I fell in love with our friend's gas-lit chandelier. Now, most times when I wanted something, John was game to get it for me (yes, I was very spoiled). But not this time. "Too dangerous," he said when we arrived back home, and that was that. No gas lighting for us. Not to be fully denied, I opted for candlelight. Here's how I got it: One day, after John had left the house, I removed the electric bulbs and wiring (no dimmer switches back then) from the elegant crystal chandelier in our dining room and replaced the bulbs with candles. I was sure John would like the new ambience, and he did. The only problem was we couldn't get ladies and gay men to leave the table, as everyone looked extra good in that soft, flickering glow.

About six months after the chandelier transformation, I had a more serious problem. I had invited an important producer and his wife to a dinner party at our house with the hope that he would hire me for one of his future shows. That week, a fierce heatwave hit Los Angeles. Heat like that in LA was unusual, so we hadn't bothered to install air conditioning. There was no easy way to reschedule the dinner. What to do? We improvised: John and I hauled the dining room table and chairs out onto that terrace with the great view of Hollywood, then set a beautiful table with silver, fine china, and flowers and hung the chandelier–candles and all–from the terrace tree. Perfect. I got the job. When it came to giving our friends a good time and impressing a client with that wonderful house, it seemed like we couldn't miss.

After nine years though, the time came to move on. John was turning 55, and he had decided he might as well retire. I was making good money, and he no longer needed to work. After a successful career as a negative film cutter for television shows, he no longer enjoyed his work. The challenge was simply no longer there. (It turned out he got out just in time, as the film industry soon moved over to using digital imagery and digital video; celluloid film was a thing of the past.) But I was worried. I had heard about men retiring without anything to take the place of work and dying within a year. Somehow, I couldn't see John doing nothing but cooking for our dinner parties and playing golf. Buying a new home that needed plenty of work seemed like a good idea, and it was.

And so, on July 3, 1980, we sold the Hollywood Bowl house for $585,000–and made a whopping half-million-dollar profit.

We bought a house at 363 South Las Palmas in Hancock Park for $680,000. Hancock Park was, and is, a rather grand area that predated Beverly Hills and is known for the cool breezes that arrive like clockwork around 8 p.m. every

323

evening. Our new home was an elegant French-style manor house designed and built in 1939 by Stiles O. Clements for Judge Lucius Peyton Green and his wife, Mildred Browning Green, an heiress from the Browning family of gun manufacturing fame. Prominent collectors of European art, the Greens had used the house to display rare French furniture and works by Canaletto, Monet, Rembrandt, and David, which are now part of the permanent collection of the Huntington Library and Art Museum, near Pasadena. It was a house I never thought I'd be invited to, and here we were, the new owners.

Our work was cut out for us, as the judge and his wife had been in failing health for 20 years and the house had been dying with them. It would take a great deal of effort to bring the dwelling back to life. The 4,000-square-foot house had a large oval entry hall with some of the most beautiful parquet flooring I had ever seen. A grand, curved stairway led to the rooms above. The doors to the living room and dining room were richly paneled and when opened, became part of the surrounding woodwork. One of the biggest projects we faced was to rebuild the 40- by 60-foot lath house that graced the backyard. This metal-framed structure had a roof made from redwood strips, or laths, set four inches apart, which provided shade for plants that needed to be out of direct sunlight. With help from our friends Jeff Leith and David Archer, John replaced every single wooden slat. The results were spectacular, with 100-year-old camellia trees and a center fountain making for a charming retreat.

Overlooking the formal flowerbeds was our garden room, where I trained the vines of creeping figs to cloak the walls and bring the outdoors inside. As we got to know the house, we discovered hidden cubbies and even small closets behind various paneled walls. Here, pieces of the past were cleverly concealed. For instance, we found a stash of Lux Soap Flakes, popular in the '40s but difficult to get during the Second World War. It turned out the Greens had been hoarding soap! In the attic we discovered some old picture lights that still bore labels inscribed with names like Canaletto and Rembrandt. Alas, the paintings were long gone.

Returning the house in Hancock Park to its former glory wasn't easy, but eventually everything came together. We loved it there. In time we added a pool, compliments of the fire-ravaged MGM Grand Hotel in Las Vegas. In front of the house, we installed a drive-in gravel courtyard measuring 70- by 45 feet; a holly hedge three feet thick and seven feet tall that came with the property framed the courtyard handsomely. On party nights we would roll out an eight-foot-wide red carpet leading from the road to the front door so our female friends wouldn't complain about the gravel ruining their shoes. We'd flank the red carpet with 80 large votive candles and hang, from the lath-house roof, elaborate Chinese lanterns found on a hunt through LA's Chinatown. These were also fitted with candles. We knew how to party. Many producers and directors were guests at this house, and I gained a reputation for being a designer with taste and style.

The next four years were a wonderful time for us, and I had hoped to live in that house for the rest of my life. Unfortunately, in 1984 our stay came to an abrupt end. We had heard stories of neighbors being held up at gunpoint or having their homes burglarized when they were out of town or at work. On her own doorstep, our next-door neighbor Billie had been forced to surrender her diamond rings at gunpoint. We were concerned that Hancock Park was in danger and became neighborhood watch captains. This didn't do us much good the night it was our turn to be terrorized.

After driving home with John and my 79-year-old mother, I activated the garage-door opener and drove into the garage. My mother was in the backseat, and after exiting the car from the left side she began walking around toward the back of the car. John mistakenly pressed the button to close the garage door, and my mother had to move quickly around the back of the car to avoid being hit by the descending door.

"Hold it!" an unfamiliar voice said. My first thought was that someone was attempting to be considerate and have us stop the garage door from hitting my mother. But then I saw that the voice came from a young man standing about 15 feet away. He was holding a gun, and it was aimed at us.

To this day, I don't know how I managed to think so fast, but without hesitation I said in a commanding voice, "Don't! . . . *Don't!*" He hesitated just long enough for the garage door to finish closing with John, my mother, and me inside the garage. We could hear him running away. John bolted out of the detached garage and into the house to get a gun (something I was very much against), while I leapt over the trunk, grabbed my mother, and pulled her down to the side of the car for protection just in case the guy returned and decided to shoot us through the garage door.

After a short while, Mom said, "Raymond, I don't care if I get shot. I have to get up. My girdle is killing me!" Then I heard words I never thought I would hear from her, "Can we go inside and have a drink?" What a night, and what a wake-up call for us.

We now knew that living in this marvelous house came at a price we weren't prepared to pay. In time, we sold the place–and then were faced with a decision. Where, exactly, would we go? After looking at more than 50 houses in safer neighborhoods and seeing nothing of interest, we passed a house under construction and I said to our patient broker, Howard Kreiger, "Gee, that looks interesting." Later, John said that at that moment he knew his "goose was cooked." Four days later we bought a lot at 13337 Mulholland Drive in Beverly Hills, where we could build a house that would be safely gated and alarmed. I used to love telling people the house we planned to build was halfway between Marlon Brando and Warren Beatty. Okay, so they were a half-mile in either direction. No matter. The lot had a stunning view of the entire San Fernando Valley.

I had never designed a house before, but I knew what kind of place would work for us. Reproducing our Hancock Park house would be beyond our budget but, in any case that house wouldn't have been right in this new, spectacular setting. The challenge in creating our new home was this: How could we do it without making any mistakes? Norton Brown, our financial adviser at the time, shared some words of advice: 1) Don't use any curves, and 2) Don't change your mind.

I developed a ground plan, and the ABC Television Studios were kind enough to lend me a sound stage that was empty on a weekend. There, John and I taped out the entire ground plan in full scale as if we were conducting a rehearsal. And, in fact, we were, as we checked out how we would move from the kitchen to the various entertaining areas in the house. In this way we were able to visualize and decide what would work and what wouldn't. I went back to the drawing board, made some adjustments, and we taped out the plan again. When all was satisfactory, we hired an architect to draw up the plans.

In the course of designing our Mulholland Drive house, we rented a condo in Studio City. One night our friend, the producer Scott Stone, came for dinner and at one point said, "Ray, I have a show for you. It's a home selling show, but you'll have to design an entire house." Ha! Talk about great timing. I took Scott up to my office and showed him the half-inch scale model I had made of our new home. Scott liked my design and hired me to do the show. Within a few months I would be taking photos of our would-be home as it appeared in the set. Everything worked out perfectly.

Back on Mulholland Drive, once we had the plans drawn up and all the bids and permits were in hand, we were ready to start construction. To share our plans with our friends, we used bright, two-inch-wide yellow ribbon to outline the proposed house on the lot. A crowd of 30 gathered to help us launch our new adventure. Our friend Ed Handler opened a bottle of champagne and poured it around the perimeter of the house for good luck. We were on our way.

While the house was in the framing stage, my thoughtful assistant Randy Blom gave us a terrific housewarming gift: a helicopter ride so we could view our property from the air. After returning to the airport, we drove to the construction site, where Randy had arranged a picnic lunch complete with two chairs and a linen-topped table: our first meal in our new home. The next week we had a housewarming party so that our friends could see our place in the framing stage. The invitations read, "Please join us for a real open house." It was important to include those we cared about in this new adventure. To us, it's what made the new house a home.

And so, in about a year we completed our dream house, which was a more casual version of a French country home. The floor was made of 400-year-old French tiles that our ever resourceful and supportive French lady friend, Jacqueline Seyrat, located and arranged to have shipped over to us. While on a trip to Paris, John and I found balustrades for our big hall staircase and other antique pieces to give the interior an authentic French feel. A handsome slate roof and exterior walls covered in fast-growing ivy (painstakingly planted by us) gave our "manor" an established look. The place turned out just the way we had planned it–and on budget. We had been careful to not change our minds, and there were no curves. I had made one compromise, however. I have always loved fireplaces, and the charming, small French mantelpiece I had found locally in Los Angeles and that scaled perfectly for the master bedroom sitting area, was simply too expensive. We opted to not include it in the construction. I was disappointed, but we were determined to be practical. It happened that around that time I was again nominated for an Emmy award (this time for my work on "The American Music Awards"), and as I was sitting in the audience with John on awards night, waiting to hear my fate, John handed me an envelope. In it was a photo of the mantelpiece and a message: "Win or lose, the mantel is yours." Well, I didn't win the Emmy that night, but I knew I had won something much more valuable: the most marvelous, thoughtful partner one could hope for.

All seemed safe and as near to perfection as life could be. Then, on April 29, 1992, Los Angeles and much of the rest of the United States erupted in riots following the arrest and brutal beating of Rodney King. In LA, the chaos lasted for six days and claimed the lives of 63 people. Many properties were damaged or destroyed by looting and fires. As John and I looked out onto the San Fernando Valley from our Mulholland Drive house, we could see the flames slowly advancing toward us. It was a strange and frightening feeling to know that our home and perhaps our very lives might be in danger. Eventually, the fires were contained, but the message was clear: Life could be turned upside down in a matter of minutes.

And indeed it was.

Two years later, on January 17, 1994, the entire house shook. We had never felt nor heard anything like it. The sound was ear shattering and the gyrations staggering. As our bed moved wildly across the floor, we held on for dear life. Since we had both been in deep sleep, we had no idea, at least initially, what was going on. Had a train rammed into our house and then barreled through it? Within moments, we realized we were in the middle of an earthquake. Later, this seismic event would be dubbed the Northridge Earthquake, or "The Big One," with a magnitude of 6.7 on the Richter scale.

Somehow in all the mess, and believe me our place was a shambles, John found a flashlight, and the reality of the disaster became more and more apparent. Gradually, we ventured into the corridor and explored the damage. As we walked down the central staircase, which had moved six inches off its base, John flashed his light around the huge cracks in the walls and said repeatedly, "Oh, my God! *Oh, my God!*" (Much later we joked that he hadn't said that many "Oh, my Gods" since our first night in Amsterdam.)

The living room was quite the sight. All the window frames had been ripped out of their moorings and had fallen either inside the house or out onto the exterior shrubs. Oddly, the windows' panes and mullions all remained intact in their frames. Because the house had been newly constructed, it had many engineering features designed to help it withstand a major earthquake. The 150-year-old, 32-foot-long wooden beam that ran down the middle of the living-room ceiling remained up. Salvaged from an old barn to become the mainstay of our living room, the beam was as solid as ever. However, the hundreds of books that had resided in the many bookcases were scattered throughout the room. I don't believe one book stayed in place on its shelf. It was as if a giant had shaken the entire house.

To secure the house, John and I spent the first day following the quake putting all the windows back into the openings in the first-floor walls. Together we lifted six large windows ranging in size from five feet by eight feet up to ten feet by eight feet, wedged them in place, and then secured them with nails. It was a huge but gratifying job. What surprised us was the elation we felt while reclaiming our home.

The kitchen was another matter. Part of what had made entertaining so much fun was the eight patterns of china, in sets for six to eighteen, that John and I had collected over the years. Now most of it, along with countless Waterford crystal goblets and vases, lay shattered in drifts across the floor. Like a bad joke, a set of everyday dishes, nothing special, sat safely inside the dishwasher without a chip on them. Ha! The warped humor of the gods! Very little else remained intact. However, inside one kitchen cabinet, I found a prized and valuable 25-inch-tall Baccarat crystal vase given to us by a dear friend. As

I pulled it from the cupboard, it slipped through my fingers and crashed to the floor. I joined it on the floor and just sat there and laughed. What else could I do? Cursing or crying wouldn't solve a thing.

Next door to us was a woman who, months earlier, had sent her gardener over our garden wall to trim one of our beloved oak trees because it obstructed her view of the Valley. Needless to say, we were no longer on speaking terms. Nonetheless, in an emergency situation like The Big One, neighbors come together. We went next door to see if she and the lady with whom she lived were okay and to help them open their electric gate just in case of fire (countless houses and apartment buildings burned in the quake's aftermath). They, in turn, let us use their cell phone (a novel toy in those days) so that we could call our families and let them know we were intact, even if our house was not.

We were alive and physically unharmed, unlike the 60 people who died that day and the 9,000 who were injured. We also called Steve Bailey, who had overseen the construction of our house, and asked him to start rebuilding our place ASAP. Poor Steve had just arrived in the Caribbean on a vacation and was making himself comfortable on the beach when he got my call. He and his wife were soon packing and heading back to LA. We were lucky to be at the top of the rebuild list. Some Los Angeles homeowners waited a year and a half for available workmen.

We were lucky, too, that our insurance policy covered the entire house, as well as some of the contents. During reconstruction, we lived on the second floor, mostly in our bedroom and its sitting area, which had sustained a minimum amount of damage, not at all the situation for the owners of three houses near us, which were totally destroyed. Six weeks after the earthquake, we replaced the immense floor-to-ceiling mirror in the master bathroom. Too soon! One week later an aftershock took it out again. In total, there were more than 10,000 unnerving aftershocks. The recovery time seemed to go on forever and, in the end, I stopped caring for this house that we had so lovingly created. We left the house in the hands of a friend who repainted it and we departed for Europe and a much-needed vacation.

When we returned, our house was back in order, but something had changed. We had a new awareness of what really mattered in life. We could see how materialistic we had been, without really appreciating what we had. When that "train" ran through our house, it changed our lives in yet another way. We now felt vulnerable to the possibility of more earthquakes and wondered if the time had come to leave Los Angeles.

In the back of my mind something else had been set in motion. Maybe now was the time to move to Manhattan and try my luck at designing sets for Broadway. And that's exactly what we did. It took a while, but eventually we sold the Mulholland Drive house and purchased two condos: one in Beverly Hills and one in New York. John was very supportive in all this. What a wonderful partner he was.

In 1997, we purchased our first Manhattan apartment, on West 95th Street. It had just one bedroom. A small place made sense, as we were on the road a lot, flying back and forth between LA and New York as my work dictated. (John would tell friends we were now bisexual, and they would roll their eyes.) Small though it was, the new apartment had charm, with a fully functioning fireplace and walls of exposed brick.

Eventually, we sold it and moved to a two-bedroom at the corner of 85th Street and West End Avenue. I was working more and more in New York and needed the workspace.

On moving day, as I was placing the first box on the floor, John announced, "We've made a mistake. This place is too small." While we now had a second bedroom that was intended to function as my office, the room would also serve as a guest room, and we often had houseguests. If visitors arrived from the West Coast, they were likely to sleep until noon. How was I supposed to work? John was right. The place was too small.

We informed the woman who managed our building that we were looking for a larger apartment, and one day she called with good news. Adam Katz, who owned many of the apartments in our building, was adding six floors on top of an existing six story building at 203 W. 90th St., between Broadway and Amsterdam. We rushed over and were the fourth party to see the new construction. We grabbed #7B, the best apartment in the addition. The seventh-floor unit measured just under 1,800 square feet and had three bedrooms, three bathrooms, a dining room, kitchen, sunken living room, and best of all, a 10- by 20-foot terrace sheltered from the wind. The place was almost too good to be true. We were delighted.

We got lucky selling the West End Avenue apartment, too. Originally, we had tried to purchase the apartment next door, with the intention of combining it with our place, but the owners wanted way too much. Now that we were looking to move, they expressed a sudden interest in buying *our* place. So, since the apartments were of similar size, we quoted the same price to them that they had quoted to us. No, they said, they wanted to pay $50,000 less. "No deal," we responded, and then remembered that by selling privately we would be saving a hefty realtor's fee. Just as we were about to call them and agree to the $50,000 reduction, my cell phone rang. Okay, the neighbors said, they would pay full price for our apartment. We had a nice celebration that night.

Creating our new home turned out to be one of our most successful, and most enjoyable, projects together. Adam Katz, from whom we bought the West 90th Street apartment, agreed to a deal: He would do work on our place for free in exchange for my services as a designer; he was looking for ways to improve a deluxe apartment he owned down the block and thus make it more attractive to buyers. And so, at no cost to us, he moved a doorway to make room for built-in bookcases in my office and added attractive moldings.

On our own, we added a handsome mantelpiece (of course!), another gift to us from our friend Jacqueline Seyrat, who had removed it to make room for a wardrobe in her Paris apartment (crazy). I designed two curved bookcases for one end of the living room and asked a carpenter with whom I had worked on Broadway to build them. The bookcases gave the space an intimate, enveloping feel without making it appear smaller. Then I called the Hudson Scenic Studio, which had built my set for "Waiting in the Wings," and bought two gallons of a custom stain I had used on that show. For $35 I was able to transform the entire apartment floor from a contemporary-looking blond to an old-world deep brown, which was much more compatible with our many antiques and period paintings. Next, we had the dining room walls upholstered in sumptuous brown brocade. I also had the room's wainscoting faux painted to mimic fine wood paneling.

335

Jane Thurn, an incredibly talented scenic artist who had worked on several of my shows, completed the job after two weeks of hard work.

For the terrace, we searched the Internet and found attractive pots and planters, which we filled with deep-green boxwood hedges and white Mandevilla, training the vines on metal trellises. In time, the terrace became a favorite place for summer drinks and meals. Over the next 16 years we added treasures from our travels to furnish this wonderful home, which would be the last I would ever share with John.

Looking back, I can see how fortunate I was to live in so many exciting places, and to fill them not just with antiques and art but with wonderful people as well. I can see, too, that no matter the place, if I am with those I love and admire, I am "at home."

Chapter 28

It's a Wrap

I n television, the term "It's a wrap" means the taping of the
show is over and everyone can leave the studio and move
on. That's basically what happened to me. I was moving
on.

By 2012 I was still working a bit, even though set
designing was no longer the challenge it once had been. Earlier
that year I had moved a production of "Boeing-Boeing" from
the Riverside Theatre in Vero Beach, Florida, to the Paper Mill
Playhouse in Mill Run, New Jersey. Frankly, though, I was
getting a bit bored. Out of habit, I continued my practice of
seeing as much theatre as possible, both on and Off Broadway.
And while John seldom, if ever, went to the theatre with me
(big, splashy musicals were an exception–he loved those) I
always attended with the hope that I might encounter
something new and exciting–something that would stimulate
me.

That summer I decided to check out "C*ck," a new Off
Broadway show coyly advertised as "the play that dares not
say its name." Was the playwright a prude, or was the show's
production company merely being provocative to reel us in?
In any case, I went to see what all the fuss was about. By the
end of the matinee, I was both greatly annoyed and greatly
rewarded.

The annoyance had to do with audience comfort–or
lack thereof. Part of the overall set, the seats were arranged in

imitation of a cockfighting ring, with hard bottoms and backs positioned at an awkward angle. They were extraordinarily uncomfortable. Clearly, the set designer did not know what he was doing. I ended up complaining to the guy sitting next to me who, without reservation, shared my opinion. We continued to voice our objections quite vocally during the intermission as well as after the show. Worse still, the show, about sexual identity, was mediocre at best. In a strange way this dissatisfaction proved a bond between me and my new acquaintance who, by the way, was really good looking and charming to boot. No matter. After the show we went our separate ways.

Six weeks later, at the Off Broadway musical based on Edna Ferber's *Giant,* the seating was normal and comfortable, and the show was marvelous. I loved it. Unfortunately, the production was too large to run for any length of time Off Broadway. Paying for a large cast is seldom possible with the smaller ticket price of an Off Broadway show, and this show had a sizable cast. "Giant" was set up with the hope that the production would be good enough to attract the theatrical investors who could bankroll the cost of redesigning and building the sets and costumes that would qualify the show to earn the typical Broadway-priced ticket. My estimate for building new sets and costumes, creating new musical arrangements, advertising, rehearsing the new and larger cast, moving the new scenery into a Broadway theatre, and lighting it would run somewhere between $10 and $15 million. "Giant," alas, never moved forward.

But I did. That man who had been sitting next to me at "C*ck" was there at "Giant," and his name was HR Nicholson. The "H" stood for Henry and the "R" for Rexon, and he shared my enthusiasm for the show. We had coffee afterward, and it was a simple beginning to a wonderful friendship. Of course, when relating this story to others, I cannot resist saying that HR and I met at "Giant Cock."

It was impossible to not be struck instantly by HR. He has the greatest head of gray hair I've ever seen, and it crowns a lean, handsome face. That hair is so perfect our friends and acquaintances sometimes can't believe it's real. His face has just enough lines to tell you he has lived an intelligent, sensitive life. More than once I've been pulled aside and asked, "Say, isn't that Richard Chamberlain?" My usual response, "He prefers to not be recognized." I leave it at that, allowing passersby the pleasure of thinking they've come close to someone famous. Like John, HR can wear clothes with an elegant flair. In John's case it was a bizarre combination that only he could get away with. For HR, it boils down to wonderful taste and an open wallet.

HR was born in Camden, N.J., and raised about 10 miles away, in Stratford, N.J. His father, Herbert Rexon Nicholson, was a very astute businessman who in the early years of the 20th century sold ice and coal. When electric refrigerators and fuel oil came into vogue, he dropped the ice and coal, and in 1907 opened a car dealership that sold Fords. That lasted until Henry Ford began requiring that all Ford dealers purchase a portrait of him for $65 and display it in all showrooms. Herbert stopped selling Fords and began selling Chevys and Oldsmobiles instead.

HR's mother, a schoolteacher named Geraldine Selina Hundt, met her future husband at a church event. Herbert, recently widowed, then invited Geri to his daughter's birthday party, as Miss Hundt had been the daughter's favorite teacher at school that year. In fact, Herbert was twice widowed. His first wife had died in childbirth, and his second wife had succumbed to Rocky Mountain spotted fever after being bitten by a tick during a church picnic. When he started dating Geri, half of his family from his first two marriages objected to the relationship. Herbert suspected his relations were concerned about being edged out of his will. That did it. He married Geraldine forthwith.

When Henry Rexon Nicholson came along in 1947, Herbert at first doted on his new son, but HR turned out to have a strong will of his own. Ultimately, the two did not see eye to eye. HR was 10 when his father died after a prolonged illness and Geraldine, who had been the principal of HR's school, went on to become the superintendent of schools in Mansfield Township, N.J.

Clearly, HR got his smarts from both his parents. It's interesting to note that while HR was born with a silver spoon in his mouth and I came from very simple roots, both HR and I had exceedingly intelligent mothers. Both of us also had fathers who didn't get along with their sons.

After finishing high school, HR went on to Gettysburg College and later, through the Air Force, earned an MBA in finance and transportation at the University of Colorado, Boulder. Before long, as part of the Armed Forces Courier Service (ARFCOS), he became the personal courier for Henry Kissinger during the Hirohito-Nixon meetings. Tellingly, HR was one of the few individuals who got along with the notoriously difficult Dr. Kissinger.

While a captain in the Air Force, HR and a group of other long-range thinkers strategized about the best way to land large numbers of aircraft in the case of an emergency.

What would happen, they wondered, if all of a sudden none of the aircraft in United States airspace could land on United States soil? The group worked with their Canadian counterparts to select Canadian airports with runways long enough to accommodate U.S. jets, then developed contingency plans and executed contracts with the Canadian government. Years later, on Sept. 11, 2001, the plan worked. That day, when two commercial U.S. jets were hijacked and flown into the Twin Towers at the World Trade Center in New York, all other air traffic–some 230 planes–was rerouted and landed safely at 17 airports across Canada. The 2012 play "Come from Away" is based on the results of that perceptive and far-thinking plan.

In 1977, HR married a woman who was also in the Air Force. He left the Air Force in 1980 and the marriage in 1987. Next, he moved into municipal transportation, specifically, transportation in Atlantic City, N.J., and later, in Monmouth County, N.J., where he served as head of the transportation department. For 20 years, he was partnered with Emile Riendeau, one of IBM's top office product salesmen. By the time I met HR, Emile was gone, having died the year before at the age of 86. I discovered that HR had been an incredibly supportive partner as Emile fought his pulmonary problems. When it became clear that John was beginning to have age-related issues, that spirit of generosity was transferred to John and me. HR fit naturally into our lives; soon we were traveling together, exploring new and unfamiliar parts of the world, and renting vacation houses for extended periods, first in Portugal and later in Greece. Some of our happiest times were spent on cruises that HR found and helped us book. Collectively, we took excursions tailored specifically to older travelers, including one to Antarctica that was tailor made for John's mobility issues.

In 2015, when John turned 89, the challenges became even more pronounced. His body just wore out, and a case of blood poisoning was more than he could handle. The doctors talked of amputating his foot, but that would most likely have hastened his demise and robbed him of whatever remained of his pride and his love of life. It was an awful time. I tried so hard to save him and simply couldn't. In hindsight, it's easy to see that part of the problem was my own lack of experience with older people. My parents had lived on the opposite side of the country and never suffered debilitating age-related issues. Consequently, I had no idea about the right way to care for John. But HR did. He helped us find the perfect motorized scooter and made sure John was admitted to the best institutions for treatment. At one point John was having trouble getting in and out of HR's Volvo, so HR traded in the Volvo and bought a comfortable old Mercedes much better suited to John's needs. HR named the "new" car Ella, after John's mother. He was there for us every step of the way during this challenging period, right up to John's death on July 7, 2017.

John didn't want a funeral, just a cocktail party, so I contacted his many friends and had gatherings in Manhattan, Sarasota, Los Angeles, and Palm Springs. I took his mountain of recipes, complete with John's astute and sometimes terse comments, and distributed them among our closest friends. Shortly after, a recipient of one of the recipes phoned and told me with delight what was written in the margin of her particular recipe: "Don't use a fucking blender for this recipe!" Even beyond the grave, John was making us laugh. How grateful I was that we had put a lot of love, laughter, energy, and thought into sharing our lives together.

After John died, I put all our furnishings into storage and rented out the West 90th Street apartment. Living there without John was just too hard. I moved in with HR, who helped me stick with my policy of always looking forward. It's hard to explain, but HR's kindness, keen intellect, and impeccable honesty were and are so extraordinary that I fell deeply in love with him and found a new happiness. While John had at first been defensive about HR's presence in our lives, he had clearly come around. After John's death we discovered he had left a great deal of money to HR, which he will inherit after I pass away.

HR has always loved real estate. As a result of clever investments, he has had homes in New York City, Atlantic City, N.J., Fire Island, N.Y., Sarasota, Florida, and Palm Springs, California–at one point, all at the same time. I have on occasion teased him by telling our friends that HR never got over playing Monopoly as a kid. He also loves boats. Most of his life he has never been without one (his first was a small sailboat, given to him when he was five years old). When we met, my own experience with boats was limited, to say the least, but after John died, I decided to go along for the ride. Together we bought a 30-foot Monterey Cruiser Modal 304 powerboat and named her *Our Adventure*. This purchase was almost our undoing. Two years later, knowing how HR had always wanted to do the Great Circle Loop (a huge undertaking that starts in Miami, moves up the East Coast, into the Hudson River and through the Erie Canal, then into Lake Erie and Michigan and on to Chicago, down the Illinois and Mississippi rivers, and eventually back to Florida), I suggested

343

we sample part of the voyage in reverse. We would cruise from Fire Island, N.Y. down the East Coast to Florida. I thought it was a loving and caring proposal. HR responded to my suggestion by saying that we didn't have enough time to buy a bigger boat–essential for the length of the trip I had suggested. In response, I foolishly said, "I was an Eagle Scout, and I'm used to roughing it." This trip gave new meaning to the word "roughing."

And so, on September 23, 2018, on Day Four of our trip, we arrived at Knapp's Narrows Marina and Inn, in Tilghman, Maryland, on the Intracoastal Waterway. The heavy rain showed no sign of abating, and the visibility was challenging. With relief we tied up at the dock. Usually HR would have cooked dinner, often in a crock pot that would simmer all day and produce a tasty stew or soup by evening, but with the terrible weather we decided to treat ourselves to some fresh seafood at the Marker Five, the marina's reportedly fine restaurant. In fact, our dinner was delicious and our waitress could not have been nicer, providing a welcome break from the foul weather. Eventually, the time came to head back to our boat on foot. After pocketing our cell phones, we put up our umbrellas and, in a downpour, walked 500 feet toward our boat, which was in full sight.

I've had a few hair-raising moments in my life, including the time I was held up at gunpoint at my own house, not to mention surviving the 1994 Northridge Earthquake, and of course the MGM fire. What happened on our way to the boat was equally terrifying. The path to our board was initially well lit, but as we walked toward our boat the walkway and surrounding ground sank slowly as the water rose. Soon the area we were walking across was one large dark reflective surface. We could, however, still see our boat, which was a short distance away. I could also see HR, who was just ahead of me and impossible to miss in his bright yellow rain slicker and orange and blue umbrella. I glanced down at my feet to avoid slipping. When I looked up, HR was gone. He had simply vanished. In near total darkness he had misjudged the walkway and fallen into the water, which was well over his head. He popped up quickly but was amazingly quiet. Was he hurt? Could he swim in all that heavy clothing? I had no idea. I had been a qualified lifeguard in my teens and my impulse was to jump in and rescue him–he was 71 years old, after all. But on second thought, I was eight months shy of 80 myself. My lifesaving years were clearly behind me. So, I threw my umbrella aside, leaned over and grabbed his hands, then held him afloat as I assessed the situation.

It turned out HR was unhurt and just shocked by the turn of events; he was trying to take stock of the situation himself. My attempts to haul him up onto the dock were futile. The angle was awkward, and I just wasn't strong enough. Moreover, the sides of the seawall were so slippery he couldn't get a foothold. It was now 11:30 at night, and the area appeared to be totally deserted. Was anyone nearby who could help us? At the top of my voice, I yelled the only thing I thought boat people could relate to, *"Help! Man overboard!"* I did this repeatedly, each time with the feeling that my calls were useless. No response. Panic slowly gripped me as I realized what I was about to lose. How many people get a second chance at happiness? And here was that chance slipping from my fingers.

Suddenly, out of the darkness appeared a young man and woman. Since they had come from the direction of the parking lot, we later concluded they must have been there necking. Each grabbed one of HR's arms and hauled him up onto the dock like a soggy whale. What a relief! What a miracle! Oh, by the way, a word of advice: If you ever submerge your cell phone in water, do not try to revive it by heating it in a microwave oven. HR recovered, but his now-melted phone did not.

We've gone on to a new life. After a long search, we upgraded to a 39-foot Silverton powerboat which we named *Our Adventure Too*. We now live in two new homes, one in Sarasota and another in Palm Springs. I have yet to regret my decision to retire from set designing, which is probably a good thing, as the technology has changed greatly. The world of television production I once knew is long gone.

Projections and other technical scenic solutions are now the order of the day, and I'm fine with that. I just don't have an understanding of or an interest in these evolutions. Having wrapped up my design career, I know the time has come for fresh adventures and new faces. I've gone from Hollywood to Broadway, and now I'm ready to explore new territories. Aboard our boat, HR and I will finally do the Great Circle Route. We'll see what's in the middle of our nation, not just what's on the coast, as we thread out way up and down North America's waterways. Who knows?" A whole new crop of characters and stories may be out there, just waiting for me.

Between 1979 and 1982,
I designed four television
specials for Lynda Carter
plus her act for the MGM
Grand Hotel. I could not
have had a better time.

In 1977, I designed the
American Film Institute
Tribute to Bette Davis.
Getting to know her was an
unforgettable experience
for me and John.

Miss Piggy, center stage,
in "The Fantastic Miss
Piggy Show," 1982

Marty Pasetta was a brilliant director known for his innovative technical expertise. We worked together from the early 70s to the mid 90s. In 1973, Marty and I did "Elvis Aloha From Hawaii Via Satellite."

Debbie Allen is one of the most powerful, dynamic ladies I have worked with in the business. It's no wonder that she was a 2020 Kennedy Center honoree.

In 2009, Charles Busch and Lypsinka (John Epperson) appeared in "Legends" for Friends in Deed at Town Hall in New York City. Multi-talented and great fun, They are the ultimate pros. Thanks to their talent, and the terrific direction of Mark Waldrop, the evening was a big success.

At home on Mulholland Drive with one of my sculptures prior to my one-man show in Tokyo at Gallery Sanyo.

In 2000, I was 60 years old, and while I had exercised for most of my life, time was catching up with me. Most likely, I would never look better than I did at that time. I hired Tom Bianchi, the well-known photographer of male nudes, to take some photos. Here are two of the more modest shots.

349

In 1980, the MGM Grand fire was a major catastrophe that killed 87 people and caused many changes to the fire regulations in Las Vegas.

A torn piece of the destroyed rhinestone theater curtain and my framed hotel room key are my souvenirs of having survived that fire.

REMEMBER YOU'VE HAD HARDER DAYS

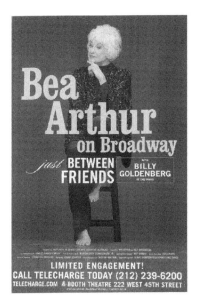

Bea Arthur was one of my favorite stars. While I didn't get to know her well during the run of our Broadway show, I was fortunate to become a good friend afterwards.

Alexander H. Cohen was a major producer and was instrumental in building my career in both television and Broadway theatre.

Noel Coward's "Waiting in the Wings" was my first important Broadway show.
Produced in 1999, it starred Lauren (Betty) Bacall who was a bit difficult, and
the divine Rosemary Harris whom I adored.

To research the set for "Brooklyn the Musical" (2005) I walked the roughest
streets I could find in Brooklyn. For once, the messier the set, the better.

This was my first version of the musical "Big River" at the Deaf West Theatre. Jeff Calhoun asked that the set look as if Mark Twain had thrown his book into the air, and that the pages had exploded into larger versions of the originals.

I adapted my original concept of "Big River" to become a full blown set at the MarkTaper Forum, this time with giant pages from MarkTwain's books.

My set for "Big River" (2003) on Broadway featured the set that I designed for the Mark Taper Forum, but with some needed changes.

In 1972 my father built this bar and bookcase from my design for the living room in our home behind the Hollywood Bowl.
Photo: Carlos Von Frankenberg

My favorite of our many homes is in Hancock Park. It's a copy of a 17th Century French country manor. An attempted armed robbery convinced us to move.

The stationery I used when I lived on Mulholland Drive. The sketch of our house is by my assistant Elína Katsioula.

My New York City apartment was great for entertaining. To hold my many books I designed the bookcases using curves instead of right angles which gave the living room a cozy yet expansive feeling.

In many ways, our 44' Silverton 39 Motor Yacht "Our Adventure Too" is a second home for us. It represents one of the many surprises that keep popping up in my life.

HR and I enjoyed many good times out on Fire Island, in the Pines.

HR and I travel a great deal. Here we are in Ciudad Vieja, Uruguay.

This is my favorite photo of HR and myself sharing time on the beach at Fire Island.

Appendices

- **Ray Klausen's Shows**
- **Glossary**
- **Assistants**
- **Acknowledgements**

Awards

Emmy Awards:

Cher 1975
The 54th Academy Awards 1982
The 55th Academy Awards 1983

5 additional Emmy nominations

Honors

The Bates Travel fellowship from Yale
The Eminent Scholar Chair at Florida State University

Two one-man shows of sculpture at the Gallery Sanyo
(Tokyo, Japan)

Credits

T   *Theatre*
TTV   *Tape Television*
LTV   *Live Television*
TVS   *Television Series*
TR   *Tour*
I   *Industrial: In-house promotional program*

2013

Vanya & Sonya & Marsha Asolo Repertory Theatre, Sarasota T
Viacom I
Burn the Floor Broadway T

2012

Boeing-Boeing Paper Mill Playhouse, Millburn, NJ T
Drama Desk Awards New York Theatre, **LTV**

2011

Shoemaker Off Broadway T
Boeing-Boeing Riverside Theatre, Vero Beach, FL T

2010

Yank Off Broadway T
The Pretty Trap Off Broadway T
Burn the Floor Longacre Theatre, Broadway T
Martha Stewart I
The Shoemaker Off Broadway T
A Funny Thing Happened on the Way to the Forum
Riverside Theatre, Vero Beach, FL T
Holiday show Bushnell Center, Hartford, CT T

2009

Burn the Floor Longacre Theatre, Broadway ᴛ
Liza's At The Palace Palace Theatre, Broadway ᴛ
Legends Off Broadway ᴛ
Inventing Avi Off Broadway ᴛ
Pig Tail Off Broadway ᴛ
Yank Off Broadway ᴛ
Rest in Pieces out of town tryout ᴛ
Cat on a Hot Tin Roof Broadhurst Theatre,
Broadway ᴛ

2008

Cat On A Hot Tin Roof Broadhurst Theatre,
Broadway ᴛ
Pig Tale Off Broadway ᴛ
Liza's at the Palace The Palace Theatre, Broadway ᴛ
The Music Man Bushnell Center Hartford, CT ᴛ
Brothers of the Knight The Kennedy Center ᴛ
Lady on a Carousel prep work for Broadway
(never opened) ᴛ
Directors' Guild Awards New York City ʟᴛᴠ

2007

On Golden Pond National tour ᴛ
My Fair Lady Avery Fisher Hall, New York City ᴛ
Brooklyn the Musical Japan tour ᴛ
The Best of Nature television Documentary ᴛᴛᴠ
Yank! Off Broadway ᴛ

2006

Brooklyn the Musical National tour ᴛ
IBM industrial ɪ
The Pirate The Prince Music Theatre, Philadelphia ᴛ
On Golden Pond National tour ᴛ
My Mother's Italian and My Father is Jewish and I'm

in Therapy Off Broadway **T**
Twin Spirits with Sting Off Broadway **T**

2005

Brooklyn the Musical The Plymouth Theatre,
Broadway **T**
On Golden Pond The Cort Theatre, Broadway **T**
Dancing in the Wings The Kennedy Center **T**
Amici Forever on PBS The Harvey Theatre,
Brooklyn **TTV**
Big River two tours, the US and International **T**
Wall Street Week with Fortune PBS series,
Owings Mills, MD **TTV**

2004

Wall Street Week With Fortune PBS series,
Owings Mills, MD **TTV**
Brooklyn the Musical The Plymouth Theatre,
Broadway **T**
Big River National tour **T**
Dancing in the Wings The Kennedy Center **T**
Pipito's Story The Kennedy Center **T**
The Night of the Hunter Willows Theatre,
Concord, CA **T**
A Few Good Men...Dancin' National tour (18
Cities) and International tour of the Netherlands (23
Cities) **T**

2003

Wall Street With Fortune PBS Series, Owings Mills,
MD **TTV**
The Weight on the Roof Court Theatre, Los Angeles **T**
The 9th Annual Screen Actors Guild Awards, Los
Angeles **LTV**
Brooklyn the Musical, Tryout at the Denver Civic

360

Theater **T**
Brothers of the Knight The Kennedy Center **T**
Pepito's Story The Wadsworth Theatre,
Westwood CA **T**
Big River The American Airlines Theatre,
Broadway **T**

2002

Travis Tritt US Tour **TR**
The 8th Annual Screen Actors Guild Awards Los
Angeles **LTV**
The Daytime Emmy Awards New York City **LTV**
Bea Arthur Just Between Friends Broadway **TTV**
Big River The Mark Taper Forum, Los Angeles **T**
The Richard Rodgers Gala The Kennedy Center **TTV**
Wall Street With Fortune PBS,
Owings Mills, MD **TVS**
Pearl The Kennedy Center and Geffen Playhouse,
Los Angeles **T**
Follies Reprise series, Freud Playhouse, Los Angeles **T**
Gentlemen Prefer Blondes Reprise series, Freud
Playhouse, Los Angeles **T**
It's Better with a Band Prince Music Theatre,
Philadelphia **T**
Jennifer Holiday Romance in the Night Town Hall,
NYC **T**

2001

The 7th Annual Screen Actors Guild Awards Los
Angeles **LTV**
Broadway Celebrates the Spirit of Harlem Apollo
Theater New York City **TTV**
A Tribute to Dudley Moore Carnegie Hall **TTV**
Pete 'n' Keely Off Broadway **T**
Three Mo Tenors PBS, Brooklyn NY **TTV**
Big River Deaf West Theatre, Los Angeles **T**

Brothers of the Knight Kennedy Center **T**
My Favorite Broadway: The Love Songs PBS,
New York City **TTV**
A Few good Men.... Dancin' New Victory Theatre,
New York City **T**

2000

Comedy College with Allen King PBS **TVS**
Soul Possessed Alliance Theatre, Los Angeles **T**
The Miss America Pageant Atlantic City **LTV**
Dreams The Kennedy Center **T**
Call Me Madam Reprise Series, Los Angeles **T**
My Favorite Broadway City Center, PBS,
New York City **TTV**
A Few Good Men.... DANCIN New Victory
Theatre, New York City **T**
I Get A Kick Out of Blue New Amsterdam Theatre
New York City **T**
The 27th annual American Music Awards Los
Angeles **LTV**
The King Faisal International Prize
Saudi Arabia **TTV**
Pete "n" Keely The John Houseman Theatre,
Off Broadway **T**
The 6th Annual Screen Actors Guild Awards Los
Angeles **LTV**

1999

The 26th Annual American Music Awards Los
Angeles **LTV**
The 5th Annual Screen Actors Guild Awards Los
Angeles **LTV**
The Daytime Emmy Awards New York City **LTV**
The Miss America Pageant Atlantic City **LTV**
Soul Possessed The Kennedy Center **T**
A Few good Men... DANCIN The New Victory

362

Theatre, New York City **T**
Waiting in the Wings Broadway **T**
Pepito's Story Orange County, CA **T**

1998

The 25th Annual American Music Awards
Los Angeles **LTV**
Brothers of the Knight The Kennedy Center **T**
A Gala for the President at Ford's Theater
Washington, DC **LTV**
Vibe Los Angeles **TVS**
The Miss America Pageant Atlantic City **LTV**
Hypnotized! Los Angeles **TTV**
My Favorite Broadway: The Leading Ladies
Carnegie Hall for PBS **TTV**

1997

Comedy College with Allen King for PBS **TVS**
A Gala for the President at Ford's Theatre
Washington DC **TTV**
The 24th Annual American Music Awards Los Angeles
(Emmy Award Nomination) **LTV**
Ira Gershwin at 100 Carnegie Hall for PBS **TTV**
Vibe Los Angeles **TVS**
The Miss America Pageant Atlantic City **LTV**
Quincy Jones - The First 50 Years Los Angeles **TTV**

1996

The 23 Annual American Music Awards Los
Angeles **LTV**
The 69th Annual Academy Awards Los Angeles
(Emmy Award Nomination) **LTV**
Pepito's Story The Kennedy Center **T**
The Daytime Emmy Awards New York City **LTV**
The Miss America Pageant Atlantic City **LTV**
Totally Animals Los Angeles **TTV**

Naomi Judd talk show pilot Los Angeles **TTV**
Celebration of President Clinton's 50th Birthday at Radio City Music Hall **TTV**

1995

The Jim Thorpe Professional Sports Awards Los Angeles **LTV**
Tony Danza's Night Club Act **T**
Lew Wasserman Dinner Universal Studios, Los Angeles **I**
The 22nd Annual American Music Awards Los Angeles **TTV**
America's Craziest Animals pilot, Los Angeles **TTV**
The Daytime Emmy Awards New York City **LTV**
The Miss America Pageant Atlantic City **LTV**
A Gala For The President at Ford's Theatre Washington, DC **TTV**

1994

The Natalie Cole Christmas Special PBS, Los Angeles **TTV**
Comedy Tonight Lunt-Fontanne Theatre, Broadway **T**
Carnegie Hall Salutes Jazz Ma*sters* Great Performances, PBS **TTV**
The 21st Annual American Music Awards Los Angeles **LTV**
America's Funniest People Los Angeles **TVS**
Love Connection Los Angeles **TVS**
The Miss America Pageant Atlantic City **LTV**
The Jackson Family Honors Las Vegas **TTV**
The Jim Thorpe Professional Sports Awards Los Angeles **LTV**
A Gala for the President at Ford's Theatre Washington, DC **TTV**
Oracle **I**

1993

Love Connections Los Angeles **TVS**
The Jim Thorpe Professional Sports Awards Los Angeles **LVS**
The 20th Annual American Music Awards Los Angeles **LTV**
The Neil Diamond: The Christmas Special Los Angeles **TTV**
A Gala for the President at Ford's Theatre Washington, DC **TTV**
The 14th Annual Cable ACE Awards Los Angeles **LTV**
The Clinton Inaugural Gala Lincoln Memorial **LTV**
Travis Tritt's National Tour **TR**
The Miss America Pageant Atlantic City **LTV**
The American Film Institute Tribute to Elizabeth Taylor Beverly Hills, CA **TTV**
America's Funniest People Los Angeles **TVS**
Kids are Funny (pilot) Los Angeles **TTV**

1992

The 19th Annual Daytime Emmy Awards Los Angeles **LTV**
The Jim Thorpe Professional Sports Awards Los Angeles **LTV**
Travis Tritt's National Tour Nationwide **TR**
The ACE Awards Los Angeles **LTV**
The 19th Annual American Music Awards Los Angeles **LTV**
America's Funniest People Los Angeles **TVS**
Love Connection Los Angeles **TVS**
Jazz Leggs A theatrical review, Berlin, Germany **T**

1991

Perfect Match (pilot) Los Angeles **TTV**

365

The ACE Awards Los Angeles **LTV**
The 18th Annual American Music Awards
Los Angeles **LTV**
The 63rd Annual Academy Awards (nominated for
an Emmy Award) Los Angeles **LTV**
Love Connection Los Angeles **TVS**
The 18th Annual Daytime Emmy Awards Los
Angeles **LTV**
Perfect Match (pilot) Los Angeles **TTV**
America's Funniest People Los Angeles **TVS**
The Chuck Woolery talk show Los Angeles **TVS**

1990

Johnny B On The Loose (pilot) Los Angeles **TTV**
The Night of a Hundred Stars Radio City Music
Hall **TTV**
The 17th Annual American Music Awards
(Nominated for an Emmy Award) Los Angeles **LTV**
The Five Minute Workout with Sandy Duncan
Los Angeles **TTV**
The ACE Awards Los Angeles **LTV**
Nighttime attraction for Disney World Orlando, FL **I**
America's Funniest People Los Angeles **TVS**
Love Connection Los Angeles **TVS**
The Kennedy Center Honors **TTV**
The 62nd Annual Academy Awards Los Angeles **LTV**

1989

Friday Night Surprise Los Angeles **TTV**
The 16th Annual American Music Awards Los
Angeles **LTV**
The 61st Academy Awards Los Angeles **LTV**
Love Connections Los Angeles **TVS**
The 50th Anniversary of Television Los Angeles **TTV**
The Kennedy Center Honors **TTV**

Dick Clark's Friday Night Surprise Los Angeles **TTV**
The Smothers Brothers Los Angeles **TVS**

1988

Super Stars and their Moms Los Angeles **TTV**
Dick Clark's Friday Night Surprise Los Angeles **TTV**
ABC Affiliates Meeting Beverly Hills **I**
The Kennedy Center Honors **TTV**
The 15th Annual American Music Awards Los Angeles **LTV**
The Image Awards Los Angeles **LTV**
The American Film Institute Salute to Jack Lemmon Beverly Hills **TTV**
The Smothers Brothers Los Angeles **TVS**
TVAM News set London **TVS**
WAC A Day - show for children London **TVS**
Kenny Rogers Talk show (pilot) Los Angeles **TTV**
Love Connections Los Angeles **TVS**

1987

"Scenario" decor for an Atlanta nightclub
*ACE Award*s Los Angeles **LTV**
Caesar's Palace 20th Anniversary Special Las Vegas **TTV**
You Are The Jury Los Angeles **TVS**
Happy Birthday Hollywood (Nominated for an Emmy Award) Los Angeles **TTV**
The Special Olympics South Bend, IN **TTV**
The Pontiac Industrial Los Angeles **I**
The 14th Annual American Music Awards Los Angeles **LTV**
Super Stars and Their Moms Los Angeles **TTV**
The ABC Affiliates Show at Radio City Music

Hall **1**
Love Connections Los Angeles **TVS**
The Most Beautiful Girl in the World Australia **LTV**
Let's Make A Deal Los Angeles **TVS**
*Mi*ss Hollywood Los Angeles **TTV**
Dick Clark's Good Times Los Angeles **TTV**
Golden Nugget Hotel Showroom Las Vegas
The Emmy Awards Pasadena, CA **LTV**
The Tony Awards New York City **LTV**
Pontiac Industrial at the Aladdin Hotel Las
Vegas **1**
Make A Match (game show) Los Angeles **TVS**
Dick Clark's Rock 'N' Roll Summer Action Los
Angeles **TTV**
AIDS Benefit The Bonaventure Hotel, Los Angeles
AGLA Awards Los Angeles **LTV**
The Kennedy Center Honors **TTV**
Rocket To The Sta*r*s Los Angeles **TTV**
Motown Merry Christmas Los Angeles **TTV**
*Dance Feve*r Los Angeles **TVS**
Value Television (VTV) Los Angeles **TTV**

1986

The 13th Annual American Music Awards Los
Angeles **LTV**
Nel Carter...Never Too Old To Dream Special
Los Angeles **TTV**
The Jeffrey Osbourne Concert Tour Nationwide **TR**
NBC's 60th Anniversary Show Los Angeles **TTV**
Miss Hollywood (beauty pageant) Los Angeles **LTV**
The 40th Annual Tony Awards New York City **LTV**
ABC's Affiliates Meeting New York City **1**
The Emmy Awards Pasadena, CA **LTV**
The Pontiac Industrial Los Angeles **1**
Love or Money Los Angeles **TTV**
The Chuck Woolery Show (pilot) Los Angeles **TTV**

Love Connection Los Angeles **TVS**
You Are The Jury Los Angeles **TVS**
The Kennedy Center Honors **TTV**
What a Year - 1986! Los Angeles **TTV**
Value Television (VTV) Los Angeles **TTV**
Dance Fever Los Angeles **TVS**
Perfect Match Los Angeles **TVS**
Let's Make A Deal Los Angeles **TVS**

1985

The 12th Annual American Music Awards **LTV**
The ABC Affiliates Show Radio City Music Hall **I**
Love Connection Los Angeles **TVS**
The Most Beautiful Girl in the World **LTV**
Let's Make a Deal Los Angeles **TVS**
Miss Hollywood Los Angeles **LTV**
Dick Clark's Good Times Los Angeles **TTV**
Golden Nugget Hotel Showroom Las Vegas
The 39th Annual Tony Awards New York City **LTV**
The Pontiac Industrial Aladdin Hotel, Las Vegas **I**
The Emmy Awards Pasadena, CA **LTV**
Make A Match (game show) Los Angeles **TVS**
Dick Clark's Rock 'N' Roll Summer Action Los Angeles **TTV**
AIDS Benefit Bonaventure Hotel
AGLA Awards Los Angeles **LTV**
The Kennedy Center Honors (Nominated for an Emmy Award) **TTV**
Rocket To The Stars Los Angeles **TTV**
Night of 100 Stars III New York City **TTV**
NBC 60th Anniversary Celebration New York City **TTV**
Super Stars 1985 Los Angeles **TTV**
You Are The Jury Los Angeles **TVS**
Dance Fever Los Angeles **TVS**

369

1984

The 11th Annual American Music Awards Los Angeles **LTV**
Dick Clark's "Animals Are the Funniest People" Los Angeles **TTV**
The Most Beautiful Girl In The World **TTV**
The Kenny Rodgers' National Tour nationwide **TR**
The Lionel Richie National Tour nationwide **TR**
Superstars and Classic Cars MGM Hotel, Reno **TTV**
The American Film Institute Tribute to Lilian Gish Beverly Hills **LTV**
The Olympics Gala Los Angeles **TTV**
The Pontiac Industrial MGM Grand, Las Vegas **I**
The Kennedy Center Honors (Nominated for an Emmy award) **TTV**
Double Platinum (pilot) Los Angeles **TTV**
Love Connection (series) Los Angeles **TVS**
The Jackson Brothers Video, Los Angeles
Kenny Rogers Golden Nugget, Las Vegas **T**
You Are The Jury Los Angeles **TVS**
Julio Iglesias National Tour nationwide **TR**
The ABC Affiliates Show Beverly Wilshire Hotel I
Let's Make a Deal Los Angeles **TVS**
Devereux Foundation Benefit Beverly Wilshire Hotel, Beverly Hills **I**
Hollywood Star Screen Test Los Angeles **TTV**
The National Conference of Christians & Jews Beverly Hilton Hotel, Beverly Hills
Irving Berlin Tribute New York City **TTV**
Dance Fever Los Angeles **TVS**

1983

The 10th Annual American Music Awards Los Angeles **LTV**
The American Film Institute Salute to John Huston Beverly Hills **TTV**

370

The 55th Annual Academy Awards (received an Emmy Award) Los Angeles **LTV**
L.A. Chamber of Commerce ABC The Century Plaza Hotel, Beverly Hills **I**
The Pontiac Industrial National Tour **I**
Lionel Ritchie's National Tour nationwide **TR**
The Magic of Christmas theatre tour **TTV**
Hollywood Private Home Movies Los Angeles **TTV**
Love Connection Los Angeles **TVS**
ABC Affiliates Meeting Los Angeles **I**
The Kennedy Center Honors **TTV**
Dance Fever (series) Los Angeles **TVS**
Dick Clark's "Animals Are The Funniest People" Los Angeles **TTV**

1982

The 9th Annual American Music Awards Los Angeles **LTV**
Inside America (4 part mini Series) Los Angeles **TVS**
Lynda Carter's act at the MGM Grand hotel Las Vegas **T**
Lynda Carter TV Special Los Angeles **TVS**
The American Film Institute tribute to Frank Capra Beverley Hills **TTV**
The 54th Academy Awards (received an Emmy Award) Los Angeles **LYV**
Texaco Salutes Broadway Los Angeles **TTV**
The Fantastic Miss Piggy Show Toronto, Canada **TTV**
The Pontiac Industrial **I**
Hollywood Private Home Movies Los Angeles **TTV**
Love Connection (series) Los Angeles **TVS**
The Kennedy Center Honors **TTV**
Magic With the Stars Los Angeles **TTV**
Dance Fever (series) Los Angeles **TVS**

1981

The American Film Institute's tribute to Fred Astaire Beverly Hills **TTV**
The 8th Annual American Music Awards Los Angeles **LTV**
"Jubilee" at the MGM Grand Las Vegas (ran for 34 years) **T**
IBM Industrial Hawaii **I**
People's Choice Awards Los Angeles **TTV**
Small World Los Angeles **TTV**
A Gift of Music Los Angeles **TTV**
Lynda Carter's Celebration (nominated for an Emmy Award) Los Angeles **TTV**
ABC Affiliates Meeting Los Angeles **I**
*Magic With The St*ars Los Angeles **TTV**
The Kennedy Center Honors **TTV**
Bobby Vinton and His All Girl Band Los Angeles **TTV**
Lynda Carter's Act MGM Grand, Las Vegas **T**
Dance Fever (series) Los Angeles **TVS**

1980

The 7th Annual American Music Awards Los Angeles **LTV**
The American Film Institute Tribute to Jimmy Stewart Beverly Hills **TTV**
The 52nd Annual Academy Awards (Nominated for an Emmy Award) Los Angeles **LTV**
The Monte Carlo Show Monte Carlo **TVS**
Omnibus (four one hour specials) Los Angeles and New York City **TVS**
The Kennedy Center Honors **TTV**
The Lynda Carter Special Los Angeles **TTV**
Doc (pilot) Los Angeles **TTV**
IBM Industrial Hawaii **I**
National Conference for Christians and Jews Los Angeles **I**
The Beatrice Arthur Special Los Angeles **TTV**

Dance Fever Los Angeles **TVS**

1979

The Muppets Go Hollywood Los Angeles **TTV**
The country Music Awards Los Angeles **LTV**
The ABC Affiliates Show Los Angeles **I**
The John Denver and The Muppets: A Christmas Together Los Angeles **TTV**
The Kennedy Center Honors **TTV**
Dorothy Hamill's Corner of the Sky Lake Placid, NY **TTV**
Dance Fever Los Angeles **TVS**
IBM (in house production - San Francisco and Hawaii **I**
The 6th Annual American Music Awards Los Angeles **LTV**
The American Film Institute tribute to Alfred Hitchcock Beverly Hills **TTV**
Best Bonner (commercial) Los Angeles **I**

1978

ABC's 25th Anniversary Los Angeles **TTV**
The 5th Annual American Music Awards Los Angeles **LTV**
The Natalie Cole Special Los Angeles **TTV**
The American Film Institute's Tribute to Henry Fonda Beverly Hills **TTV**
TBM In-house industrial Phoenix & Hawaii **I**
Gino's Pizza (commercial) Los Angeles
Second half of MGM's *"Hello Hollywood, Hello!"* Reno **T**
Dick Clark's Good Old Days Los Angeles **TTV**
The Joe Namath Special Los Angeles **TTV**
The Johnny Yunn Special Los Angeles **TTV**
Super Night at the Super Bowl Pasadena, CA **TTV**

1977

Dick Clark's Good Old Days Los Angeles **TTV**
Sammy And Company (Sammy Davis' TV Series)
Los Angeles and Mexico **TVS**
The United Way Special Los Angeles **TTV**
The American Film Institute Tribute to Bette Davis
Beverly Hills **TTV**
New Year's Rocking Eve (Pre-tape and live)
Los Angeles and New York City **TTV**
Paul Anka... Music My Way Los Angeles **TTV**
The 49th Annual Academy Awards Los Angeles **LTV**
Eddie and Hubert (TV pilot) New York City **TTV**
The Photoplay Awards Los Angeles **LTV**
The Pontiac Industrial Los Angeles **I**
The John Davidson Christmas Special
Los Angeles **TTV**

1976

Sammy And Company (Sammy Davis' TV series)
Los Angeles **TVS**
Super Night at the Super Bowl Pasadena, CA **LTV**
The Dorothy Hamill Special Toronto, Canada **TTV**
The 4th Annual American Music Awards
Los Angeles **LTV**
The Ted Knight Musical Comedy Variety Special
Los Angeles **TTV**
The American Film Institute Tribute To William Wyler
Beverly Hills **TTV**
The 50th Anniversary of Television Los Angeles **TTV**
The 48th Annual Academy Awards Los Angeles **LTV**

1975

Hollywood Star Screen Test Los Angeles **TTV**
Cher (won an Emmy Award) Los Angeles **TVS**

Sammy and Company (Sammy Davis series) **TVS**
Los Angeles
The Werewolf of Woodstock (TV Movie) Los Angeles
The 3rd Annual American Music Awards
Los Angeles **LTV**
The John Davidson Christmas Show Los Angeles **TTV**
The American Film Institute Tribute to Orson Wells
Beverly Hills **TTV**
The Way We Were Los Angeles **TTV**
The Democratic Telethon Los Angeles **I**

1974

The 2nd Annual American Music Awards
Los Angeles **LTV**
Sandy in Disneyland (starring Sandy Duncan)
Anaheim, CA **TTV**
The American Film Institute Tribute to James Cagney
Beverly Hills **TTV**
The 46th Annual Academy Awards Los Angeles **LTV**

1973

The Perry Como Winter Show Los Angeles **TTV**
One More Time Los Angeles **TTV**
Up With People Albuquerque, NM **TTV**
Elvis Aloha From Hawaii Hawaii **LTV**
The 1st Annual; American Music Awards
Los Angeles **LTV**
Bing Crosby's Sun Valley Christmas Sun Valley, ID **TTV**
The American Film Institute tribute to John Ford
Beverly Hills **TTV**
The Helen Reddy Show Los Angeles **TTV**
Helen Reddy's Act at the MGM Grand Hotel,
Las Vegas **T**

1972

Christmas with the Bing Crosbys Los Angeles **TTV**

375

Dick Clark's New Year's Rocking Eve
Los Angeles and New York City **TTV**
Bing Crosby and Friends Los Angeles **TTV**

1971

Bing Crosby and the Sounds of Christmas
Los Angeles **TTV**
The Pearl Bailey Show Los Angeles **TVS**
The Perry Como Winter show Los Angeles **TTV**

1970

Hooray for Hollywood (my first TV special)
Los Angeles **TTV**
Worked as an assistant for Spencer Davies on
The Dean Martin TV Series Los Angeles

1969

Worked as an assistant to Jim Trittipo on:
The Hollywood Palace Los Angeles **TVS**
The Frank Sinatra Special Los Angeles **TTV**
The Mitzi Gaynor Special Los Angeles **TTV**
The 41 Annual Academy Awards Los Angeles **LTV**

1968

The Moths The Mark Taper Forum Los Angeles **T**
The Dance Next Door The Mark Taper Forum,
Los Angeles **T**
Rosebloom The Mark Taper Forum, Los Angeles **T**
The Golden Fleece The Mark Taper Forum, Los
Angeles **T**

1967

Master's degree from Yale School of Drama
Bates travel Fellowship to Europe Yale University
The Miser The Loretto Hilton Theatre, St Louis, MO **T**

376

The Caucasian Chalk Circle
The Loretto Hilton Theatre. т
The Time Of Your Life The Loretto Hilton Theatre,
St Louis, MO т

1966

Designed the following summer stock theatre for the
John Drew Theater, NY:
The Subject Was Roses
Gypsy
The Fantasticks
A Funny Thing Happened On The Way To The Forum
Mary Mary
Beyond The Fringe
You Can't Take It With You
How to Succeed in Business Without Really Trying
Life With Father
Oh Kay! Yale School of Drama т
The Revenger's Tragedy Kirby Memorial Theatre,
Amherst College, MA т

1965

Summer And Smoke Connecticut College т
Johnny Johnson Yale School of Drama т
Nature's Way with Jayne Mansfield, Lake
Whalom Playhouse т
Tartuff Yale School of Drama т

1964 to 1967 Yale School of Drama, Master's Degree in
Theatre Design
1963 Master's Degree in Fine Arts, New York University
1962 Bachelor of Arts, Hofstra College

377

Group and Solo Shows of Ray Klausen's Sculpture

Eva Cohon Gallery, Chicago, IL
L.J.B. Gallery, New Port, CA
Paris Gibson Museum, Great Falls, MT
Hunter Museum, Chattanooga, TN
Plattsburgh Art Museum, Plattsburg, NY
Multiples Gallery, Los Angeles, CA
Mc Kenzie Gallery, Los Angeles, CA
Gallery Moos, Toronto, Canada
Zantman Gallery, Carmel, CA
Wade Gallery, Los Angeles, CA
Gallery Sanyo, Tokyo, Japan
Ruth Bachofner Gallery, Santa Monica, CA
Florida State University Museum and Gallery, Tallahassee, FL
Palm Springs Desert Museum. Palm Springs, CA

My assistants…. My backbone

Over the 50 or so years since I left Yale, I have been first an assistant and then had to hire many assistants of my own. I don't know how the training at Yale is today but in my day, there was no instruction as to how to interact with people who were one's assistant. It was kind of a learn-as-you-go set up, and I think I eventually acquired a pretty good approach. I tried always to be fair and honest but I was a bit of a perfectionist, and because I worked hard, I expected the same of anyone who was my assistant. I'm sure I was very difficult in the early years but hopefully I got easier to work with in the latter part of my career. Because I don't want to favor any particular assistant, I will list the outstanding ones in alphabetical order and make comments about them accordingly. If I slight anyone or fail to adequately compliment him or her, I apologize. I've been always grateful for the wonderful support and contribution each and everyone made. They helped me achieve the success I aspired to.

Rebecca Barkley

I interviewed Rebecca for the job of assistant. She was on a par with a man who also wanted the job. I always favored women because they had a harder time breaking into the business. Rebecca turned out to be Jim Trittipo's cousin. She got the job. In addition, to her considerable style, Rebecca had a sly sense of humor. She made me laugh. Also, she was damned good at her job. I loved working with her. Rebecca also taught me to be more open to new ideas, to be less rigid in how I saw things. On July 13th 1978, she was no longer working for me and came for lunch as I liked staying touch with my assistants , and Rebecca was one of my favorites. She arrived with her cute new baby boy Griffin and she had pink hair! In the past, I might have been judgmental of the latter but she had loosened me up. I loved both her new additions and how she had changed me a bit.

Randy Blom

Randy came to me with an architectural background which was perfect for me in that he drafted beautifully and quickly learned the ins and outs of the business of good set designing. Like many of my assistants, he has a fantastic sense of humor. It seemed like he was always laughing which is something I valued a great deal while dealing with the intensity of the work we were in engaged in. What separated him from many people I worked with was his generosity of spirit. His gift of a helicopter ride that took John and me over our new home was an amazing present. After, he provided us with a picnic set up in the framework of our house while it was still under construction. Our first meal in our new home! That gift was indicative of his thoughtfulness and largesse. Eventually Randy moved to Palm Springs where I lost track of him. One day, HR and I were getting estimates for some construction work on our new house there and guess who appeared out of the blue? There he was, all smiles and with a new set of credentials. Smart man, Randy. I was so grateful to have reconnected with this marvelous man.

Joe Cashman

Joe brought something special to the office. He was excellent at drafting and model making, but the thing that I valued the most were his smiles. He always seemed to be in a good mood which I valued because I was always under tremendous pressure as I tend worry things to death. Joe's smiles and overall good humor were highly valued by me. Joe went on to be the art director on numerous shows including The Ultimate Toy Awards, The DVD Exclusive Awards and America's Millennium plus, he was the set decorator of Night Stand (television series.)

Michael Corenblith

Michael had an architectural background when he came to me. He was terrific when it came to drafting. He could really nail down a design so there were no problems when the set was being built in the shop. I never had to worry if something would work or not. I would have kept him as my assistant forever but there was one problem: Michael really wanted to be in the film business. He was meant to be a film production designer. So, one day I reluctantly sat him down and discussed my thought that he should move on and work in the film end of the business which is what he did. Ten years later, in 1995, I was setting up the Academy Awards show and there in the audience along with all the showcards indicating where the nominees would be sitting was Michael's name. He had been nominated for an Oscar for his designs on "Apollo 13." I left a note taped on his seat congratulating him on the nomination, and while he didn't get the Oscar, he certainly had come a long way and in the right direction. To me he was the real winner that night.

Paul Galbraith

Paul probably did more to make me look good than any other assistant I ever had. I was doing a Bing Crosby Christmas special and I was trying to use paper sculpture (a system of cutting and folding thick paper to form marvelous shapes.) I knew little about how to make the most of this terrific medium. A friend told me about Paul who had extensive knowledge in this. We met, talked about what I hoped to do, and Paul, who was in charge of displays for Bullocks (a large department store in Los Angeles) said he would quit his job and help me. I was horrified that he would give up his job just to help me out on this one show. Well, he ended up working with me for decades and made me look more talented than I ever was! When I got my first Emmy, I gave him a miniature gold Emmy charm as a thank-you, plus many photos of all the terrific work he had done. He was an amazing talent and a wonderful friend. He died a few years ago and I greatly miss him.

Elina Katsioula

In 1985, I had set up a modest scholarship at Yale for set design students to help them pay for art supplies. Elina was the first recipient. When I visited Yale and met her, I was impressed with this tall, beautiful, smart and modest young woman. Imagine! She was born in Greece and didn't speak English until three years before she entered the Master's program at the Yale Drama School! We really hit it off, and she suggested that she try to come to Los Angeles for a visit to check out the TV end of the business. Well it turned out that I suddenly had a rush job for a show that came up and I was able to put Elina to work with the end result she made a lot of much needed money, and was hooked on working in Los Angeles. She ended up working for me for a number of years and she was one of the best assistants I've ever had.

Steve Moore

I inherited Steve when I took over the "Cher" television series as he had worked as Bob Kelly's assistant the year before. Steve was incredibly helpful in showing me how the show ran. In the process, I learned a great deal, including how to run an office. At the time, I was very inexperienced about how to treat an assistant, and in retrospect I admire the fact that he didn't quit on me. Thank you, Steve.

Tobin Ost

Thanks to my dear friend Leigh Rand, I met Tobin at a rally demonstrating in favor of the controversial Off Broadway play "Corpus Christi" by Terrence McNally. We got talking as we stood in support of the show, and I quickly got to like this smart young man who aspired to be both a set and costume designer. As luck would have it, I soon needed an assistant and Leigh wasn't available. We started working together and it was wonderful because Tobin is a very gifted designer in his own right. We worked on the Broadway show "Brooklyn the Musical" where he did the costumes and I did the sets. It turned out that his contribution to the show's sets was such that I arranged for him get co-set designer credit. It has been a pleasure to watch his career take off. He's a smart man who is charming, gifted and has already gone far in the business.

Randy Parsons

Randy worked on many shows with me. He was an incredibly reliable and talented assistant. He not only can make the most remarkable models of the sets I've imagined, he was excellent at intuitively understanding what affect I had in mind when we developed a look for a show. He was a great help on "Brooklyn the Musical," "Big River," and "On Golden Pond," both on Broadway and the National tours. Even now that I'm no longer designing, we have remained good friends. He has a fun sense of humor. Just ask him about firemen. He has been an important part of my life.

Leigh Rand

Leigh was a classmate of mine at Yale and a very important friend, like the sister I never had. Leigh was a smart, gifted designer and a loving friend. When I went off to Los Angeles to build my career in television, I kept in touch with her and tried to use her as my assistant whenever I worked in New York City. Leigh aided me on my first two Broadway shows "Comedy Tonight" and "Waiting in the Wings," and guided me through the ropes making me look much better than I deserved. Sadly, she died in 2000. She was way too young. I miss her to this day.

Bob Rang

Bob was great fun and a terrific talent but I almost didn't hire him. I first met Bob when he was working in the CBS Shop. He approached me for a job, and I actually laughed at the idea. Here was this kid who was a mess. He had two chipped front teeth and was wearing a rumpled T-shirt that had the following emblazoned across his chest "FAT JACK'S, THE BEST MEAT IN TOWN. IF YOU CAN'T EAT IT, BEAT IT!" Now you may have gathered from this book that I have always aspired to be a class act and this kid certainly wasn't projecting that image. However, what he did have was an incredible drive. He mirrored me in that area. After being pressured by him over and over again, I reluctantly said "OK, if you can take a week off from work, I'll let you hang around while I set up The Academy Awards." Well that week turned into two and eventually I hired him because not only was he smart as a whip, he was funny and at that point in time I was way too serious for my own good. He lightened me up and made the work much more enjoyable. Yup, he's the guy with me in the red Bob Mackie drag! Well I helped Bob by paying for fixing one of his teeth and he fixed the other one. He worked with me for years and became a fine designer. He eventually codesigned shows with me and went on to do many shows on his own. Helping him get into the business is one of my proudest accomplishments.

Keaton Walker

I loved Keaton. He passed away in May of 2020 and was very special to me. I first met Keaton when he was working in the ABC Carpenter Shop as a foreman. Because he had worked as a carpenter, he was remarkably well suited for assistant work, and was one of the best in the business. He was smart, warm, fun and one of the best associates I've ever had. I knew Keaton for over 50 years and loved his dry sense of humor and his fine honest approach to life. I developed an incredible amount of respect and love for this wonderful, fun and talented man. I was so blessed to have had his support and friendship over all those years.

As I've said, my assistants have been the backbone of my career. I could not have had the degree of success I attained without their support and help. I was continually blessed by their presence

Rebecca Barkley (l)
with John Denver and me

Randy Blom

Joe Cashman

Michael Corenblith (r)
with me, Miss Piggy,
and Frank Oz

Paul Galbraith

Elina Katsioula

Tobin Ost

Randy Parsons

Leigh Rand (l)

Bob Rang (r)

Keaton Walker (l)

389

Glossary

Air Wagons

A platform that has air blown in between the wagon and the stage floor so that it floats and can be easily moved by a minimum number of stage hands.

Bidding a show

Generally the designer and his assistant or assistants visit three or so shops at their various locations. Often there is a model in 1/4" or ½" scale to illustrate what the set should look like. A set or sets of blueprints of the construction drawings along with paint elevations that show how the set or sets should be built and painted are shown to the shop and reviewed so that they can work up a bid. Ideally it is a bid and not an estimate.

Costume Designer

Is the person who designs, rents and shops for the clothing worn by the performers on a show. Coordinating the look between the sets and costumes is extremely important.

Cyclorama (Cyc)

Usually a surface that provides the background for production looks. While it can be a hard surface, it usually is made out of two layers of fabric with the front layer being of a gauze like material which is usually made of scrim in either white or light blue and occasionally black and backed with a second layer of white muslin fabric. These fabrics come in large sizes often 30 to 36 feet high by up to 100 feet wide and are usually attached to a traveler track so it can be moved around the stage at will.

Dino White (paint color)
This is a color that was developed for the Dean Martin show in the 1960's and was a "tech" white color that was grayed down so it wouldn't flair or appear too "hot" when the cameras saw it.

Extras (actors)
These are actors who are hired to be used in TV as background atmosphere. Usually they only provide an additional look for a scene and do not play a pivotal part in the scene being shot.

Fly in
A term mostly used in theatres. Scenery is often stored up high and out of sight of the audience but is lowered into view or "flown in" by a system of pulleys when needed usually on pipes that are part of the backstage equipment.

Fly out
After a piece of scenery is no longer needed, it is "flown out" by a stage-hand(s) using a system of ropes and pulleys.

Freelance
While some set designers are on salary by a studio, many designers work as freelancers and use agents to arrange to secure work for them and to help to deal with their contracts. It is unusual for a designer to work without a written contract.

Gloss Black Flooring
In the old movie studio days when a shiny black floor was needed, the only solutions were either use a painted surface which required repainting when it got scuffed and unattractive,

or use 4'X4' black tiles which needed polishing or buffing when scuffed during a dance number. I developed a system using 4'X8'sheets of shiny black Formica or similar material backed by a ¼" phonelic backing which makes for a very durable surface that looks attractive on camera. (see Chapter 16 and Ann Miller)

Lighting Designer

The designer who decides what instruments are needed to illuminate the scenery and the actors, order them up, decides where they should be hung (located), focused which refers to aiming the lighting instrument so that it illuminates the set and and actors to the best advantage and then determines when the lights should be turned on and off, often with a degree of how fast or how slow and how bright to illuminate what needs being lit.

Load in

The term for when the set is brought into the location and set up to be lighted and shot by the cameras or in the cased of theatre, seen by the audience.

Pad

When working out a budget, it is a good idea to incorporate a "pad" (or extra money set aside) in the budget so that when unexpected expenses arise, one can stay on budget and not go over budget.

Producer

The person who often conceives of a show, sells it to a studio or network, often raises the money to execute the show, hires the stars and other performers, the production team (the writers, production designers, costume designers, lighting designers, the musical director, etc. as needed.

Prop man
The man or woman who handles the props or set dressing.

Props
This term can also be termed "Set Dressing" and covers the items called for in the script such as those handled by that actors, furniture, pictures for the walls, etc. and in general items that make the look of the set supportive to the script and or the production.

Prop houses
These are businesses that have a stockpile of items to rent that help the set designer, production designer or prop man "dress" the set so that visually the set is supportive to the needs of the director and the script.

Scene Shop
Is where the sets are built. Having a good working relationship with the shop that builds the set is essential and choosing the best shop for the specific production is very important.

Scrim
A gauze like material that comes in an assortment of colors usually in white, black or light blue and sizes up to 30 and 35'X100'. These are often used for studio cycloramas (cycs.)

Series
This can be a show that is story driven such as "Dallas" or "Dynasty" or a weekly show that covers any number of subjects.

Set Dressers
People who "dress" or furnish a set with the appropriate props which are supportive of the script.

Set Dressing
The "props" that the set dressers use to visually support the production.

Special
A "special" is usually a program that deals with a subject or that highlights a star such as Bea Arthur or Lynda Carter, a subject such as an event like an American Film Institute Tribute or an awards special.

Special Effects Person
This person creates and is supportive to the look of the show and whose job is to solve any technical problems that the script might call for be it smoke, an explosion, a break-a-way prop that can be broken on camera, etc. They are the ones that come up with the special effect that the script writers have dreamed up.

Sound Man/Woman
The person who handles the sound recording of the actor via microphones.

Stage Left
An onstage term that refers to the area to the left of a performer when he or she is facing the audience.

Stage Right
The area to the performer's right when facing the audience.

Stage Manager

Stage managers are very important to the workings of the entire show. She or he "calls" the lighting and sound cues as to when the lights, sound and special effects integrate into the show's actions. They also are responsible to see that the actors are where they are supposed to be at specific times. In the theatre, they are responsible to make sure the actors adhere to the script and the director's intent. It is a hugely responsible job.

Star Drop
A drop usually made of cloth with small electric lights in it to create a star-like look. Lately the use of fiber optics has pretty much replaced the use of electric bulbs.

Strike a Set
The term "strike" refers to dismantling the set after a TV shoot or after a play or musical has ended or "closed". In the case of a TV show the set is dismantled and any pieces that were used from the studio are then returned to the studio's sock storage area. The rest is generally thrown out. In the case of a theatre set, unless the set is going on tour, it generally is destroyed.

Trucking
Sets are generally trucked from the shop to the studio or theatre. The set needs to be designed to be constructed so it will fit into a truck and in rare occasions if the set needs to fit into an elevator before getting to the studio or stage, that limitation needs to be taken into account.

Touch up Scenic
A standby scenic artist is used to touch up the scenery and refers to the need to clean up any scuffs or scrapes that are incurred in the process of trucking and setting up the set.

Turntable

Turntables are sometimes used in the design concept of a show. Some venues have a turn table existing as part of the facility. If not, there are rental houses that carry turn-tables of various radiuses.

United Scenic Artists
Is the union that represents set and production designers. It establishes the minimum fee that a designer should expect however many designers can command a larger fee. Compensation for productions that run over a period of time needs to be negotiated by one's agent.

Variety Series
Is a television term and refers to a musical show that usually (but not always) airs once a week.

The above areas generally refer to tape television and live theatrical productions and not movies.

I wish to acknowledge the following people who helped to shape my life and to make this book possible:

Sandy Wernick

Ane Kathrine Jensen Klausen

Tony Adams

Donald Oenslager

Patton Campbell

Fran Dwyer

Jo-Ann Geffen

and especially, Rebecca Sawyer-Fay

Made in the USA
Columbia, SC
12 September 2021

44615475R10217